Evan Bloom is a British author with a professional background in the language industry. Having spent most of his life in London, he currently resides in France with his partner. Evan wrote this book based on his experiences growing up homosexual in an orthodox Jewish environment.

# Dedication

This book is dedicated to my family, who has been through an equally difficult journey as I have and whose ultimate love and faith in me has made this work possible.

Evan Bloom

# THEY SAID I WAS MISGUIDED

AUSTIN MACAULEY PUBLISHERS™
LONDON · CAMBRIDGE · NEW YORK · SHARJAH

Copyright © Evan Bloom (2017)

The right of Evan Bloom to be identified as author of this work has been asserted by him in accordance with section 77 and 78 of the Copyright, Designs and Patents Act 1988.

All rights reserved. No part of this publication may be reproduced, stored in a retrieval system, or transmitted in any form or by any means, electronic, mechanical, photocopying, recording, or otherwise, without the prior permission of the publishers.

Any person who commits any unauthorised act in relation to this publication may be liable to criminal prosecution and civil claims for damages.

A CIP catalogue record for this title is available from the British Library.

ISBN 9781788230230 (Paperback)
ISBN 9781788230247 (Hardback)
ISBN 9781788230254 (E-Book)
www.austinmacauley.com

First Published (2017)
Austin Macauley Publishers Ltd.
25 Canada Square
Canary Wharf
London
E14 5LQ

# Prologue

It's hard to know where to start really. Sitting down and writing about the events and experiences that have shaped my life and character so far is no mean feat. To narrow down an otherwise mammoth task, I have decided to concentrate on my adolescent years, providing my childhood as a context and finishing at the age of twenty-one because I went through such an extraordinary journey during that time and have so much to say and so much I need to get out about that period of my life; almost like a personal therapy session, in order to make sense of it all.

These are the memoirs of my life as a boy and a teenager, living within a strict religious community and trying to make sense of the world and my place within it. As I faced the usual challenges of adolescence, I was also forced to deal with fundamental issues of sexuality and spirituality side by side that most people could never imagine having to contend with. It is a story of real life, through my own eyes.

I grew up being both Jewish and gay, and therefore representative of two long persecuted minority groups. However, this story will resonate with all those that have experienced issues of sexuality whilst being brought up within any strict religious environment. Ironically, the two communities I represent are at complete odds with one another, the result of which has been an often bewildering experience for me. The Jewish culture is based on the importance of procreation to ensure the continuation of the religion, as it does not encourage people to convert from other faiths. As a result, Judaism inherently condemns gay activity in the strongest possible terms.

The gay community has evolved as a strong and proud worldwide movement, which through political lobbying and engendering a sense of 'pride' amongst its members, actively supports them and attempts to protect them from the prejudices of the outside world. However in the main, the gay community shuns any notion of a religious institution, believing that a more hedonistic and liberal lifestyle is the key to happiness. There are many gay people who in fact believe that religion has been the cause of most of the marginalisation and malice directed towards homosexuals throughout history.

There are then the people who seem to be stuck in the middle. Deeply attached to their faith and culture yet in no doubt about their homosexuality. These are the people struggling the most to work out how they can fit into both aspects of their life at the same time. I fall squarely into this category. Although these days in the Western world gay people enjoy more basic freedoms than at any time in the past, there still remains much oppression and intolerance of homosexuals within many religious groups, Orthodox Judaism being one of them. The main problem for me was that I spent my teenage and young adult years struggling to somehow reconcile my gay self with my Jewish self instead of being able to simply get on with life and the normal preoccupations of youth. I tried for a long time to find a way of living a life true to my sexuality whilst remaining a part of my community and with the full acceptance of my family, but unfortunately I discovered that just by being who I was, my lifestyle would always be considered fundamentally unacceptable by the Jewish culture at large. To make matters more interesting, I have never actually felt truly connected to either the gay or Jewish communities, which has led to my need for inclusion in some area, being a driving force in my life ever since.

The search for meaning has led me down several paths, some of them enlightening and beneficial and some of them dangerous, yet I have nearly always followed these paths alone. I have made countless mistakes along the way and have learned so very much at the same time. Fundamentally though, I have had to rely on my intuition to steer me through complex and unknown waters as I did not feel I had anyone to look up to as a source of inspiration or guidance; most figures of authority I turned to in my times of need simply wanted to change me rather than understand me. Most seriously, the support of my family unit which is normally one of the biggest sources of comfort people rely on when going through troubled times, eluded me at a critical turning point in my life. If this was not enough, I then had to deal with the shocking betrayal of my closest friend, which together with my family problems at the time, led to a prevailing sense of disharmony with my surroundings. The effect of all this on me personally, was a distinct lack of self-confidence and a feeling that I needed to justify myself and my actions in the world, on a regular basis. These issues continue to hound me to the present day.

There may be people out there who, on reading this memoir, will be able to relate my experiences to the ones they have been through in some way and realise that they are not alone. In fact there are countless people in my situation around the world and if I can provide a connection to even just a few of these people, this memoir will have been worthwhile. There are numerous others who until now may have never understood what it was like to live with the issues that I have dealt with and who on reading this may get some insight into the troubled world often faced by people like me. This may then foster further understanding and tolerance of those that are different. If that proves to be the case, then so much the better.

Ironically, I have finally reached a point in my life where the only person left who is still capable of making me feel like an outsider in my own world is myself, having achieved acceptance from all those around me, one way or another. I have come so very far, but the final hurdle, although under my complete control, remains the hardest of all my struggles. But that's another story.

# Chapter 1

I was brought up within a family of five children, comprising an eldest girl and four younger boys. I am the second child. We grew up in a mainly Jewish suburb of North West London, a traditionally orthodox Jewish family of modest but comfortable means. My parents have always practiced a religious lifestyle, following all the main Jewish laws and customs including only eating kosher food, going to the synagogue every Saturday which is the Jewish holy Sabbath day and celebrating all of the Jewish festivals. As children, we were taught that this was the only acceptable way to live our lives, and throughout our primary and secondary education at strict Jewish schools, these values were reinforced heavily.

My father's name is Malcolm. He is a dentist and throughout most of my youth, owned a couple of practices; one being attached to our house which he worked from at weekends, and the other situated somewhere in the West End of London. My father is quite a placid person, happily leading his Orthodox lifestyle with a set routine for pretty much every aspect of his life. He is definitely from the old school and seemingly a supporter of Victorian values including not displaying any overt emotions or discussing any matters of an intimate nature in front of others, even within our family unit. My father has always been very practical and scientific in his approach to things, which made it somewhat difficult for us to establish a real emotional connection to him as children. He has always had a complete head of grey hair and an older-than-his-years appearance ever since I can remember, and he also used to look quite gaunt when we were young although his kindly eyes and warm smile made up for it to some extent. My mother has often told me that his appearance in those days was probably due to the fact that he is a celiac, meaning he is allergic to gluten, which was a condition he was not diagnosed with until he was around forty and therefore spent many years being quite ill without knowing why. I remember once, when I was probably about six years old I was running along the street with my sister, then about eight with my father following along behind. An elderly gentleman passed us, and called out something along the lines of "Now make sure you both look after your granddad!" I can only imagine now that my father must have felt mortified by such a comment.

My mother is called Karen and has always been a very attractive woman, her eyes sparkling with life and with a beautiful smile to match. Throughout my youth, she had afro-like hair always in the same style of a well-groomed fuzzy mop. It has only been in more recent years that she has straightened and styled it and coloured it to make it look more interesting. I have always thought that she looked good for her age despite having given birth to and raising five children. She is certainly the passionate driving force of our family and in terms of her personality, a polar opposite to my father. From a very young age, my mother instilled within us all the fundamental values of the Jewish family unit and the need to be supportive of one another through thick and thin. This particular value has proved to be controversial for me at times. I suppose you could say that whereas my father represented the practical duties of living a Jewish life, my mother provided the nurturing aspect, trying to help us develop a sense of emotional engagement with our culture and heritage. When we were younger, my mother had various jobs that she seemed to juggle all at once; helping my father as his dental nurse at our home practice at weekends, managing a French student exchange company followed by working at an insurance firm full time and being a doting mother to us all. How she managed everything I still do not know to this day, suffice it to say that she is a truly remarkable and resourceful woman.

My childhood up to the age of about ten was mostly spent in a hyperactive state. I suffered from several allergies to different foods and additives and before I was finally diagnosed and treated with a carefully managed diet, I would cause complete havoc with my family as I was unable to sit still for long and ended up exhausting everyone around me. During these years, a lot of my time was spent trying to include myself in my older sister's activities, attempting to join in with games she would play with her friends and generally trying to be part of her group. I had no real interest in what my three brothers were doing as I considered them to be far too young to bother with, although whenever we were stuck at home together on Saturdays, which is the Jewish Sabbath day, we would find ourselves playing various different games to pass the time, which mostly ended up with fights that my parents had to try and calm down.

My brothers' names are Lewis, Daniel and Jonathan and there is approximately two to three years' age difference between each of us. People have often said that we all look extremely similar, with dark hair and eyes and big smiles, although I never used to see the similarity myself. I really just thought my brothers were annoying brats most of the time. It was my sister that I looked up to and I was fascinated by her world.

My sister's name is Eva. When we were both younger, we were regularly mistaken for twins. She has beautiful brown eyes with long lashes, wavy brown hair and a smile that would light up any room. She has always looked very much like my mother in that sense. As a child, she had a tight-knit group of friends, all of whom were full of personality in their own right. Her role amongst this group appeared to be that of the bossy, organising type, whereas most of the others seemed more laid back to me. I believe she resented me for trying to involve myself with her friends, hanging around them and listening in on their conversations. If they were playing skip rope games which was one of their favourite pass times, I would ask to join in and despite being brushed off by my sister, one of her friends would always take pity on me and I would end up helping to hold the rope so that my sister could show off her acrobatic jumping skills.

They used to sit together in our lounge or garden, talking about the latest chart music and free jewellery that they would get from girls' magazines and I would stay there, far enough away to not be seen as an intrusion, yet close enough to take in every word. I would find myself eavesdropping outside her bedroom where she would sometimes be huddled with her clan gossiping about something or other and I with my ear pressed against the door, would strain to hear what they were saying. On several occasions I would wait until my sister was out somewhere and take the opportunity to go into her room and play with her wide selection of dolls, dressing them and playing with their hair. Her dolls interested me more than any other game or activity. I wanted her life and to be in her world, it was as simple as that.

I guess looking back on it now, I should have realised that such an interest in a girl's environment was a direct precursor to my development into a gay man. However at that age, such thoughts were beyond my comprehension. More importantly, it was around this time that my feelings of not truly belonging anywhere and feeling that I was quite different from others around me, started to become ingrained within my character. My parents were busy trying to keep the family going as well as managing the pressures of their own careers and we, the children, tried to find things to occupy our time outside of school. For me, I wanted that to be involvement with my sister's life. Unfortunately she had other ideas. The more my sister made me feel I wasn't welcome, the more I desperately wanted to be included and accepted. She would often accuse me of having taken something from her room and to keep away from her, or tell me to get my own life and stop interfering with her friends. However I simply became more and more intrigued with her, somehow fuelled on despite knowing that I was not really wanted.

As the next few years went by, my fascination with my sister largely remained, although faded with time, and any continued attempts to be included in her life were met with disdain. A sense of loneliness pervaded everything around me because I was finding my own relationships with school friends somehow limiting and had not managed to find a group that I felt I truly belonged to. At primary school, the children were mainly either brainy and studious or cooler, more athletic types obsessed with football (otherwise known as soccer). I didn't fit into either category and instead would look on in admiration as other boys at break time would run around the playground showing how good they were at scoring goals. I wanted them to want me as their friend but I felt I had nothing to offer them that they did not have already. Watching the popular boys at school being confident and surrounded by admirers actually stirred something within me which I did not understand. It felt like a kind of deep admiration coupled with a kind of desire that I could not put my finger on. It was a strange feeling for sure. I grew used to my own company and tended to have conversations with myself when I was alone, taking on the role of my own best friend. Nobody else understood me like I did after all. It was not so much that I was happy being alone with only myself for company, it was just that the others around me were simply either not interesting enough or if they were, they would not give me the time of day. Therefore the possibility of somehow discovering new friends and experiences that I could connect with was what captured my imagination. Amazing what goes on in the head of a pre-pubescent boy!

Sometimes, on a whim I would simply decide to go out on a little trip and would leave the house and wander off to an unknown destination, mostly just somewhere across the other side of the suburb where we lived. I would walk along the tree-lined streets, gazing into the windows of other people's houses and wondering what their lives must be like. I would go into sweet shops and simply look around at the goodies on display, sometimes daring myself and then managing to steal a few penny sweets which gave me a buzz of excitement. It almost seemed a challenge to do this, knowing that I was being watched but finding just the right moment when the shop staff were otherwise occupied to grab something, stuff it in my pockets and walk calmly but purposefully out of the door. This was solely for the aim of providing some kind of adventure and often I had no real interest in what I was stealing. I suppose to an extent, I was tempting fate and wondering how long it would take for people to focus attention on me, even for the wrong reasons.

There was a large park situated about fifteen minutes' walk from our house, which I had discovered once by chance on following a carnival procession that was passing by. I had gone into the park, which was the destination of the carnival, because there was a funfair that had been set up there. It was great to just look at the rides and the different entertainment stalls and see families and couples laughing together and enjoying themselves. My parents did not really take us on outings of this nature and anywhere we did go, ended up being a big mission with at least one of my brothers throwing a tantrum as they did not want to come with the rest of us. This would then lead to us all being bundled into the family car, an old Peugeot estate model, where someone or other would be moaning and whingeing all the way to wherever we were heading. Family outings were definitely not much fun.

My spontaneous trip with the carnival to the park as well as various other wanderings alone, ended up with my parents frantically worrying where I had disappeared to and calling the police to help find me. Looking back, maybe in some way I felt I needed to do something drastic to make them realise I was around, but if this were the case, it was certainly a subconscious thought. As far as I was concerned, these were just little trips I was taking and I always intended to come back home afterwards. I really just wanted to go and find an interesting environment for a while where I could lose myself in another world. At the time I had never stopped to think about the effect on my parents if I disappeared somewhere, and clearly I had shown no consideration for their feelings, but the look of pure relief coupled with sheer anxiety on my parents' faces when I managed to find my way home is something I will always remember. Strange how despite being part of a large family, I could not find any fulfilment within it, which is ultimately what directed me to go elsewhere.

When a Jewish boy reaches the age of thirteen, it is considered an extremely important stage in life. It is called becoming 'Bar Mitzvah', which represents the official passage from child to adult and is when you are expected to take on the full responsibility of living a life that is true to the ethics of the Jewish religion. This process is marked by a very large celebration, where the whole family and often most of the local community is invited to celebrate the coming of age experience with you at a party. Being one of the youngest boys in my school year, whose birthday always fell a few weeks after the end of summer term, I had already attended a few Bar Mitzvah celebrations before my own and had witnessed the sheer joy that surrounded my school friends on these occasions. Mostly, their families would hold parties at extravagant venues with fantastic entertainment and sometimes at least half of my class would be there. This was an opportunity for anybody that was popular, to show off the true extent of their friendship network to everyone they knew and for the proud parents to use the event as an excuse to promote their influence to the wider Jewish community. It was all about who you knew and the amount of respect and admiration you received in public and from this point of view, such events had a shallow and self-ingratiating side to them. Nevertheless I enjoyed occasions like these as it meant that I could be part of something big, exciting and often extremely opulent, whilst remaining almost anonymous. My fellow schoolmates would acknowledge my existence briefly and sometimes hang around me for a while, but then would mostly stay within their cliques and effectively shut me out of any further involvement with them. I was always thankful that at least I had good food to indulge in.

For me, my own Bar Mitzvah party was quite a bewildering experience. Not having ever been remotely popular at school, I was suddenly the centre of attention amongst several hundred people who I mostly did not know, or who had never spoken a word to me previously; people from my local synagogue, relatives that suddenly appeared to have come out of the woodwork, a selection of family friends and a very small group of my own schoolmates that I had invited but really did not expect to turn up. Most of them were no more than acquaintances really, but I had thought it best to invite them as I had at least had some interactions with them at school and certainly did not want to put myself to shame by being seen to have no friends.

One of the boys that had been invited to my party was the nephew of one of my parents' friends. He was called Ephraim and he came from New York. I had never met him before, and I found him strangely fascinating. It could have been that he was American and I had never spent any time with an American until now. Out of all the boys my age who were there, he seemed to be the most interested in me, and we spent quite a long time chatting to each other. Something inside me stirred while I was in his company, but I could not make out what it was. I assumed it was just the fact that he seemed exciting and different, and from another place. Yet the interest he showed in me, made me believe that I was his sole focus. It was something I had never felt before in my life. This effect he had on me was so strong that after my Bar Mitzvah celebrations were over, I attempted to follow him back to New York, going as far as the airport and trying to board a plane without a passport or ticket. Another of my follies, that again caused havoc with my family as my parents had no idea where I had gone and were called by the police to come and collect me, as they had taken custody of me at the airport.

Back to my Bar Mitzvah party – it was strange to be congratulated constantly by random people filled with mirth, most of them quite drunk on a variety of alcoholic beverages, being given gifts by them and being told that now I was becoming a man I needed to start thinking about my responsibilities in life. Some of the guests also said they were looking forward to sharing the next big celebration with me at my wedding!

Of course I remained extremely polite, smiling and thanking everyone for their kindness but inside, there was nowhere else I wanted to be any less. Why on earth were all these people really here? Had they come simply because my parents had put on a big party and they wanted to be seen, or did they in fact care at all that it was about me as a person? I was certain that it was the former. It was a very long evening and as part of the proceedings,

I was required to read out a speech that my father and a family friend had hurriedly written on the car journey to the venue, extolling the wisdom of the great Jewish Sages, quoting some of their most famous words and explaining how my actions would now be counted amongst the actions of the entire Jewish world. I read the speech with as much confidence and conviction as I could muster, this having been the first time I was required to speak in public in such a formal way. I did not really understand much of what I was saying, but seeing the appreciative nods and smiles of those seated in front of me, I thought that at least I was doing myself and my family proud.

One thing was for sure – this was the biggest and most important time of my life so far and I was expected to now actively participate in and contribute to my community; a group of people who I did not really know and who I felt so different from. Was this really MY world? Were these people *really* part of my community? I had never felt so alien to my surroundings. Yet this indeed was my life and these people represented my environment; the Jewish environment. So warm, so welcoming and so inclusive – as long as you continued to fit the mould. And therein lay the problem, as I was due to find out.

# Chapter 2

It was now the late 1980s. When the stirrings of puberty hit me at around thirteen or fourteen years old and the first feelings of sexual awakening and desire developed, it was an incredibly unsettling time. As a child, I had sensed I was different somehow, without knowing why. As a teenager, these feelings were heightened immensely and led to a series of crises I had to deal with, trying to reconcile my lack of self-worth, my apparent sexuality which began dawning on me, and my religion which was something that overarched my life. I now know that I am not unique in this aspect, and that there are countless people who have a similar struggle on a daily basis to make sense of their world and their role within it.

Along with my brother Lewis and my older sister Eva, I attended an Orthodox Jewish high school in London. My youngest brothers Daniel and Jonathan were still at primary school at the time. Our school was an all boys' school, with the girls' equivalent being on a separate site nearby to avoid the 'danger' of teenagers of the opposite sex meeting and getting up to all sorts of prohibited pleasures. I suppose my parents thought it would be a suitable grounding for my siblings and me to continue into adulthood and live good, religious and meaningful lives. Every day, one of my parents would ferry us all to our respective schools, often running late due to my younger brother Daniel's regular tantrums and refusal to get dressed in the mornings. By the time we arrived, we had endured him screaming, kicking and often vomiting out of the car window which left us almost always frazzled, miserable and suffering from car sickness ourselves.

The school was considered a real institution and had been around for many years, going back to the 1940s. Although almost certainly in its earlier days it would have been regarded as a place of high achievement and somewhere to be proud of attending, it was by now the butt of jokes and suffered from a distinct lack of respect from many of the pupils that went there. The head teacher was an extremely austere Rabbi who although very learned, did not once attempt to foster any kind of relationship with the students, resulting in him being seen as a scary, distant figurehead. The lessons were in fact run mostly by Rabbis with the odd 'normal' teacher thrown in for good measure to teach subjects of a less academic nature such as Physical Education and Art. There was a real mix of quite religious pupils and those who had no interest in religion, but whose parents wanted to transfer their responsibilities for religious education onto the school.

The school buildings themselves consisted of the original old and by now slightly decrepit structures, with bolt-ons of modern portacabins that looked like they had been placed there as an afterthought (and most probably were). The original old building at the centre housed most of the classrooms and a large assembly hall-come-dining room which had very high ceilings and wooden panelled walls, with what I am sure was meant to be fashionable wooden edging when it was built, but which was now rotting and badly in need of refurbishment. The lino-floored corridors reeked of a history of damp rot, old books, stale sweat and failed discipline. Every classroom told its own story, traces of graffiti scrawled on desks or on the walls by pupils clearly bored to tears during lessons and bits of chewing gum having been stuck under the chairs and tables. One thing was for sure, you could tell that this school had seen some real action and was not exactly run like clockwork. Pupils would run along the corridors, only to stop suddenly with fake reverence as a Rabbi or two walked past, chastising them for unruly appearance, lateness for lessons, munching on non-approved snacks or any manner of other so called infringements. As soon as the rabbi turned their back, the pupils would often just snigger, make fun of the unsuspecting victim and carry on as they were. It was almost like a Jewish version of St Trinians except slightly watered down.

At break-time the playground, desperately in need of some kind of landscaping or at least resurfacing, became filled with boys playing football or a game called 'hand tennis'. This was basically a game where teams of maybe four or five boys would gather in front of the various walls surrounding the old building and take turns to hit a tennis ball against the ground with their bare hand. The aim was to hit the ball at a certain angle so that it hit the wall and bounced off in such a way that the next boy couldn't return the serve. Each boy in the team would take it in turns to try to return the previous player's shot until someone missed the ball or hit it wrongly straight onto the wall instead of it bouncing on the ground first, meaning they were out. The game continued with the remaining team members until it came down to the last two. The ultimate winner would be the one who's shot the opponent could not return. Other boys would be sitting around gossiping, some would bully some of the smaller boys for fun and some even tried to study or finish off last minute homework for their next lesson.

An overall macho environment pervaded the school, where several pupils would make fun of others that seemed somehow feminine, or different. Gangs of 'hard lads' would roam the playground and abusive terms would often be spat out at poor unsuspecting individuals who had no chance of ever defending themselves. Most of the offending terms that were used related to homosexuality, as if this was the lowest form of address possible and being gay the worst thing to be considered as.

Many of the less religious boys would walk around boasting of conquests with girls and comparing their own probably fake experiences with their peers in an attempt to be seen as the coolest guy in the group. These were the most popular boys, and they were always surrounded by admiring followers lapping up their every word. As if by chance, this group of boys was also far and away the most attractive group in the school. There were several large groups of more religious types too, whose parents often knew the teachers personally on a social basis. As a result, these boys would seem to always get away with murder, and most of the teachers would turn a blind eye to any rules they broke. The religious pupils had an uncanny knack of being seen just at the right time by the head teacher or other senior figures, discussing various biblical concepts and religious questions which made it seem that they were serious about their studies. Only the other pupils really knew that they were just as badly behaved as anyone else and therefore resented them enormously. Unfortunately, the concept of favouritism was certainly alive and well at my high school and it was all based on how you looked and who you were seen with.

It was within this environment that I spent my most defining years, never belonging to any specific group and realising with ever growing certainty that I was simply not like the other boys around me. It was an unsettling feeling that I lived with on a daily basis.

My best friend at school, Simon, was my constant companion. Simon was a short, olive-skinned boy with enormously oversized glasses and a mop of frizzy black hair. He was a strange looking creature in fact, but was my moral support and confidant. We must have looked quite strange together, me being quite tall and lanky, and him so short. We would spend time just talking about teachers, other pupils, life in general, TV shows, books we had read and new things we had bought. Simon came from a family who on the surface did not seem to be overly wealthy, yet he was always telling me about his new purchases of designer labels and expensive items. I always thought that he lived a more luxurious life than I did and he also seemed far more in tune with the latest trends and aspects of popular culture than I could ever grasp. I often wondered why he was so interested in our friendship at all, as unlike him I had no real conception or appreciation of pop star culture and fashion, my entire wardrobe and that of my siblings having been furnished mainly by market stalls. It simply did not occur to me that wearing Ralph Lauren instead of 'Maxi Fashion' would be a more acceptable option amongst my peers. Ultimately, despite feeling more comfortable in Simon's company than anyone else's, I still had a sense of being separate and not quite on the same wavelength. It's strange how you can be there and yet not quite be there despite your best efforts to fit in.

From about the age of fourteen, my feelings of attraction to other boys really took on a life of their own. I would find myself developing an interest in anyone that smiled at me or said something friendly, and would then start to build up hopes of them becoming close to me. I would end up imagining all sorts of romantic scenarios with them – nothing really sexual, but rather the sense of being wanted by them and being the centre of their world. Any kind of physical contact I received, such as an arm round my shoulders or warm handshake gave me shivers of pure longing. I just needed to feel wanted emotionally by another boy and it was a yearning that stayed within me throughout high school. I always knew that such feelings were considered wrong and were not the normal way that boys felt about each other, but I had no idea how to stop them. While I lived with these feelings on a daily basis, Jewish studies lessons at school taught me that the acceptable way to live was something very different. Apart from learning about Jewish history and sacred texts from the Bible, our religious lessons were aimed at equipping us with the knowledge and conviction required to live respectable and spiritual lives as adults. At the centre of all this was the purity of marriage between a man and a woman, and the importance of continuation of the faith through procreation. Any other lifestyle was deemed simply inferior or unacceptable and to be looked upon with disdain.

Despite all of this, I knew without a doubt that my feelings were directed towards other males and felt a sense of frustration that I would probably never have the opportunity to have my feelings returned. I suppose I already knew I was gay, although did not yet understand what it all really meant. I did not in fact have a problem coming to terms with being gay per se; I was who I was at the end of the day and my feelings were my feelings regardless of whether they were considered right or wrong. Rather, I struggled to understand why I was evidently created this way whilst having been brought up in an environment that fundamentally disapproved of the feelings I had. Why had God done this to me and made me as I was while at the same time, making it perfectly clear that I was never allowed to be true to myself? Was this some kind of sick game? I started to question my culture, wondering whether I was honestly supposed to respect a religion that played with innocent people like this and fostered intolerance and derision towards people that were not like the majority. Yet I believed entirely in the notion of God as the all powerful Creator of the universe. I was however, completely baffled as to what my relationship with Him should be. It felt like a no-win situation for me. And aside from dealing with this struggle, my yearning for another male's intimate and emotional attention continually became the overriding desire in my teenage life.

Unfortunately for me, my high school days were also the period where adolescence took its toll on my appearance. I was incredibly lanky and thin, reaching almost six feet tall by the time I was fifteen. I also had a horrendous shock of black curly hair that was uncontrollable. It came from my mother's side for sure. Looking back at photos now, I realise I resembled a *Jackson 5* reject. The worst thing for me however, was my ongoing acne problem. Despite every effort, I would wake up in the mornings with a rash of new oversized pimples somewhere or other and any products I bought to alleviate the problem seemed to prove ineffective. I even went so far as to visit my family doctor for antibiotics, which again were useless. I had super acne! Clearly this did not do wonders for an already delicate self-esteem. I would tend to look at other boys in my school, many of whom were blemish free and fresh faced and think how attractive they were just because they had clear skin. I would often pray fervently to be like them, and agonise over the fact that I seemed to have the worst of all worlds.

I mainly responded with unexpected surprise if a boy at school showed me attention or even said a friendly "hello." I would rarely know what to say back and felt that if they started up a proper conversation, I would soon be found out as a complete bore.

Once, I attempted to join in a conversation some of my classmates were having before a lesson. It was about a recent cinema release that was the hit of the month and which I really wanted to see. Most of this group had already seen it and were describing some of the thrilling aspects of the plot to the others. Being interested in this, I had come up with:

"That sounds so cool. I wouldn't mind going with someone if they want to see it?"

The looks I received in response were all the answer I needed.

"Are you even allowed to go out?" commented one of the group. "This was a private conversation anyway, go and find your own friends – oops, I forgot, you don't have any!"

This was followed by sniggers from the group. And that was it, I was not welcome as usual and apparently had nothing to contribute. I wondered if it was because I looked weird with my unmanageable hair and spots, or if it was because the others could sense I was just not like them. It was the story of my life so far in any case. In the end, I had actually gone to see the film alone, thankful that at least in the darkened cinema nobody would see that I was not sitting with anyone. Simon had already seen the film with one of his sisters the previous weekend so I really didn't have much option.

I would often wonder why on earth anyone would want to talk to me or be seen with me anyway, and what could I possibly offer them? I felt I had nothing to add in conversations, as most of my peers would be discussing football (which I had no interest in), girls (as with football) or latest clothing gear from the hot designer of the moment (which I was not privileged enough to have experienced wearing). I simply felt that I may as well be on a different planet.

Sometimes, before going into school, I would stop off at the local newsagent down the road and buy several kinds of sweets for break-time. It soon became apparent that this enabled me to attract attention from other pupils, who would come up to me with friendly smiles and pretend to take an interest in me. Clearly, the only reason they would approach me was because of my sweets, but at least it meant I got some attention even if for a brief moment.

I was in a strange place emotionally – I was from a religious Jewish background yet I did not feel connected to the core beliefs that my family and community were built upon; I was surrounded by testosterone-filled boys obsessed with girls, yet I could not relate to that at all and struggled to keep my attraction to other boys under wraps; I had only one true friend I could rely on, yet I felt continually socially inferior to him and furthermore I considered myself to have a physical appearance that was well below par…

So, with all these issues to contend with, what on earth was a teenage boy to do?

# Chapter 3

It was now the year 1990. It was just before my senior exams and fast approaching sixteenth birthday, in a period where I was supposed to be revising hard for subjects that mostly did not interest me, that my attentions were drawn quite seriously to a boy at school for the first time.

His name was Jamie. He was probably in the year below me and for some reason, I had not really noticed him before now. He was of average height, with quite pale skin and almost black hair with a slight quiff at the front. His eyes were the most astonishing shade of hazel and I was simply mesmerised by him. He seemed to suffer from eczema around his mouth, or at least very dry skin, which in fact only served to interest me more. The first time I noticed him properly was in the playground when I overheard him laughing with some friends. His laugh was quite raucous and hearty and it grabbed my attention even before I took his appearance in.

It was almost like an epiphany. Seemingly from nowhere was this boy, this beautiful yet flawed creature, who enchanted me without me even knowing why. What was it about him exactly? I had seen several boys that attracted me before yet none who had quite this effect on me. I certainly did not even know what he was really like so could not possibly judge his personality. It was that laugh, so alive, so full of character that seemed to answer all my questions at once. I knew instinctively that this was a person who could change my life somehow.

Of course, it was one thing to have noticed someone, but quite another to get them to have any kind of interest in you. What was I really after anyway? This was a religious Jewish school, where the concept of same sex love was considered completely abhorrent. What would I even say to this boy who could be no more than fifteen years old, while I was almost sixteen and in schoolboy years, one year may as well have been five? All I knew was that suddenly, I started seeing him everywhere and could not stop thinking about him. It's like when you pay attention for the first time to a particular car on the road, and then see the same model all the time afterwards.

I also realised that while I had no real friends to speak of at school except Simon, Jamie seemed to be continually surrounded by friends, people who laughed at his jokes, begged to hang out with him at lunchtime and make arrangements to see him at weekends. Why on earth would he even want to speak to me? Yet somehow, I simply had to make that happen.

Each morning, I would wake up and immediately think about the day ahead, my heart beating faster simply at the thought of catching a glimpse of Jamie. I would concoct scenarios in my head about how we would eventually meet properly, what I would say and what he would say. My mother was certainly quite surprised about my sudden enthusiasm for going to school. I would even hurry my siblings along to make sure we could just for once, leave on time and therefore arrive before morning registration. My world seemed to suddenly make sense, I had a purpose and it was propelling me along.

The reality was however that once I saw Jamie at school, courage failed me and I had no words to say. I would just stand there, in the corridors, in the playground, in the dining hall, watching him and his every move, every interaction he would have with others. I would often get told off by Simon for not paying attention in conversations and for seeming distant. It was certainly some kind of obsession that I had developed, based on a person I had never even spoken to. But I so desperately wanted to be part of Jamie's world. Maybe that's what it was. He represented such an interesting, attractive and fun world to me, that maybe it was more about that than about who he was as a person. Nevertheless I simply had to talk to him.

One day, I engineered a situation where we literally bumped into each other in one of the corridors between lessons. He looked at me, directly into my eyes, the flecks of hazel colour burning through my brain.

"Sorry mate," he said.

"I really should look where I'm going I guess" was my pathetic response.

And then came the smile. A wide, tooth-filled smile which made his eyes light up, and made me feel that I would pass out right there.

"Errm, hey, I'm Evan," I managed. "I'm in Year Eleven."

"I'm Jamie, Year Ten. I was meant to be in Year Eleven but my birthday's in the summer so I just missed out and was put into the year below."

So, that would make him closer to my age than I first thought. I felt a surge of hope.

"I see you around sometimes, you know, with your friends and stuff," I continued.

"Yeah, we mostly hang out in the playground and watch the losers trying to play football. I play in a five-a-side team twice a week in the evenings and I'm pretty good."

"That sounds great. I have always loved five-a-side football," I lied, knowing that I had never had any interest in the sport.

"Really? Because we could do with one or two new players at the moment," said Jamie, beginning to show some real interest.

This was it! My opportunity to get fully onto his radar and maybe even become part of his inner circle! But the very thought of having to play football, something I had no experience of at all, filled me with dread. What if I joined his team and made a fool of myself? He would almost certainly lose any interest in me then. But what else could I do? I had lied to him and he was now showing me attention.

"We play again tomorrow after school, you can come and try out if you want," said Jamie.

"Umm, well, I actually have some plans tomorrow but would really love to come another time," I hastily replied, the very thought of actually having to play football scaring me to the core.

"Okay, sure no problem."

"So, er, I gotta run now or I'll be late for a study session," I managed.

"Yeah, cool. See you around," said Jamie, as he strolled off.

I had never felt so uncomfortable. I realised that he was clearly out of my league and who was I kidding anyway, thinking I could be part of his world, talking about football with him and his friends and generally being accepted? I didn't even just want to be his friend, I wanted him to fall in love with me! But who on earth was I kidding? Jewish boys simply did not fall for each other and any hint of being gay would immediately cause you to become the focus of derision and a target for bullying. I realised I had nothing to offer anyone, I did not share the same interests as other boys my age yet so desperately needed to fit in somehow. Maybe I should just have gone back to my sister's dolls.

I spent the rest of the day defeated, feeling terrible and certain that the next time I saw Jamie, he would simply ignore me. Simon remarked that I was quieter than usual and asked if there was anything wrong with me. I could not bear to even explain myself to him.

I wondered what it would be like the next time I saw Jamie. At least we had already broken the ice, but my first attempt at pretending to share his interests had not exactly been successful. I was now well and truly hooked, I just had to see those eyes and that smile again and get close to him, even if it meant hiding any of my real feelings.

My next encounter with Jamie was during break time a few days later. I saw him with a couple of his friends, laughing about something. That laugh again, I wanted to be the one that made him laugh like that. I heard him say that he would love a game of hand tennis but did not have a ball. I had always carried a ball in my bag, just in case an opportunity arose to play with someone.

"Hey," I exclaimed as I walked slightly nervously towards Jamie and his friends. "Anyone fancy a game of hand tennis?"

"Yeah, cool! That's just what I was talking about," answered Jamie, showing me those amazing white teeth of his.

"Okay, so, erm, who wants to start?"

"Well, you can start as you brought the ball," said one of Jamie's friends who I learned was called Benjy and who seemed to have permanently rosy cheeks, with a freckled face and short hair that was on the verge of being ginger.

As the first player in hand tennis, it can be quite stressful. All eyes are on you, and you need to try and start with a really good serve to set the pace for the game and prove that you are a worthy player. If your serve isn't strong enough, or at a difficult enough angle as it comes off the wall, the returning player has every chance of hitting back a truly powerful shot using the ball's momentum and making it far more difficult for subsequent players to hit back. Obviously, the most important thing is that you don't end up on the receiving end of one of these powerful shots, and that you are able to return the ball successfully.

As I bounced the ball on the ground in preparation for my first shot, I realised that looking good in front of Jamie was of paramount importance. Clearly it had not mattered to him that on the previous occasion I had shown myself up by pretending I was interested in football when clearly I had no idea about the game. My hand went back as I aimed for a low shot and I hit a great one, coming off the wall at high speed and at such an angle that Benjy tripped over himself to return it. Success! His shot went straight in the air and was counted out, meaning that only myself, Jamie and his other friend Aaron – a short stocky guy with dark hair and a nose that had clearly been broken at some point in the past – were left in the game. As I had won the previous serve it was my turn again, and feeling much more confident this time, I attempted another dazzler. This time it was more of a mediocre shot as my hand had slipped slightly, and Jamie easily returned it with a great strike of his own meaning that Aaron had to run backwards a bit to get to the ball and hit his shot. Aaron's return was even more powerful however, and as the ball came off the wall I realised that the only way to get to it in time was to dive in Jamie's direction. This I did with all the dignity of a rhinoceros and I ended up hurling myself right into Jamie's stomach, almost winding him.

"Oh, so sorry, really sorry," I blurted out, a feeling of dread coming over me that I had actually hurt my beloved Jamie.

"Goodness, watch it will you!" he shouted, clearly suffering a little from the impact.

"Maybe we should stop the game for now," I said, worried that he would hate me for what I had done to him.

"Yeah, let's just rest a couple of minutes, it'll be okay," said Jamie. Unfortunately for us all, the bell rang for lesson time causing an abrupt end to anything further.

"I'm really sorry about that," I said as I walked back into the school building with Jamie, while Benjy and Aaron followed behind chatting to each other.

"It's fine, comes with the territory I guess. Hand tennis can be a rough game at times but well played! You're pretty good!"

"Really? I mean, thanks, I don't actually play often," I responded, feeling elated that I had received a real compliment from this wonderful creature.

I was set up for the rest of the day now, and simply could not wipe a smile from my face. I was sure that I now had enough of a basis to build something further with Jamie. Simon caught up with me just as I was entering the classroom for our maths revision lesson. Maths was probably one of my weakest subjects ever, but all pupils were forced to take it for their senior exams so I did not have much choice.

"Where were you at break time?" he asked, in a slightly accusatory tone.

"Oh, well, er, I decided to do some last minute revision alone so that I could concentrate," I replied sheepishly.

"We always do things like that together though. Why didn't you ask me? I could have done with revising too instead of wandering around looking for you!"

"Sorry, I just didn't think, but we definitely will next time," I offered.

"Well, it's not like you just to disappear like that. I could have actually hung out with Daniel Hart, who is boasting to anyone who will listen about the new LA Gear trainers he is wearing today and I really wanted to check them out."

"That sounds cool, I'm sure you'll get to see them later," I said, trying to move away from the subject of my apparent desertion.

The truth was that for the first time, I had actually forgotten all about my so-called best friend, and my pursuit of the wonderful Jamie had clearly become an all encompassing preoccupation.

"Okay, well let's just forget it and next time, find me before you go off somewhere, especially if it's for revision – I would much prefer to study with you than listen to the boring teacher droning on."

"Yeah, of course. Speaking of which, here comes Rabbi Lowe looking more miserable than ever. Do you think he ever grooms that awful beard? I think we're in for a long tedious hour…"

# Chapter 4

During the rest of term at school, my friendship with Jamie grew. We would spend more time together at break times and I also got to know his friends better. I once tried to introduce him to Simon, who simply looked down his nose at Jamie and later asked me why on earth I was paying this kind of attention to a boy in the year below us.

I was also supposed to be revising hard for fast approaching exams and although I still put some effort into that, my mind would always wander to Jamie. I think Simon sensed that I was beginning to distance myself from him and so started to develop more of a friendship with some other boys. We would still hang out together at weekends and also get together for revision sessions, but there seemed to be a more relaxed feel to our friendship now.

As far as I was concerned, I was in love with Jamie and any amount of time I could spend in his company made me feel wonderful. Ostensibly we were simply friends, and the reality was that he did not treat me any differently to anyone else in his group. Yet for the time being it was enough for me and I felt happier than I had remembered feeling for a long time. That is, until Jamie did not show up at school for a week. I had realised he was not there when I went at break time to the area we had come to hang out in, to chat with his friends and play hand tennis.

"Hey, where's Jamie? Has he been held up?" I asked Benjy.

"No, he's ill. I think it's the flu. He called me last night to tell me that he wouldn't be able to come to school as he had a temperature and had to stay in bed."

"Oh no!" I exclaimed, as my heart sank. "I really hope he gets better soon."

What on earth would I do without Jamie at school? And more importantly, he was ill and I wanted to be there with him, looking after him instead of his mother who was probably doing the job. I realised then, that I could no longer bear just being Jamie's friend. I simply could not contain my feelings and keeping them repressed was only making me more obsessed with him. But that would certainly mean an end to any kind of friendship, as surely if I told Jamie how I felt, he would recoil in horror. Another boy in love with him? Unthinkable! Yet I simply could not go on like this any more.

I spent the rest of the week forcing myself to revise and just about managed to sit through an English Literature exam. Back at home, I would spend the evenings in my room, trying to compose a letter to Jamie expressing how I felt. At first I thought I would write the letter just as a way of getting all my feelings out on paper so that they were not all trapped inside me. I had no intention of actually doing anything about it afterwards. However after a couple of evenings of writing, I decided that sending him the letter would be the best thing to do, as it would mean I could tell him how I felt without having the embarrassment of doing it to his face. Sending a letter would also give him time to digest everything I had to say and then realise in his own time that he felt the same way. At least, that was how I dreamed it would be.

In reality, what did I really expect? At least he would know my feelings and then hopefully come to terms with it all and still want to be my friend. The very notion of us becoming sweethearts however was something I knew was extremely unlikely. It still did not stop me spending every night in fervent prayer, asking God for Jamie's heart to be opened to me and promising that if my wish came true, I would try to be the best Jew ever despite loving another boy.

By some stealth, I managed to find out Jamie's address and decided, on the Sunday before his expected return to school, to go to his house and post the letter personally through his mailbox. I chose this option as opposed to simply putting it in the mail, so that I could see where he lived. When I found his home, I was initially a little surprised. He was clearly from a family of very modest means. The house was in a road filled with mainly shabby terraces. Jamie's house had an unkempt front garden and a rusty gate at the entrance. A good coat of paint was needed to brighten up this house, as a minimum. I wondered where Jamie's bedroom was and if for some reason he could see me out of his window? There was no sign of any movement at any of the windows however.

I very tentatively opened the gate and trod carefully towards the door. The intention was to simply drop the letter, clearly addressed to Jamie, through the mailbox and then make my escape. This would then give him time to read it and take it all in before returning to school, so that by the time he saw me the next day, he would not be in a complete state of shock and we could then have a conversation about what I had written and why.

As I put the letter through the door, a light came on in the front hall. Slightly startled, I turned to leave but the door then opened and a middle-aged woman appeared. She wore a headscarf with some stray greying hairs protruding out and some kind of quilted housecoat, with a high neckline and long sleeves.

"Yes young man, can I help you?" she asked curiously.

"Oh, er I'm a friend of Jamie's from school and just wanted to give him that letter. Can you make sure he gets it? I must go now as I need to get home."

"Jamie's not been well but he is feeling a lot better now. Are you sure you don't want to come in? He would probably be happy for some company, he's been confined to his bedroom all week."

As much as I wanted desperately to see Jamie and see what his room was like, I realised that it would be a very bad idea especially as I could not face him reading the letter in front of me.

"Oh, no that's fine, I really must go," I replied with a smile. "But thank you so much!"

"Okay dear, God bless you on your way."

So Jamie's family was clearly quite religious. He certainly did not appear to be so at school, but maybe that was his way of trying to assert some individuality away from his home environment. Now that I had met his mother, somehow it made Jamie seem all the more human to me. At least now he would have the letter and would finally know my true feelings.

Unfortunately, I was not prepared for the reaction I got the following day...

I had arrived at school feeling rather anxious about seeing Jamie as I was not quite sure what he would say, but was hoping for something positive. I did not actually see him until lunchtime in the dining hall where he was eating with his friends, and when he noticed me all hell broke loose.

"You faggot!" he spat, coming towards me and shoving me violently outside the main hall, pinning me to a wall. "I can't believe you did this to me!"

"Wh... what do you mean?" I managed, hoping desperately that nobody else could hear or see what was going on.

"Your love letter, you freak!" he hissed. "My mum read it and started interrogating me asking if I was gay. I didn't know what she meant until I read it myself! She's really nosy and nothing gets past her. Last night was hell for me, having to explain that I didn't know anything about it and must have a crazy stalker. There's NO way I'm gay!"

I immediately went a bright shade of crimson and wished there and then that the ground would swallow me up. Jamie's eyes, usually filled with laughter, now only radiated hatred. Those beautiful hazel flecks were now daggers of pure contempt.

"Can we go somewhere else and talk about this?" I begged.

"I NEVER want to see you or speak to you again, you poof! Don't you know that gays go to hell? You're disgusting!"

I twisted myself free from his grasp and ran straight into the nearest toilets, where I locked myself in a cubicle and burst into tears. What had I done? I felt like I could never face Jamie or any other boy from school again. I was certain that Jamie would tell his friends about the letter and that they would all start spreading gossip about me and treating me like I had the plague. My life was ruined, and the worst thing of all was that Jamie, the beloved centre of my world, could no longer stand the sight of me. Did I honestly think I was ever anything special to him anyway? I simply wanted to die.

The rest of the day passed in a haze for me. I did not dare to look anybody in the eye and was certain that I was now a laughing stock. Oddly, Simon seemed unaware of the incident earlier or at least he was acting like his usual self. I told him I was not feeling well, as my excuse for being uncommunicative.

That evening, at home, I lay on my bed and thought about what had happened and what I was supposed to do now. My exam period had now started and thankfully, I had the option of taking study leave and staying at home, only going into school for the exams. Until now, being at school was the highlight of my day and I had not wanted to stay at home when I knew I could see Jamie, but now clearly I needed to stay as far away as possible.

I knew that my whole infatuation with Jamie was purely in my own head. Due to my need for belonging somewhere and for being close to someone I had fallen for, I had allowed everything to take on a life of its own and for my desires to run rampant. Of course Jamie would never have considered me as anything more than a friend. Why would he? I was obviously the only boy in the school that liked other boys, or at least that was the case as far as I was concerned. Even the boys who were often picked on and called gay were probably not, in reality.

Jamie was right – it was against the Jewish religion for a male to show love to another male, and for that, I would go to hell. What had I done to deserve this? I had not chosen to be how I was although I knew I must have been created this way for a reason. A reason that I simply could not fathom. Was I destined for a life of unrequited love, surrounded by people who would never understand me? I prayed that it would not be so.

# Chapter 5

My senior exams had passed by and for a couple of weeks in the summer break, I went on holiday to Israel with Simon and two other friends from school who had somehow involved themselves in our plans. I had relatives in Israel, and had been there a few times to see them all with my family whilst growing up. This was the first time I had gone there without the rest of my family, and the thought of being free to do what I wanted was quite exciting. Simon's parents had an apartment in Tel Aviv, which we had been able to use while we were there so that made the whole trip worthwhile as we would have struggled to afford a hotel room, even if we had all shared it. We spent most of our time basking in the glorious Tel Aviv sun and generally relaxing on the golden sandy beaches or checking out local restaurants and shopping in the famous Dizengoff centre. Israel really was a magical place, infused with history and a perfect mixture of Middle Eastern and European culture, with a large dose of American commercialisation thrown in for good measure.

I was very thankful that I at least continued to have Simon for company and that I could always rely on him despite anything else. It was Simon that had suggested coming here, as a welcome break after the pressures of the exams and a far preferable option than hanging around in

London. The only thing I continued to hide was my sexuality, which by now was threatening to overtake me. Everywhere I turned while on holiday, there were semi naked men; in tiny bathing trunks on the beach, wearing skimpy t-shirts and shorts while walking along the streets. You simply could not escape them. The hot and humid Israeli weather did something to you; it made you feel continually aroused, which, especially for a young man of sixteen, was very hard to deal with. At least the ever present sun had helped to clear up my acne somewhat, which made me feel for the first time, relatively confident in my appearance.

On one of the evenings, we were supposed to be checking out a new bar that had opened on the sea front. There did not seem to be an age limit for getting into bars in Israel which meant as long as you generally looked old enough, you would be allowed in. I had a bit of a headache and decided that I would actually just take it easy instead, so Simon and the others went out for the night without me. After a while, I became quite bored stuck in the apartment and decided I would take a walk through the city. It was a balmy evening, and even at night, temperatures in Tel Aviv rarely dropped below twenty five degrees in the summer. I decided to walk down to the end of the beach front and for a minute, hesitated over whether I should go to the bar and try and find my friends. But in fact I was enjoying myself just being alone, taking in the gentle sea breeze. After walking for a while, I came across a small park that was situated behind one of the bigger hotels on the coastal strip. I decided to walk through the park, which graduated upwards to a kind of summit, on top of which I imagined was a nice view of the beach. As I wandered through it, I could see silhouettes ducking in and out of bushes, and some other figures hovering by a large monument in the centre of the park. At first puzzled by this, it suddenly dawned on me that I had stumbled into a whole new world. I instinctively shuddered, for I realised that these figures were all male, and that this park clearly acted as some kind of gay cruising ground at night.

I had never imagined that Israel, the Holy Land of the Jewish people, would harbour any kind of 'deviant' sexuality. Even though Tel Aviv itself had always been pretty cosmopolitan and was considered to be the most liberal and diverse of all Israel's cities, I still had not appreciated that gay activity could take place here, at least not so publicly. This was clearly a very naïve view, as I should have realised that there are gay people within any given community, who somehow or other will always find a way to express their needs. I decided to turn and leave the park as I was far too nervous to even try and go any further. As I turned around, I came face to face with a man. He was probably around twenty-five years old, tall, with dark skin, sparkling eyes and a lovely smile. In fact, he was probably one of the most attractive guys I had ever seen.

He reached out his hand and said in a smooth deep voice in Hebrew, "Hi, my name is Oren."

I took his hand and allowed him to shake mine gently.

"My name is Evan," I replied back in Hebrew, nervously.

"Where are you from?" Oren asked, his smile still pasted across his face.

"London. I'm here on my holidays with some friends," I said.

"Nice to meet you," replied Oren, who was now starting to stroke my hand gently with the tips of his fingers.

I was immediately overcome by extreme excitement and extreme nervousness at the same time, the result of which was feeling that I may actually throw up.

"I really have to go now, my friends are waiting for me," I managed, as I gently took back my hand and with a small awkward wave, turned and left the beautiful Oren behind.

I found it amazing that I had experienced such a situation in the park, but with the nervousness abating as I walked back along the seafront, my sexual excitement remained and when I returned to the apartment, I had to relieve myself before going to sleep.

For the rest of the holiday, my eyes were well and truly opened. I continually wondered if I would somehow bump into Oren whilst out with my friends somewhere and how many of the men walking around the city were actually gay. I simply could not believe that in an essentially Jewish country, gay men felt that they were able to act on their needs apparently without much guilt, whereas within the London Jewish community, I could not imagine any such kind of scenario. On one level, due to the mixture of the stifling heat and my sexual desires running rampant and overtaking any rational thought, I really had wanted to be able to do something further with Oren in the park. However in reality, I guess I was simply not ready to take that step and I knew I had made the right decision to leave when I did. In fact it would have been far better to have been able to talk to Oren more and ask him several questions about how he lived his life as a gay person in Israel, as a Jew. There was so much to understand and this had been the first opportunity for me to find some answers. Yet it was clear that he really only had one thing on his agenda. It did not actually cross my mind for a second whether or not it was even legal for a boy of my age to be having sex with anyone, let alone another male. Nevertheless, I now knew that if I needed to, I had a place to come back to where I could hopefully meet somebody to talk to and gain a better understanding of what life could be like for me in the future.

On arrival back in London where the sun rarely troubled you for long, I knew that my ongoing internal struggle would go on but that the far cooler weather would at least not make my libido go into overdrive. I also knew that although life in the Jewish suburbs of London seemed to offer me little hope of meeting any other gay people, I would always have the option of going back to Israel, and this buoyed me slightly. On receiving my exam results, I was very relieved that my grades were in fact pretty good considering that my attentions were truly elsewhere for the latter part of my exam year. I was now back at my school, my parents having convinced me that it was the best place to remain for my higher exams.

My feelings for Jamie had pretty much faded over the summer as well, as I seemed to have forced myself to get over him. The incident between us also now seemed like a distant memory, although it had left me with an indelible sense of shame, for allowing myself to have even gotten into such a situation. It was all for the best anyway, clearly nothing whatsoever could have happened with him and I knew that my attentions for any boy were not welcomed within my school environment. I was now fully aware that I was a gay male and knew that by its very nature, anything I did to act upon this would lead to condemnation from on High. I could never imagine telling my parents about my sexuality, or Simon or anyone else. It was a secret I had to live with, and I knew it would mean that if I wanted to live a life true to myself, I had to lead two separate existences as a result.

For the next few months, my thoughts turned more and more to my need to connect with other young gay men, if nothing else, to at least be able to meet someone who I could relate to. I knew this meant that I would need to find people who were not of the Jewish faith because at the time, I simply could not imagine how to find anybody within my community that was also gay. The fact was however, that this was far more difficult in practice. I had been brought up solely within a Jewish environment and did not even know anybody on a personal level that was from outside the faith. In fact, the Jewish religion discouraged any undue socialising between its members and those of other religions, for fear of assimilation. This meant that any friendships I might openly have with non-Jewish men would be strongly disapproved of by my family and friends, or at least lead to worries that I was somehow going off the rails. All of this only reinforced the fact that I would need to start leading a double life.

I was certainly far too nervous to start going out into the West End of London, where abundant night life and opportunities for liaisons presented themselves in their droves. Who would I be able to go with anyway and what would I do if I went to a gay bar or club alone? No, that was out of the question and far too scary. If I could not even handle a conversation with Oren in the park in Israel, how would I cope amongst a crowd of men, all probably looking for a hook up? I realised that the best option at this time would be to find some kind of gay youth group where everybody would be a similar age to me and would be in the same boat, taking their first steps into the gay world.

My father would often bring home from work a daily newspaper. Until now, the thought of browsing through it did not even enter my mind. After all, it was only full of boring news stories which I had no interest in and in any case, I would catch the evening news on TV if I really felt inclined. However one day after my father had brought the paper home, I decided that I would actually check it out. I skimmed through most of it, and then came to a section towards the back that ran some advertisements. Within this I spotted a heading entitled 'Adult Services'. These listings were mostly for massage services and consisted of images of women in lingerie, looking very suggestive with a number to call underneath. I was hoping to find some kind of listing for a gay community group, but then an advert caught my eye. It was an advert entitled 'Relaxing massage – man to man'. Could this really be what I thought it was? Even though I had told myself it was too soon for a sexual encounter, I nevertheless started to shiver with excitement.

At the age of sixteen and a half, sex between two males was still illegal in the UK. The current age of consent was eighteen years, something that the then Conservative government had voted on as a 'compromise' between the previous age of twenty-one, and the consensual age for heterosexuals which was sixteen. If only I was not permanently filled with desire for other males, I would not be thinking so much about actually doing something about it, legal or otherwise. I wanted so much to experience sex and yet, it still seemed an overwhelming thought. Should I call this number in the paper, or would it be a big mistake? Would the man at the other end be happy to just sit and talk to me? Surely if I told him I was not ready for sex, and simply wanted to be in the company of another gay male, he would understand? Looking through the paper in more detail, I also noticed a small handful of listings in the lonely hearts section which were under the heading 'Men seeking Men'. However these seemed to be people looking for either a relationship, which I was in no way ready to consider, or 'fun times'. I knew what that meant.

Feeling slightly disheartened, I closed the paper. After all, what was the point in trying to connect with a complete stranger who was blatantly only after one thing? At least I had my own imagination and right hand to help me release my sexual frustrations on a day-to-day basis, but I just needed someone to relate to on all levels, someone who would know what it was like to share my sexuality, and someone who was happy to accept me regardless of anything. I knew that I simply could not risk bringing any of this up with Simon, and risk damaging the friendship I relied on as much as I did. The worst part about all of this was that there was absolutely nobody in my world who I could talk to about any of it, and this was very difficult to live with.

I would often look around me and see other people happily going about their business; my sister, by now over eighteen, going out frequently with her friends and talking about boys; my younger brothers, mostly preoccupied with football, chart music and action movies; my parents working hard and looking wearier as time went on whilst keeping the household running as smoothly as possible, and then there was me and my world. Simon was by now completely obsessed with fashion labels and would phone me almost daily to describe in detail how fantastic his new shoes/shirt/jacket/belt was and how much it had cost. A few other friends from school would mostly be preoccupied with the opposite sex, music or even their studies for their higher exams. As for me, none of these things were of major interest. For some reason, I seemed to have no other real focus apart from my continual struggle to make sense of my life. If only my biggest problem was simply how to attract a girl from school, or how to get to grips with my latest essay, or how to find a way to earn money to buy the latest CD, gadget or item of clothing. My problem was much more fundamental than this. How do I work out how on earth I fit into this world and why have I been cursed with being a gay male in a religious Jewish community?

My seventeenth birthday was quite a fun experience for me. I went out with a small group of my friends, including Simon and a girl called Alex who I had gotten close to. Alex was in the same year as Simon and I, and attended the same school, on the separate girls' site. She was what you would call 'big boned', and had a long mane of thick, dark and very curly hair. The most prominent feature on her face was her nose, which was rather unfortunately quite hook-like. But she had a personality that was larger than life and she always made me laugh. Our first proper meeting was the result of my mother's efforts to get me to start spending time with nice Jewish girls from the local community. My mother, always hopeful that I would meet someone nice, had spoken to Alex's mother and arranged a date between Alex and me. We had gone to the cinema and shared popcorn and generally got to know each other. We clicked almost instantly in fact, but definitely in no more than a purely platonic way. After that, we spent more and more time together at weekends, which was made especially easy because we happened to both live round the corner from each other.

It was Alex who had suggested the venue for my birthday, which was a bar in Leicester Square, called the 'Zoom Bar'. It was a very popular venue and had a dance floor downstairs where a resident DJ played the latest hits. Although we were not yet legally allowed to drink alcohol, we had a great time dancing the night away, sipping soft drinks and generally having a laugh. I honestly felt freer than I could remember in a long time and for a few hours at least, my inner conflict did not trouble me.

After that, on most weekends and sometimes during the week, I would start hanging out with Alex, Simon and some other friends at various people's houses. We fast became a close-knit group and this suited me perfectly as I was now much more occupied in social activities than ever before. I also for the first time ever, felt like I might in fact belong somewhere. Alex was a bit like a whirlwind, as she always had random friends popping over to her place while I was there, with on-the-spot decisions being made about where we would go out. I found it all quite exhilarating. Of course, conversations would often turn to relationships and as it happened, most of the group would be dating someone or other at various points, so would relate their current dramas/problems/sexual shenanigans to the group. I found most of this fascinating, but never had anything to share on that front. It transpired that everyone except for me, had in fact at least had some kind of experience with the opposite sex, and were not ashamed to talk about it. Such conversations however, would always be out of earshot of anybody's parents who would almost certainly have disapproved of any pre-marital sexual activity.

Whenever it came to me, I would simply make up some excuse as to why I did not have any information to share. Mostly I would say that I preferred not to just date anyone, and that I was hoping for someone special. I would often get strange pitying glances from the rest of the group, as if to say that I was too uptight and needed to let my hair down like they were doing. It was as if I was the prude of the group. It was at times like this that I realised I still did not fit in with these people when it came down to it. It was all very well hanging out with them and enjoying their company, but at the end of the day, a huge part of me would never be able to express itself, and that was a soul-destroying feeling. To make matters worse, it had become common amongst people my age to tease others that were never seen to have a girl or boyfriend, calling them 'gay', 'queer', 'bender', 'lezza' – in fact any number of spiteful taunts. The utter humiliation on the faces of the poor victims only made it more apparent that to reveal yourself as a gay person would be the biggest mistake to make, and would lead to a sure social death.

As my seventeenth year rolled on, I knew I had a choice to make. Either I needed to bite the bullet and finally take the step to meet another gay male, or else try to conform fully with my group of friends in the hope that maybe I would, in fact, meet a girl and could convincingly pretend that something was happening between us. I did not have to think about this dilemma for very long. One evening, when we were all going out ice skating, Alex mentioned to me that a girl would be coming along who she had recently become good friends with at school. The friend would be meeting us at the ice rink and we would then all go in together. When we got there, I was introduced to her. Her name was Claire, which I found to be a beautiful and interesting name. She was quite tall and slim, with a pretty smile and long brown hair. There was a kind of inner warmth that radiated through her and I felt comfortable in her presence straight away. It did not take long for us to become engrossed in conversation, and while the rest of the group enjoyed themselves on the ice rink, we spent most of the time sitting and chatting away, with only the odd attempt to join the others skating.

Claire came from a small family and had one younger brother. She was certainly very intelligent and liked to read all manner of English literature, which was one of the subjects she was studying for her higher exams. Over the following few weeks, we would spend more time together, sometimes within the group but often alone, going out on what I suppose you would call a series of dates. Everything remained purely platonic however and there was no attempt on her part to initiate anything overtly physical with me, which suited me down to the ground.

One day, I was at Alex's house after school just relaxing and catching up on some gossip. Out of the blue, she asked me how I felt about Claire.

"Um, well, she's really nice," I replied. "We seem to get on really well and I like her company."

"So why on earth haven't you tried to kiss her yet?" asked Alex, looking at me rather quizzically. This took me by surprise, and I realised that Claire had obviously been talking to Alex about us.

"Er, I don't know really. I guess I'm just not ready for that yet."

"You're nearly eighteen years old for goodness sake! All of us have had at least one boyfriend or girlfriend by now, yet you never seem to talk about anyone, and we certainly haven't noticed anything. What's the problem? Claire is gorgeous and she really likes you."

Struggling to know what to say to this, I managed "I just don't know if I want to do anything yet, and anyway it's between me and Claire."

"Well, don't you know that she tells me everything? She's starting to wonder if there's something wrong with you. Is there?"

At this point, I became incredibly uncomfortable. Clearly there was a very good reason why nothing had happened so far, but there was no way I could explain this to Alex, who was looking at me as if I had just come from the moon.

"Well, I'll speak to Claire and we'll see," I said irritably. "Some things can't be forced you know. There's nothing wrong with me, so just leave it will you!"

"Fine, but she's waiting for you to make a move so I suggest you get on with it," Alex shot back.

When I got home, I began thinking about the conversation with Alex, and realised that there was no point in stringing Claire along. There was no way I could take it any further and although I really liked her as a friend, it was clear that she expected more. But how on earth could I explain myself to her? She was certainly an attractive girl, one that my parents would definitely approve of, yet I had no interest of a sexual nature in her whatsoever. I wished that she could have been a boy. I started to imagine myself in a parallel world, one in which my desire for other males was not an issue and that any attentions I may show someone, had every chance of being requited. It was a world where somehow, the Jewish religion was accepting of who I was and where my parents encouraged me to meet other boys. If only that were the case, I would have been happy and fulfilled a long time ago. What a cruel world I lived in. Having to guard my secret was killing me every day and trying to act just like the others in my group of friends was clearly not working. Nervously, I picked up the phone and called Claire.

# Chapter 6

Things were never quite the same within the group after I had told Claire we could only be friends. I had tried to explain myself as best I could to her, assuring her that it was me and that I enjoyed our friendship so much that I did not want to risk ruining anything by taking it further. She had told me she was disappointed in me as we could have had something great together and I was clearly too short-sighted. What was that supposed to mean? Although we continued to see each other within the group, things certainly cooled between us. I felt disappointed in myself in fact, for having let Claire down but I knew there was no other way it could have continued.

Alex also was not overly impressed with me, for a while continuing to tell me that I had lost a good thing there and that I probably had some issues that I should sort out. I became very paranoid as I was not sure if anyone may have picked up on something about me. All I knew was that things seemed to have changed somewhat. Simon was becoming quite close with a girl called Jenny and a guy called Adam, who were both trendy types, and were considered the ones that lead the way in the group in terms of knowledge of fashion and anything cutting edge. Simon, always interested in anything to do with fashion, would lap up their every word and attempt to develop a look that mirrored their own. It even led to him dating Jenny for a while. I started to feel that we were moving in opposite directions and that I was no longer of much interest to him. I suppose thinking about it, I did not really share his main passions, so there would be less and less for us to talk about.

Once again, I felt alone and despite being in a group of friends who were generally happy to hang out with me, I did not feel connected to what was going on. It was time for me to finally get on and pursue my ever more pressing need to connect with other gay men. It was just a question of finding the courage to take the first step into the gay world with the belief that surely after that, I would be able to meet people easily enough that would help me on my journey. As my higher exams were coming up shortly, I decided to try and concentrate as much as possible on revision so that at least I could get decent grades and try to make my parents proud of me. That would hopefully alleviate some of the guilt I would no doubt feel after having done something to feed my desires.

A couple of months later, my higher exams finally arrived. I had chosen to study English Literature, French and Economics. Although the exams were quite difficult, I found that I was relatively confident in being able to do well as I had put quite a lot of effort into studying. I had actually spent a meaningful amount of time with Simon again leading up to the exams, as we had always found each other helpful for revising, and worked well together. It was good to get closer to Simon again especially as I realised I quite missed his company on a one-to-one level. In between study sessions, he would update me on things he had done, mostly with Jenny and Adam, new clothes designers he was interested in and what he thought about new music in the charts. I continually marvelled at how he managed to keep apace of developments in the celebrity and fashion world. I suppose that whereas with me, my sexuality and reconciliation issues had taken up my time and concentration, he would not have had such issues and could therefore concentrate on the kinds of things that most regular teenagers were interested in.

On thinking about my relationship with Simon, I actually realised that as we had gotten older, the things we would speak about together had become more and more frivolous. I had always thought that Simon was quite a deep person but ever since we had turned sixteen, he had certainly become a slave to transient teenage pleasures. This probably had a lot to do with our group of friends I suppose. Maybe it was just me, but I had started to wonder if I had become entirely too caught up in my own issues, big as they appeared to be, instead of just trying to relax and have fun with whatever life threw my way, hence making me come across as too serious to others. It was something that made me feel resentful about my religion and my relationship with God, because if such issues had not been thrust upon me in the first place, I would have been far more able to integrate with my friends more fully and be more relaxed like they were.

It was now the summer of 1992. After having taken my higher exams, my parents told me that they wanted me to consider a summer programme being run at a seminary in Israel by one of the local Rabbis, who was trying to encourage young adults to engage more with their heritage. The programme was aimed mostly at less religious young men who were interested in getting more to grips with their culture and who for whatever reason, did not feel connected to it on a day-to-day basis at home but it also attracted several religious guys who felt the experience would be valuable. I decided that in fact this might be an interesting opportunity for me to kill two birds with one stone as it were; it would enable me to go back to Israel and hopefully find a way to rediscover the lost opportunities of a couple of years ago, whilst also doing something that my parents wanted for me. Maybe it would even do me some good in the process by bringing me back to a healthier place in my relationship to God. I also realised that by going on the programme, it would mean I would be spending my eighteenth birthday in Israel, without my group of friends. I had no real desire to hold a big party with my friends in London anyway and quite relished the thought of just letting my birthday go by with no fuss.

When I told the group about my decision to go on the programme in Israel, I received a mixed response. Alex told me that she had been thinking of going somewhere in Europe for a relaxing beach holiday, and why on earth would I want to spend my well-earned break holed up in a seminary with a load of Rabbis? Especially as surely I would have had enough of that whilst at school. Simon told me that he may actually consider coming along just for a week or two because his parents had also mentioned the programme to him, and would then probably spend the rest of the time with Alex or Jenny. This heartened me somewhat, as it meant I could at least have someone with me for a while that I knew well. The remainder of the group made noises about it being a waste of time and that they were all intending to take their own trips abroad at various points over the summer in any case.

Before I left for Israel a couple of weeks later, I received a few birthday cards in advance from the group, all wishing me a good time and sorry they would not be with me to celebrate on the day. As far as I was concerned, I was quite looking forward to just getting there, seeing what lay in store for me at the seminary, and best of all seeing if I had the courage to finally go out and meet some men. I had not in fact done much towards that goal before my exams, as my studies had ended up taking most of my time, but mentally I felt more ready than ever before. My memory of that experience in the park a couple of years previously had stayed with me ever since and I knew that I would be going back there as soon as I could. Yet again, just the thought of this gave me shivers of pure anticipation.

When I arrived in Israel, along with a small group of others who would be attending the seminary programme, we were met by our Rabbi at the airport. His name was Rabbi Levine and he was responsible for looking after our welfare throughout the term of the programme. He was considered a representative of 'Modern' Orthodox Judaism. That meant that he had a very inclusive approach, and spoke to people on their own level, thereby drawing them in as a friend as much as anything else. This was markedly different from the approach most other Rabbis took, of being almost aloof, unwavering and intolerant of any deviations from the code of conduct as laid down by the religion. I felt that Rabbi Levine was in fact a breath of fresh air and that maybe he and others like him at the seminary could re-galvanise my interest in Judaism. It also crossed my mind that I may have an opportunity to talk to him in private at some point about my ongoing struggle and see if he would be open enough to help me make sense of it all.

Over the next couple of weeks, I immersed myself in the programme and got used to my surroundings. The seminary itself was in the historic capital of Israel, Jerusalem. The complex had a very large building with a flat roof, laid out in a square shape, with a huge courtyard at the centre. The building was made of white stone slabs, called 'Jerusalem Stone', whose main properties were the ability to reflect the sun's rays rather than absorb them. This was extremely common throughout Israel and gave most of the buildings a distinctive architectural look and feel. The students were put up in rooms, mostly sharing with a couple of others. It was a very dormitory like existence. I also met a number of other young adults some of whom had come from countries such as the USA and Russia, and it was quite refreshing to get to know people from such different places. A typical day for us would include waking up for morning prayers at about seven in the morning, followed by a hearty breakfast and then attendance at a number of lectures and seminars covering a whole range of different topics, broken up by lunch and relaxation time. In the evenings, a huge buffet was laid out in the dining hall which everybody would enthusiastically tuck into, and following that there would be communal evening prayers before being able to retire or simply go out and explore the surrounding area. Every few days, there would also be a trip organised where anybody that wanted to go, could visit some of the other holy cities around Israel, and learn more about Jewish history and events that had occurred during biblical times. It really was a fascinating programme.

On one of the weekends, which I was spending at the home of some of my cousins in Tel Aviv, I decided that I would go back to the park I had been to on my previous trip. It was quite a warm evening and very humid and I just did not feel like going to bed or spending time with any of the others. Thankfully, I had my own key to my cousins' apartment and was able to come and go as I pleased, so I had no worries about being questioned later. As I made my way towards the beach front in the direction of the park, I started to become very nervous again at the thought of what might happen there. Maybe I would see Oren again? Despite being so nervous, I decided that I would definitely take the next step this time as it was long overdue. I had not even kissed anyone before now!

I found my way eventually to the park and tentatively went inside. Once again, I could see a few shadowy figures roaming around, with the large monument appearing to be the main centre of all activity. I took a deep breath and strolled with as much purpose as I could muster, up towards the large structure. When I got there, I realised that there were a few openings at the side, and that if you ducked your head, you were able to step inside the monument which seemed to be pretty black. I wondered how anybody could see anything when they went in there. I had not yet realised that this was in fact the point! I hesitated, unsure of what to do. Then I looked up and I noticed a man staring at me intently. On checking him out, I saw that he was in fact rubbing his crotch and smiling at me in a lewd fashion. I froze with fear. What should I do? Does he want me to go up to him and touch him, or go with him inside? I was not quite expecting this. I turned and slowly walked away, deciding that despite my best efforts, I was still not ready for such an anonymous encounter. As I continued walking, I felt a hand on my shoulder. I turned around and saw that it was the same guy that had been rubbing himself in front of me just before. He smiled at me again, and at this close distance his mouth revealed a couple of crooked front teeth, which gave him quite a quirky cuteness.

"Uh, sorry, I don't want anything," I said in Hebrew.

"You are cute, why don't we take a little walk together?" he replied.

"Sorry, I'm really not sure…"

Before I could continue, the man leant towards me and kissed me full on the lips. It took me completely by surprise, but also awakened something in me. Before I knew it I was responding to him, and we ended up in full embrace. I had never experienced such euphoria before! Just the feeling of this man's mouth on mine, his warm breath and hands that caressed me as he kissed, was quite overwhelming. I became extremely excited, and as his hand started rubbing gently on my groin, I exploded in my pants. Now this was extremely embarrassing!

I pulled away from him and as he noticed what had happened, he simply smiled at me again, shrugged his shoulders, turned and walked away back up towards the monument. I was not sure what to think; was this all I had been good for? It would have been nice to at least have been able to talk to him properly without any of the sexual pressure and ask him questions I had about how he felt being a gay man in a Jewish country. Leaving the park, I thought that at least I had experienced my first kiss with a man, something I had only imagined for so long. Then a thought struck me. Would this mean I would now go to hell and have my soul cut off for eternity? Jewish scriptures called homosexuality an 'abomination', with the punishment being death and having your soul cut off from God's source. I started to panic. What had I done?

What was going to happen to me? I spent the walk back to my cousins' apartment praying fervently that God would take pity on me and that I was only doing what I needed to do, and that it was God's fault anyway for having created me this way. I ended up spending the whole night in restless sleep, with bizarre dreams of being tortured somehow for my grave sin.

Three weeks after I had started the summer programme, Simon, true to his word arrived at the seminary. I was extremely happy to see him because I was actually missing the group somewhat and nobody more so than Simon. He told me that he had been spending the last few weeks hanging out with Jenny, Adam and Alex mostly, and they had been on a weekend away to Paris too, which by all accounts was a very enjoyable time. I felt sudden pangs of jealousy as I realised that I had not been part of such a fun experience and that my friends were happily doing things without me. Although I certainly had enjoyed my time at the seminary so far, I was still unsure what it would actually achieve in the end. I had not attempted to speak to Rabbi Levine about my ongoing issues and most of the lectures and seminars were focused on areas of Judaism such as love of God, making relationships work between a man and a woman and the spiritual meanings behind the Jewish laws and practices. Although interesting enough in their own right, I needed to have my burning questions answered and until that was the case, anything else would always seem to fall short.

Simon stayed for two weeks, during which time we mostly stuck together and I introduced him to some of the other people I had met. He did not seem that interested in developing any new friendships however, although at least I had him to myself again. Afterwards, he told me that he had done enough to keep his parents off his back and he was going to return to London where he and Alex were then planning on going to Spain on a cheap deal she had managed to find. It struck me that Simon had not even asked me if I wanted to join them which brought back a pang of jealousy. Was I no longer considered important enough to be included in my friends' activities? I then thought that maybe he assumed that I would want to spend most of the summer at the seminary, so I decided just not to bring it up.

After Simon had left, I decided I would speak to Rabbi Levine. One day after morning prayers and breakfast, I approached him and asked to speak to him in private. He happily agreed, probably thinking I would want to engage him in an interesting theological discussion. There was certainly something about Rabbi Levine that made you feel comfortable in his presence and like you could almost tell him anything, which certainly made it easier for me in a way. We went into one of the offices, a sparsely decorated room with stone walls and a couple of tapestries hanging up, an old solid wood desk with some papers, books and a telephone on it, a long filing cabinet and some chairs. This room was clearly only used for administrative purposes.

We sat down, face to face.

"So Evan, how are things going for you here? Enjoying yourself I hope?"

"Yes thanks, I am really very grateful that you have looked after us all so well and I'm learning a lot already," I replied, attempting to sound as positive and enthusiastic as I could.

"That's wonderful," gushed the rabbi. "So tell me, what is it I can help you with? Is there a specific question you would like me to answer?"

I was suddenly overcome with the seriousness of what I was about to bring up and this made me feel quite queasy. Nevertheless, it was now or never, and I simply had to get this out of the way.

"Erm, well, I have this really big problem and I've been keeping it to myself for as long as I can remember. I actually don't even know where to begin…"

"Well, just begin however you want, and the rest will simply follow," the rabbi said reassuringly.

This was it, I was about to tell someone the truth about me for the first time! I felt an overwhelming sense of pure nervousness and fear.

"I'm attracted to other guys," I blurted out, my heart beating so fast I thought it would burst right out of my chest.

Rabbi Levine sat there, his face expressionless. I was not quite sure what to make of this; was he taking in what I had just said, was he in total shock or was he just waiting for me to continue and explain myself further? I decided that I should just continue, especially now that I had dropped the bombshell.

"Well, you see, I have known since I was little that there was something different about me that I couldn't put my finger on, and as I've grown older, it has become clear to me that I was born gay, but I know that Judaism doesn't accept this, and I have no idea what to do about it."

It was at this point that the rabbi spoke again, his face suddenly taking on a very serious expression.

"Do you really think that you are the first person who has had such a problem, the first person that has had issues with their sexuality?"

"Er, well, I don't know…" I began to answer, but was cut off by the rabbi.

"In life, every person endures several tests. These tests are set by God, who wants us all to fulfil our utmost potential in this world. We can be tested on absolutely anything, and this helps us to overcome obstacles and barriers to true spirituality and true connection with the Divine source. Homosexuality is one of these tests and those who are set the challenge must use it as an opportunity to break through their animal desires and truly embrace the sanctity of relationships between men and women and the holy gifts of marriage and children."

Was I hearing this correctly? Did my sexuality simply boil down to sexual activity alone and was it just a test, something which I should view as a challenge to get over? Surely the way I had been feeling all my life and the internal struggles that had plagued me since the start of my adolescence were so much more than just sex. Surely this was not just some cruel trial imposed on me by God?

"Rabbi Levine," I replied, trying to stay as calm as I could, "if I understand you correctly, you are telling me that homosexuality comes down to physical desire and that this is something that can be controlled somehow like any desire. With all due respect, looking back on my life I have known that I was gay since childhood, from an age where the physical aspect of sexuality did not even figure in my mind. How can you simply bring it all down to animal desires, when for the most part, it is far more fundamental than that and is part of my very nature?"

The Rabbi suddenly looked at me even more seriously, his eyes boring directly into mine. I felt suddenly like a tiny creature, about to be devoured by a fearsome predator.

"Do not think for one minute that homosexuality is an acceptable lifestyle, Evan. At its essence, it is against the order of creation as God intended. The Jewish religion encompasses the values of marriage and children, on which the foundations of the religion can continue and flourish through education to future generations. As you are no doubt aware, our sacred Torah expressly forbids homosexual acts and condemns them in the strongest possible terms. Of course, we are commanded to love our fellow man and this is certainly a requirement between males, although the kind of love the Torah refers to is platonic love, showing the highest amount of mutual respect for one another. Anything more than this is simply a perversion of our natural inclinations. As I have mentioned just now, we are all faced with tests in life, and it may be that you feel this is the biggest test you will have in your life. I am happy to recommend some people you can speak to further to help you if you want?"

I was simply stunned by this response, not quite knowing what to say next. Had I really kidded myself that Rabbi Levine might in fact understand where I was coming from and somehow try to reassure me that I could still be who I was and be accepted within my religion? I felt almost a sense of derision now for this man sitting opposite me, someone who I had thought was different from the rest but who clearly, underneath it all, was just the same. I stood up.

"Rabbi, I came to you because I honestly believed I could talk to you about anything, that somehow you would understand things that other Rabbis show no tolerance of. I have just told you that ever since I can remember, I have essentially been gay, which is something that encompasses my entire being and is not simply a sexual desire, although obviously I also have those desires. I have had emotional feelings towards other males for so long now, a need to be loved and wanted by them in the same way as I believe heterosexual males feel about women. I was born this way, I am convinced of it, and for you to just say that it's some kind of base sexual instinct that needs to be overcome, shows that you don't actually understand what I am going through. How would you like it if just by being who you are, you were told you could never act on it or be true to yourself? That you had to live life being lonely because you were never allowed to show any love that you felt to a female partner? This is not just about sex, it's about everything that matters in life! You simply don't understand what it's like for me and I'm sorry I came to speak to you." I then turned and ran from the room.

# Chapter 7

After my eventful meeting with Rabbi Levine and managing to calm down somewhat, I decided I needed to leave the programme. After all, his view was his view, he was simply defending what was already expressed in the Torah and I guess it was his job to do that fundamentally. I just felt a deep sense of loneliness once again, knowing that I had nobody that understood me or who was willing to help me find a path in life that I could be fulfilled in on every level. I had learned many things during the programme and had enjoyed it on the whole but now knowing that I would have no support or understanding whatsoever with regard to my situation, what was the point in staying? It had already been six weeks and I realised that I was also completely out of the loop with regard to what my friends were up to.

I decided to head back to London where my parents would no doubt be proud that I had lasted this long at the seminary. It also meant I could catch up with the group and also finally take the first step into gay life. I simply could not afford to be scared any more, nobody was going to live my life for me and it was up to me to make things happen. The small taste of possibility I had experienced in the park this time round was more than enough to tempt me on.

After calling home and explaining that although I had enjoyed myself it was time to come back, I made my travel preparations. There had been two more weeks left in fact, but I realised my departure was already overdue. Before I left, Rabbi Levine came to bid me farewell, and reminded me that I should think very seriously about his offer of some help. Exactly what kind of help he had really meant had never been made clear although I had not given him the chance to go into that in any detail. I waved Israel goodbye, knowing that I would be back again soon, but on my own terms.

Before coming to Israel, Simon and I had both applied for a couple of Universities in London to study Modern European history, politics and literature, with an emphasis on France and Italy. It was a degree that seemed to interest both of us and I was very happy that it would mean we could potentially study together at the same place. Acceptance was dependant on getting certain grades in my higher exams but I was sure I had done well enough to at least get in somewhere. I knew that Simon certainly would not have a problem as he had always achieved slightly higher grades than I had at school. I was in fact quite excited, because I also knew that this would be the first time I would be mixing with the wider world and the possibility of meeting some like-minded gay people at university filled me with anticipation. On arrival back home, I had some mail waiting for me, amongst which was a letter from my school confirming my grades. Holding my breath, I opened it to discover that I had done pretty well, achieving an A, B and C grade. This was more than I needed to get into university, and when I told my parents, they were extremely happy. My preferred choice was University College London otherwise known as UCL, right in the centre of town and very prestigious. I had chosen not to leave home and experience a University in another city, because I felt that London probably had the most to offer in terms of gay life and that I really needed to start exploring the possibilities on my own doorstep. With another month or so to go before the start of the university term, I decided to focus all my efforts on moving forward with realising my gay self.

One day, after having caught up with Simon, Alex and a couple of other friends for lunch and exchanging exam results, I decided I would head into the West End and venture into the vibrant gay district called Soho. Although the idea of doing this alone still made me nervous, I was nevertheless rather excited and knew that I just had to take that step. I also thought that it would be better for my first experience to be during the day as opposed to at night, when I imagined things might be more full-on. Whilst travelling there on the underground, I imagined all the things that might be waiting for me in Soho: shops and bars to visit and friendly people to talk to. I shivered expectantly.

Soho was a very interesting place for sure, and not quite like I had imagined it would be. Just on the edge of Chinatown, itself a sight to behold, Soho stood there proudly; proud to be different from its surroundings and proud to be the centre of a liberal, fun-loving and party-focused community of people. Colourful shops abounded, selling all manner of different things from revealing underwear to what seemed to be more overtly sexual paraphernalia. There were also several restaurants dotted along the streets and a number of bars with rainbow flags hanging outside, which I understood to be the universal symbol of the Gay movement. I had imagined that the area would be filled with men wandering around hand in hand or kissing each other. Although there were a few obvious male couples roaming the streets, it seemed to be quite a relaxed and mixed type of area albeit with a more characterful presence than most places. There were at least as many heterosexual couples as gay people, hanging around and mingling effortlessly with each other, some chatting away and laughing together. This at first took me by surprise as my only experience of heterosexual people's attitudes to gays was that of hostility. I had an immediate sense that this was a world I could truly get lost in, somewhere I could remain anonymous if I wanted to but at the same time, have as much fun as I could handle. The real question was where to start?

I decided to go into what was ostensibly a bookshop, to try and find a gay guide or something similar. On browsing the shelves, it became apparent that most of the literature in here was of a pornographic or erotic nature. I reached and took down one of the larger books, which was entitled *Adventures of Tom the Sailor*. On the front cover was an animated drawing of a hugely muscled man with a sailor outfit and a moustache. He was smiling broadly and I noticed that his erect manhood was protruding from his pair of tight breeches. I became immediately excited, and embarrassed that I had reacted so quickly to a picture like this. I opened the book, and realised that it was mainly filled with images of 'Tom the Sailor', in all manner of sexual situations with other men. My eyes became glued to the pages, as hard core positions unfolded in front of me. Thinking I might explode if I continued, I put the book back on the shelf, counted slowly to ten and then headed towards the staircase of the shop that led down to another floor below.

On this floor, I could not quite believe my eyes. On the walls hung various sex toys including different sized dildos, some monstrously huge. I could not imagine what people would be able to do with them. On the other wall were shelves stacked with videos of pornographic material, and by the cashier desk was a balding guy of probably around forty years old, nonchalantly checking his nails as a hard core film played on the screen behind him. My excitement stuck in my throat. I wanted so much to buy something here and examine it in detail in the privacy of my room at home. But would I have the courage to actually take something to the desk and purchase it? My heart beat faster as I thought about it. If I did buy something, would I be able to successfully hide it from my parents, or even my siblings? They did not go into my room normally so at least that was something, but would I feel confident enough that whatever I bought would be well enough hidden just in case? After a few moments, I went back upstairs and left the shop, deciding that at this point it was simply not worth the risk of being discovered. The problem being however, that I had become so very turned on by everything around me that I needed more than ever to be able to do something about it. But what, and how?

Walking back along Old Compton Street, which appeared to be the main thoroughfare in Soho, I decided to go into one of the bars that seemed quite empty. I had noticed at the entrance that there was a stack of papers and flyers which I wanted to check out. I was sure that some of this must be information telling me more about the facilities around here. I picked up one of the papers. It was called *Boyz*, and I noticed on the back cover of the paper, a picture of the 'hottie of the week', which was essentially a naked man in a seductive pose. I went up to the bar and ordered a soft drink, then sat down to look through the paper in detail. Most of it contained articles about gay life and culture and celebrity trivia, which I found pretty interesting. It had a section with bar and club listings, showing several photos of people at various club nights, which I told myself I would love to experience soon. Towards the back was an agony uncle column called 'Dear Daniel'. It had a small photo of Daniel himself, with a kind smile and welcoming eyes. The problems that week covered topics such as 'My boyfriend is cheating on me, what should I do?', 'I'm secretly in love with my straight best friend' and 'I really want to go all the way but I'm scared'. Daniel's answers to these problems were thoughtful, open, frank and non-judgemental. I found myself thinking what a breath of fresh air this was, and so different from the emotionally pressurising and guilt-inducing way that a Rabbi might handle a controversial issue. After this, was a listings page featuring several help lines for various sorts of problems. Looking down the list, I came to a phone number for a 'Coming out help line'. The description explained that it was a number especially for young gay people to call if they had coming out issues or wanted to experience the gay scene for the first time. This was exactly what I was after! Someone I could just talk to on the phone, who would listen to everything I had to say and maybe even point me in the direction of a gay youth group. Feeling much better about things, I tore out the section of the page with the number on it and made my way home.

Throughout the evening, my mind remained focused on the help line number, and after dinner when I had the opportunity, I went up the road to the nearest phone box and dialled it. I certainly did not want to risk anyone in my family overhearing me. The man that answered the phone had a very gentle and calming voice. I thought that he must have been chosen mainly for this voice, which made me feel instantly at ease as I was sure it did for others too. Unlike with Rabbi Levine in Israel, I did not have to worry about telling this man anything, as he was there to listen to me specifically about issues of my sexuality. I explained my background as a religious Jew and the fact that I had trouble dealing with that and my sexuality at the same time. I also wanted to know if there were any groups I could join where I could meet people of my own age. Surprisingly, the man at the other end told me that he too was Jewish. He was from a more liberal background however, but after having come out to his parents, they had such trouble dealing with it that he had decided to stop speaking to them altogether. I found this quite extreme, as even though I could not imagine what my parents' reaction might be if I came out to them, I still could not think of cutting them out of my life. The man, who told me his name was Alan, then said that in fact he knew of someone who ran a small group where young adults like me, met up once a week and discussed all manner of issues together. The group apparently also went out to visit bars and clubs together, where the young guys could experience gay nightlife yet feel secure and protected if they needed to. This sounded ideal! I simply could not believe I had struck it so lucky. Alan then told me that it would be nice if we met up, so that he could introduce me to his friend and I could talk to them further to become more comfortable about joining the group. I thought that sounded like a great idea, and we arranged to get together that weekend.

Over the following couple of days, I spent time with Simon and Alex who both told me that following their exam results, they had decided what they would do next. Simon told me that he was indeed going to go to UCL, which meant that we would get to study the same degree together. Alex had decided not to go to university and that she would in fact do a diploma in psychology at a college and then try out teaching. I was very happy for both of them and thought that as long as we stayed close friends, that was what counted. On several occasions my mind kept wandering to the forthcoming meeting I would have with Alan, and the whole new world I would finally become part of. I must have been smiling to myself because at one point, Simon asked me what I was thinking about. Not daring to tell him the truth, I simply said I was so happy that we had all done well so far in our studies and I was excited to be going onto the next stage of life. Thankfully, this seemed to be a satisfactory response.

The weekend finally arrived, and I found myself nervously awaiting Saturday night, which was when I was scheduled to meet up with Alan. He had told me that often, he would get together with his friend's group and accompany them out on the town at weekends which meant that after we had our initial meeting, he could come with me to meet the group. I felt very honoured that a man I had not actually met was prepared to focus on me in this way and I certainly was not used to this kind of attention. We had arranged to meet outside an underground station in north London called Hampstead at eight o'clock and then go to a bar just across the road called King William IV. It was one of the only gay bars in the North West suburbs of London and apparently very popular. I left my house at seven-thirty and eagerly went to the station to catch the underground. I arrived a little early in fact and so waited outside the station. It suddenly occurred to me that we had not given each other a proper description of ourselves and would we be able to recognise each other? However before long, a man approached me. He was of average height, probably around his mid-thirties, with short dark hair and dark eyes with several crow's feet at the sides.

"Are you Evan?" he asked, a kind smile on his face.

"Yes I am. I guess you're Alan?"

"That's right. Really good to meet you," he said warmly as he shook my hand.

"Come on, let's not stand outside, it's getting a bit cold. The bar is just over there," he pointed, and with that we headed inside.

After we entered the bar, which was quite big and old but with a warm, inviting atmosphere, Alan bought us some drinks. I had decided that seeing as I was eighteen now, I should try something alcoholic which was not normally of much appeal to me, having been brought up in a mainly non-drinking environment. On being asked what I wanted, I ordered a vodka and tonic as I had heard someone ordering this as we came in. I glanced around me and saw various men both young and older, seated happily whilst chatting away, some of them looking a little more intimate. I marvelled at the fact that a gay bar existed in this area, outside of the West End and relatively close to where I lived. Maybe I could come here more often?

Once both seated with our drinks, we began to talk in more depth. Alan asked me about my life, my experiences so far and what I was most interested in discovering about the gay world. We ended up chatting for what seemed like ages about my thoughts, feelings about my religion and my need to find like minded people I could relate to. I felt more connected to Alan because he was Jewish and this was a big bonus for me. However it turned out that Alan did not have much interest in the religion and to all intents and purposes, was an agnostic.

"I have never really believed that there was a God, ever since I was a teenager," he explained. "I'm sure there must be something up there and I'm happy to be proved wrong but I don't feel any real connection to it. For me, life is about what you make of it and the experiences that you have are what shape you and drive you forward in a certain direction. I don't believe in a pre-destined fate of any sort."

"Well, that's fine," I replied. "I was brought up quite religious, so God has always been at the centre of everything for me really. That's why I have found it so hard to deal with my sexuality while living a religious life, because I haven't been able to find any answers anywhere."

"I can tell you are a good soul, Evan," said Alan reassuringly. "I'm sure that absolutely nothing bad will happen to you. You are also incredibly cute, which I'm sure you get told often."

"Erm, well actually I don't," I replied as I started to blush. I had not expected a comment like that from Alan and in any case certainly did not consider myself cute.

"Well, we must have been in here for at least a couple of hours now. Do you want to go for a walk in the fresh air, and we can talk some more?"

"I thought we were going to meet your friend and the group at some point?"

"Well, yes of course we will. It would just be nice to get some air first."

"Well okay, sure, that would be cool," I responded, thinking that I had finally met a guy that could understand me and was happy to just listen and help me feel better about things. The feeling that he may also be attracted to me after his comment, hovered in my mind but I knew I could trust Alan and was not worried in the least. In fact meeting the group did not seem quite as important for the moment.

As we walked along, I realised that we were heading away from the High Street. I was not sure of the direction we were taking, but was happy to simply chat away and take in the fresh evening air. After a while, I noticed that we were walking into what was clearly some woodland. This seemed slightly strange to me although maybe there was a nice view or something somewhere that I was going to be shown. We walked further into the woods and I realised that this must be Hampstead Heath, a place that I had read about and where apparently several gay men went to cruise for sex at night. I started to notice random figures roaming in and out of the bushes and trees – in a way this reminded me of the park in Israel. What were we doing here? It then dawned on me that Alan probably wanted to try and have sex with me here. I stopped walking suddenly.

"Er... Alan, is there something you are trying to tell me by bringing me here?" I asked hesitantly.

"To be honest," he replied, "I really wasn't sure how to bring up the fact that I find you extremely attractive and hoped you got the hint earlier. I thought that if we walked through here you would work it out for yourself."

He then looked at me with a strange, almost lewd expression. Was he getting excited? Was this the sort of thing he did with other young guys? On one hand, I thought that I should feel disappointed and shocked that Alan would attempt this roundabout way of coming onto me when he was supposed to be in a position of responsibility and someone I could talk to about sensitive and fundamental issues. However just by looking at him and his obvious excitement, I began to respond, my constant underlying sexual frustration rapidly coming to the fore. On a whim, I decided to let myself go. I had also had a few drinks which certainly helped to make me feel more carefree. Alan grasped me and began to kiss me against a tree. His kisses were soft yet persistent and for a moment, made me feel like I was being transported to another place. As his hands travelled over my body, I felt myself pressing further against him, my own hands starting to roam. I pulled away after a while to draw breath, and it then occurred to me that should anything further happen, my first real time with someone would have been outside, against a tree in Hampstead Heath. Whereas in Israel, the thought of doing anything in the park, in the heat and overlooking the beach had an exotic feel to it, in the cold night air in an English park was a totally different matter. Is this really how I imagined it would be? It was hardly the most romantic setting, or even very private!

"Look, Alan." I began. "I didn't expect this to happen and I thought we were just getting to know each other. I would rather wait until I feel more comfortable if that's okay. I just don't feel right being outside in public like this. I can see people wandering around and it makes me a bit nervous."

"Don't worry, if anyone comes near us I'll sort them out. Just enjoy the moment," he replied breathlessly, immediately attempting to kiss me again.

"No, stop... can we maybe go somewhere else or to your place or something and just talk some more?"

"Don't be silly, we've spoken enough already and besides you've got me all excited now, so let's carry on," he said breathlessly as he started to manhandle me again, this time more roughly.

At this point something snapped inside me. Alan's persistence had become a bit scary and he clearly had no intention of stopping anything regardless of what I wanted.

"I said I really don't want to continue, I just want to go now in fact," I asserted, removing his hands. I was worried that a note of fear had started to creep into my voice and the last thing I wanted was to come across as a frightened, vulnerable person.

"You're all the same you young ones, you play the tease and then think you can just stop when you've got me all excited? You want this as much as I do," he shot back, now with a slightly menacing look on his face, still full of intent. Before I knew it, he had pushed me back against the tree and was attempting to unbutton my jeans while holding my head back with one of his hands. Fear started to grip me. Was I going to be raped? I was in the middle of nowhere in the pitch darkness by now. I thought that if I screamed, some of the other random men roaming around may come and help me, but I had no idea if they were even dangerous types themselves and if I did anything, what would Alan then try to do? My mind was all a blur, yet I knew I had to get away from him. My jeans were now halfway down my legs and Alan's persistent hands continued to grope me. What if he in fact had a knife or something and stabbed me right here if I tried to struggle? Who would even know? I would be left for dead right here on Hampstead Heath, remembered only by an article in the local paper explaining that I had been cruising at night and was unfortunately murdered by some psychopath. Is that the sort of thing my family deserved to deal with? With a single burst of effort, I shoved Alan as far away from me as I could, pulled up my jeans quickly and started to run for my life. I had no idea where I was running to, but stopping would be the worst decision to make. I did not even dare look behind me. As I ran, I almost barged into someone, a man that seemed to be happily strolling around alone.

"Sorry, please can you help me?" I begged. "I've just been attacked and I need to find my way out of here back to Hampstead Station. Do you know where it is?"

"Oh dear, I'm sorry mate," replied the man, who on focusing more on his face, was probably about fifty years old and with a bald head. "I don't see anyone chasing you. I take it you managed to get away before anything too serious happened? If you remember what this man looked like, I can come with you to the police and you can report it. You really can get some dubious types out here at night. Most of us just come here for a bit of fun really. Shall we go to the police then?"

"Oh, no that's okay, I really just want to get to the tube station."

"Well, just ahead of you is a path and if you take a left turn then it will lead you to the road where you will easily find the High Street and the station. Are you sure you will be alright?"

"Yes, thank you so much. I just need to get out of here," I replied and immediately hurried on to the pathway and made my way out of the Heath.

I had never been so scared in my life. The fear I had experienced on initially going into the park in Israel was nothing compared to this. Someone who I honestly believed I could trust had tried to take advantage of me and in the end I had no idea what he was truly capable of. I could have gone to the police, but then I did not want myself linked to any kind of official report or proceedings. What if my parents ever found out? It would be a nightmare. When I finally got home, I went straight to the bathroom and took a shower to wash off any trace of my experience that night. A night that had ended in a truly disturbing way. Did Alan's friend's gay youth group actually exist after all? Had he lead me on simply to try and take advantage of me? It was all so confusing. I then went to my room and went to bed, where fitful sleep eventually arrived.

# Chapter 8

Following my experience with Alan, I became wary of what in fact the gay world would be like for me. If at the end of the day everything came down to sex and the focus was always to find partners at whatever cost, then I would have a problem as this was still an intimidating approach for me. Certainly my sexual desires were very strong, but I was hoping I may be able to meet someone who was at least nearer to my age and who I could honestly trust and build a relationship with of some sort. If I was going to finally do the deed, it had to be in a situation where I was completely comfortable. I realised that I was actually really looking forward to the start of university, if only to be able to meet some young people I could relate to. I was not sure if I wanted look for further opportunities to meet gay people for the remainder of the holidays especially following this latest experience, so I decided to spend the rest of the time trying to earn some money. It was also good to be able to hang out with Simon, Alex and the others, even if it meant having to continue repressing myself.

In the last couple of weeks of the summer break, I took up a part time job in a cafe, serving food and being the general dogsbody. I realised I needed a focus of some sort so that I was not constantly thinking about my sexuality issues. It was a welcome relief in fact as it meant I could meet and talk to lots of different people. My parents were quite happy that I had found a job, and that I would not be reliant on them for money to pay for my leisure activities so it seemed to work all round. Simon had a part-time job working at a clothes shop which he seemed to enjoy, especially as it meant he could literally be surrounded by his beloved fashion labels. He would tell me of the funny situations he often experienced with customers and how he sometimes ended up advising people on things that they would look good in. I believed he had found his vocation. My own work stories were centred around serving greasy food to a variety of workers, and snippets of conversation I had overheard mainly from manual labour types who frequented the cafe in the mornings and at lunchtime.

Finally, the first week of university arrived, marked by the famous 'Fresher's Week', where all the newly enrolled students could meet each other and join the various societies that the university had to offer. It was quite a confusing experience really, so many students walking around, and various stalls having been set up offering a vast array of literature to aid with studies, or groups inviting you to join. Simon and I wandered around the impressive main hall, littered with pillars, statues and plaques of all sorts and avidly checking out everything on offer. It was quite overwhelming. I ended up being given several different leaflets and booklets covering all manner of things, which I told myself I would pay due attention to in the comfort of my room at home. I wondered how many of these other students were on our course, and what they were all thinking about being new students at one of the most impressive London universities? On one hand the thought of it all was quite daunting, but I just knew that this was the start of a new chapter in my life, with many new opportunities to consider.

Once I had the chance at home, I scoured through all the literature I had been given with interest. One of the booklets was all about the different societies that had been set up at the university, to cater for almost every affiliation I could think of. Interestingly, there was a Jewish Society which seemed to be quite prominent and well-established, and lo and behold, a Gay and Lesbian Society. Well, now I could join both of these groups which would mean being able to mix with other like-minded students and maybe enable me to broaden my circle of friends in every aspect of my life. I wondered what kind of people there were in these societies; was the Jewish Society mainly religious or a real melting pot of different levels of observance? I sincerely hoped the latter as it would mean they would have more of an open mind. As for the Gay Society, would the members be regular types of people who happened to be gay or real militant types? There was so much to look forward to and discover. It really did seem to be a world away from my High School days, with my shameful memories of the experience with Jamie feeling like another era. I also wondered how I would hide my association with the Gay Society from Simon, or if in fact it was time to finally come out to my oldest and closest friend. Would being at university help to open his mind? I really hoped so.

A week after the start of the semester, Simon and I both joined the Jewish Society, affectionately known as 'JSoc'. On attending the first meeting, we discovered more than a hundred other students were there, many of whom seemed to know each other already. We were welcomed warmly by a bright and bubbly female student called Natalie who I gathered was one of the organisers of this group. We got speaking to a number of other people, who were all studying different subjects and who told us that fundamentally they wanted to maintain their sense of belonging to their own community whilst being thrust into the wider world. I found all of this quite reassuring and felt that these people were the types I could relate to and who just possibly, I could come out to about my real self- one day. I wondered if I would actually feel this comfortable being involved in the Gay Society, but knew that in any event I had to join it as soon as I could.

A few days after having experienced the first JSoc meeting, I managed to locate the venue where the gay contingent met. I suddenly became very nervous at the thought of going there and officially introducing myself. It would be the first time that I had publicly affirmed myself as a gay person as part of an official movement. Did they publish member's names anywhere, I wondered? What if anyone I knew found out I was part of this Society? How would I deal with it then? I decided that my need to discover what lie in store here was far greater than any other preoccupation I may have and so I went ahead and found the venue. The Gay and Lesbian Group, or GLG as it was known, apparently met twice a week at the Student Union. When I arrived, feeling as nervous as anything, I was met with a complete cross section of people. There were possibly about fifty or so in attendance, comprising guys that seemed quite regular and were not too dissimilar from myself, more outlandish camp types and several lesbians many of whom looked more like guys than the guys did. It seemed a strange world for sure. I was welcomed by a friendly male student called Peter, who was actually rather camp but certainly seemed very genuine. He asked me if this was my first time here, and when I told him it was, he nodded reassuringly and said that I would be made to feel right at home in no time. Peter then personally took me around, introducing me to several others who all seemed to be very friendly. At one point, I thought I noticed a guy that had been at the JSoc meeting a few days earlier. So it was quite possible that here in the wider world, you could actually find gay Jews who seemed happy being part of both communities. I felt a sense of hope as I went over to speak to him.

"Hi, I'm Evan. Were you by any chance at the JSoc meeting on Monday? I thought you looked familiar."

"Yes, that's right! I'm Nathan. I don't really go to the JSoc meetings much as I am not at all religious, but I thought that seeing as it's the start of a new year, I would check out any new friendly faces. You look familiar to me too. Are you a freshman?"

"Yes I am. I've just started my course here in Modern European Studies. It's all rather daunting so far, but I'm sure I'll get used to it," I replied, trying to sound positive.

"I know, I remember when I first started! I'm in my second year now, studying Geography. I was in the closet throughout most of my first year, but after making loads of friends here and starting to go out on the scene, I realised that this was the life I wanted and I simply had to be open about it to my family."

"Goodness, that's brave! I'm not out to anyone and I'm quite scared about the whole thing really. How did your family take it when you told them?"

"Well, at first it was quite difficult especially for my mum, but after a while my parents became quite supportive. We're not a religious or practicing family, so I guess my parents don't have any major hang-ups on that front, but I'm the only boy with just one sister, and so they were rather hoping for me to continue the family line if you know what I mean."

"Yes, sure I get it. My family is quite religious. Not in an extreme way, but completely observant and very traditionally minded. That's why I'm quite nervous about the thought of telling them. Also, my friends are all straight too and from traditional orthodox Jewish families and I've been too scared to even talk to them about anything. I've actually been looking for people I can identify with for ages, who can show me the fun and relaxed side of gay life."

"Well, stick with me, Evan. I'll look after you, no problem! You shouldn't feel pressured into coming out unless you are ready anyway, but in the meantime, there's lots of fun to be had, and I can introduce you to my friends. I just know you'll all get along really well!"

I was so happy to have met Nathan. He was of average height with thick, curly brown hair, brown eyes and a wide toothy grin. He was not attractive in a typical way, although certainly had something warm and welcoming about him, which made me feel very comfortable. He was so friendly and seemed so relaxed about being both Jewish and gay. I envied the fact that he did not come from a religious family as I was certain that this had a part to play in his parents' relatively quick acceptance of him. I simply could not imagine what it would be like with my own family. We continued to chat for a while and he then introduced me to a couple of his friends who had just arrived, another guy with ginger hair called Toby and a slightly overweight, butch-looking girl called Mandy. They were both friendly enough, and neither of them Jewish. I thought how great it must be to have a mixture of friends of different religions, or even no religion at all. Just some young people who enjoyed each other's company and had a good time together. I knew that my experience at university would certainly not be a lonely one.

For a few weeks afterwards, I managed to successfully keep my involvement with the Gay Society secret from Simon. We would stick together most of the time as we also had exactly the same lectures. However, having both started to make some new friends on our course to hang out with, it was easy enough for me to invent an excuse about going somewhere or other when I needed to. I was becoming friendlier with Nathan as well, who had started asking me if I would come with him to bars or clubs in Soho at the weekends. I was still hesitant about this for some reason, probably because I had been used to spending Saturday nights with Simon, Alex and the gang and it would seem weird if I suddenly wasn't available. As well as this, I still was unsure as to what it was really like on the gay scene. Did everyone just take drugs, or try to have sex with each other? I had been too nervous to ask Nathan these questions as he may think I was really stupid and the last thing I wanted to do was to show myself up. However on the other hand, the thought of going out in Soho was extremely tempting as I would be safe with Nathan and surely did not need to do anything I was uncomfortable with?

One weekend, I decided I would just go for it. I decided to pretend I was ill to avoid having to go out with the gang, and instead arranged to meet up with Nathan and his friends to try the Soho nightlife for the first time. I met them outside the nearest underground station and Nathan said there was a really great bar we could go to, to get the night started. It was called Ku Bar on Charing Cross Road, and as we went in, a whole different world enveloped me. Loud pop music was blaring out from speakers in the corner of the bar, and it was quite packed with mostly younger guys and some girls, all chatting, laughing and dancing away. Behind the bar, men with crop tops and muscled arms served all manner of drinks, their smiles plastered on their faces constantly. I felt like I was in one big party that I had gate-crashed. Nathan led Mandy, Toby and myself to the bar and offered to buy the first round. I opted for an orange flavoured alcopop which seemed like an interesting drink, and stood there sipping away at the sweet fizzy liquid whilst scanning the bar properly. Several guys looked at me and smiled, a couple of them winking cheekily at me. I felt so embarrassed, was I supposed to wink back? I really wished I was not such a novice at all this.

"Ooh, good for you," said Nathan with a sly grin on his face. "Looks like you've got lucky there!"

"Really?" I answered, surprised. I was not used to this kind of attention at all.

"Oh yeah, there's a few of them that want you it seems. Don't act all surprised, you're a really good looking guy, you'll have to get used to this kind of thing!"

Was I really good looking? Nobody had ever told me that before, except Alan who had tried to molest me and then also my mother on a few occasions, who would often boast that all her children were beautiful. Before having started university, I had got my hair cut in a much shorter style than in the past, which meant that I no longer looked like a semi-afro mop head. Although I still suffered from spots, this too had slightly calmed down and so all in all I realised that maybe I had started to look acceptable. I still would never have considered myself above average though, all the years of having looked at myself disgustedly in the mirror having only deepened my lack of self-confidence. Before I knew it, one of the guys that had been looking at me started to come over. Glued to the spot with fear, I was not sure what to do.

"Hello," said the guy, with a broad smile. He was quite tall, with almost black short hair, gelled to a slight quiff at the front. He had olive skin, which looked smooth and perfect, and the most beautiful shaped eyes, which looked like they were green in the light of the bar.

"Hi," I replied slightly awkwardly.

"My name's Tom. I saw you as soon as you walked in, you have a striking face."

Did I really? I simply couldn't understand what other people saw in me that I was obviously missing.

"Err, thanks," I managed. "My name is Evan. It's my first time here. In fact, it's the first time I have ever been out like this in Soho."

"Wow, you're new to the scene then," said Tom, continuing to smile and looking directly into my eyes. "I promise I don't bite. Wanna chat some more?"

At this point, Nathan and his friends must have known what was going on, because they surreptitiously managed to make themselves scarce so as not to cramp my style. I stayed against the bar, not quite knowing what to do, but liking the look of this friendly guy and wanting to get to know him better. After agreeing to talk more with Tom, we headed upstairs to a mezzanine, where there were several tables and chairs for people to sit with their drinks and look down over the balcony at the goings on below. We managed to find a couple of chairs and sat down.

"So," continued Tom, "I didn't think I had seen you anywhere around Soho before. You seem a little nervous, but there's really no need to be. I'm actually a bit fed up of the people that come up to you in bars and act all friendly just to get you into bed. You seem like a breath of fresh air."

"Oh, I'm so glad you said that," I replied, feeling a lot more relaxed suddenly. "I have only had a couple of experiences before and they were with guys who clearly were only interested in trying to have sex with me. It's made me nervous about meeting anyone else because I don't know what they are after."

"I can understand that," said Tom reassuringly. "Not that I am surprised at all, that's the way most gay men operate on the scene. Plus you are really good looking of course. It's always nice to just be able to talk to someone and get to know them, and then whatever happens after that will be when both people feel comfortable."

"Exactly! That's how I've been feeling but I never thought I would meet someone that was happy to go at my pace. I had a really bad experience recently with a guy that I thought I could trust, and he took me to Hampstead Heath and tried to attack me. It put me off things for a bit."

"Oh, I'm sorry about that. He sounds like a real idiot. I just want to get to know you a bit that's all. I can't pretend I don't find you sexually attractive but believe me, I would never try anything you weren't happy with."

Feeling much more reassured and in fact rather liking Tom in general, we stayed and chatted away. At one point, Nathan came up to us and told me he and his friends wanted to move onto another bar called 'The Village', and that I could stay here if I wanted but that they would be in The Village if I felt like heading there soon. I thanked Nathan, and told him I really wanted to hang out with him and his friends more and was it okay if I came over with Tom? He said it would be absolutely fine and then headed off, leaving Tom and I together alone again on the balcony. We continued talking and soon, we were holding each other's hands and had begun kissing. It was an experience that ignited something deep inside me. Just having another man's tongue and lips on my mouth, feeling his warm sweet breath, made me tingle with excitement. It was not quite like the kiss I had experienced that time in the park in Israel, and certainly not like the more forceful kiss that Alan had thrust upon me. This time it was extremely tender and soft. What was even better was that not once did Tom attempt to do anything beyond simply enjoying our embrace. As we pulled away from each other, I looked into his eyes, and saw them smiling kindly back at me. Tom was truly the kind of guy you would stop and look at twice, or at least he was for me. Despite what he had told me about being attractive, I could not imagine what he really saw in me. I suppose beauty is in the eye of the beholder after all. Just being able to speak to him about things and explain how I felt so far about being gay with him listening intently to every word, was a truly fulfilling experience. This was the kind of life I imagined having in the gay community, one where people just wanted to support each other and respected each other for who they were.

"Let's go and meet up with my friend Nathan," I suggested, not wanting my new friend to think I was now abandoning him just because I had met someone.

"Sure," agreed Tom. "It would be nice to get to know your friends more. I came with a couple of my friends and I'm sure they'll be more than happy to be left to their own devices. I just need to say goodbye to them on the way out."

With that, we headed out of the bar, having been briefly introduced to Tom's friends along the way. Walking up Old Compton Street, Tom took my hand in his. This was a strange experience for me. It was one thing to hold his hand in a crowded bar, but on a public street? I decided to just try and relax. It was actually quite nice to be able to do this, where nobody even batted an eyelid or seemed to notice. I wondered how many people Tom had been with before. In fact, it occurred to me that I had no idea how old he was. On asking him, he told me he was twenty-eight. Ten years older than I was! That seemed such a huge gap, and yet he did not seem to be that much older than me. Neither did he flinch at all when I told him my age. After all, it was just a number, wasn't it?

The rest of the evening was spent with Tom, Nathan, Toby and Mandy all together. We had a few drinks in The Village watching some dancers show off their moves and extremely toned bodies gyrating on the bar tops while everyone else looked up at them in admiration. It certainly seemed to be a place to come and forget all your cares. Afterwards, we went to a club called GAY. This was a huge club, with what seemed to have an endless number of people. I had never come across anything like this before and it was quite overwhelming. The place was enormous, with a dance floor and several bar areas over two other floors. I was scared that I would lose the others, but Tom held my hand as we pushed our way through the crowded areas. We drank and danced for ages to the extremely catchy music. This night was turning into one of the best nights I could remember!

At about three o'clock in the morning, I decided I was too tired to carry on and wanted to go home. Nathan then offered me a pill, which he told me was called ecstasy and would make me want to keep going. The thought of taking anything like this made me extremely wary and I declined and said I really just needed to leave. Nathan told me he would catch up with me at the next GLG meeting and that he was really happy I had had a good night. Tom gave me his number and begged me to call him as soon as possible. I had every intention of doing just that. I had actually met someone I could really trust and who I liked not only personally but sexually too. I decided that it would probably be Tom who I would finally give myself to, something I had been thinking about most of the night in fact. I took the night bus home and tried to be as quiet as possible when I entered the house. As I went upstairs to my room, I unexpectedly passed my mother on the landing.

"This is a bit late for you coming home, isn't it?" she asked.

"Er, well I was just out with my friends and we got carried away," I replied, quite surprised that she was up at this time, and hovering around just as I had come home. "It is the weekend you know!"

"Why do you smell of smoke? I hope you aren't doing anything stupid, young man!"

"No, no we just went to a club in town and it was a smoky environment that's all. You know I would never do that."

"Well, you smell disgusting. Put your clothes in the wash and I suggest you have a shower before you go to bed."

"Yes, Mum. By the way, what are you doing up at this time anyway?"

"Oh, I just needed to go to the loo, that's all."

"Okay, Mum. Goodnight and I'll speak to you in the morning."

"Goodnight darling."

After having taken a quick shower, I climbed into bed full of thoughts of my wonderful first night out on the gay scene, and more importantly, of the lovely Tom whose attractive face and kind eyes stayed with me until I drifted off to sleep.

# Chapter 9

Over the next few weeks, I spent a lot of time with Tom, going out during the week and at weekends. He would take me to different places like cafes, the theatre and the cinema which he would mostly offer to pay for, and we would often spend time just sitting and talking about many different things and what we thought about life. I realised that I was probably in love with Tom; he was so gentle, sweet and passionate about what he believed in. I really thought there was a lot I could learn from being with him and each day the thought of seeing him again excited me beyond measure. He would often call me at home as well, and we would end up chatting away for at least an hour each time. Sometimes one of my family members would answer the phone and would remark that it was 'that Tom guy', for me. Having told them it was a new friend I had made at university, I still wondered who they really thought he was, as the frequency of his calls far surpassed that of Simon, Nathan or any of my other friends. However as long as nobody questioned me any further, I was happy to leave it at that.

I realised that as I was becoming closer to Tom and spending more time in a gay environment, I was less and less engaged with my spiritual, Jewish self. At times I stopped and thought about this, and realised that I had to make a concerted effort to keep the balance right. I was eighteen years old and embarking on adult life. I had no intention of forsaking God, yet I was frustrated with Him. I blamed Him for not being able to merge my two existences and have each side live together in harmony. I was still at a very sensitive age. Decisions that I made now, would probably shape the way my life evolved in future. What did I want my life to be, and more importantly, how would I be able to make it happen?

As someone who was brought up with a strong, family-centric culture, I also acknowledged that I was not putting much effort into my family. It was not their fault, as they had no idea what I was now getting up to in my life. I was hiding my real self from them, and distancing myself from everything I knew because I felt it was not conducive to what I was now seeking. Sometimes I would watch my family interact, either at Friday night meals where Jews officially welcome in the Sabbath, or at random times when we were all together. I almost felt like I was watching people from another world, with me as an outside spectator. I loved my brothers and my sister deeply, in a way that I did not even have to think about. Yet I did not feel connected to them, or their lives. I felt a sadness that I did not really have anything in common with them and that I could not really relate to them in the way I would have liked.

As for my parents, I felt this even more acutely. My mother especially, was someone who I loved with my very soul. I seemed to be the only one that was interested in talking to her in any depth and who genuinely cared about her feelings and thoughts as a person in her own right, not just as our 'mother'. We sometimes used to sit together and chat about all manner of things, like good friends do. I felt so close to her yet, I could not even think of sharing the biggest and most important aspect of my life with her. It felt like a sham somehow, withholding all of this and pretending that I was leading a normal life with normal preoccupations. I loved the new life I was discovering, yet I also hated myself at the same time. I was changing and my priorities were shifting. I started going less and less frequently to the synagogue on the Sabbath, because all I felt when I was there, was a deep sense of loneliness and I was very much disconnected from everyone around me and what they stood for. I felt like being in such a holy and community-led environment made me feel dirty, as if I was riddled with a disease that was secretly contaminating everyone around me and they were not yet aware of it. I was jealous of my fellow Jews. They seemed to be content with their husbands/wives and families, protected by the community, accepted for who they were and never having to question themselves or justify their lifestyles. I could not bear being amongst these people who seemed so pure while I felt like a leper.

So what could I do about it and how could I keep my connection to my culture and God in a way that worked for me? It seemed clear that I was separating communal Jewish life and the institution of Judaism, from my own personal relationship with God, but I thought that if I could just keep Him with me whilst establishing my new environment, then things would work out in the end somehow. I was reinventing myself as I went along.

I also found myself spending less time with Simon at university, which funnily enough did not appear to bother him too much as he had made his own small group of friends who seemed to all be into the same things as he was. In fact to me, he seemed to be developing more and more of a superficial personality, making judgemental comments about people purely based on the clothes they wore or their general appearance and deciding if someone was even worth talking to, based on the same criteria. It puzzled me and also disappointed me that he should be this way and somehow this made it easier for me to deal with any guilt I had about our gradual distancing from each other. I also found myself barely spending any time with Alex or others in the old group of friends, as they were well and truly involved in their new lives, studying or working at different places. Only random get-togethers about once a month enabled us all to reconnect with each other. It felt as if my life as I knew it before university, was taking on a whole new direction.

In the meantime, my new close group of friends had become Nathan, Toby and Mandy and of course, Tom. I would often thank God for having allowed me to meet someone so special, so seemingly perfect. I felt happy that despite being a gay person, I was not being punished for having a boyfriend, as I had so often feared in the past. Could it be that I was finally able to find the perfect balance to my life, the perfect situation? I felt for the first time in ages, like I truly belonged somewhere with this new group and was truly connecting with people that understood me, all parts of me. We would hang out most weekends, going into Soho and enjoying ourselves at various bars, nearly always ending up at GAY and dancing the night away until the early hours. Then on returning home, I would often find my mother apparently just going to the toilet at the same time as I went up to my room, the obviousness of the fact that she was waiting up for me not escaping me in the slightest.

Something that puzzled me quite a bit however, was that despite my ever-increasing closeness with Tom, we had still not reached the point of going all the way sexually, although we had kissed each other and fooled around on numerous occasions. Once, when I had suggested we go to his shared apartment for the night, he had seemed hesitant and made an excuse about it not being private enough. I certainly could not bring him back to my house, and so this left me with the option of suggesting a cheap hotel room for a night. Again, he had come up with some kind of excuse. I started to wonder what it was and if it may be something to do with me. I had never felt more comfortable and content with anyone and so now it just seemed more natural to take the next step.

One night after we had finished having dinner with Nathan and the others, I suggested that, rather than go on with them to a bar, Tom and I should just sit somewhere and talk for a bit. Tom in fact seemed to be slightly on edge that evening and I was feeling incredibly aroused and wanted more than anything to just be able to take Tom somewhere and ravage him, so this made me want to address the apparent issue of sex with some urgency. We walked along Old Compton Street together and then found our way to Soho Square, a small park area nearby where we sat on one of the benches. I was not quite sure how to bring up the subject, but before I managed to formulate my first sentence, Tom began to speak.

"Evan, you know I like you more than anything, don't you?"

"Yes, I guess so. And you know how much I like you too."

"Yes, I think I do. Which is why I need to explain myself to you."

I suddenly had a very unsettling sinking feeling inside that refused to go away.

"Explain yourself? What do you mean?" I managed.

"I know that you really want us to have sex and I also know that you are basically a virgin, which is why I think your first time should be with someone who really deserves you."

What was he saying? I didn't understand? It sounded like he was about to dump me.

"Why are you saying that, Tom? I've wanted to have proper sex with you for a while now and I just don't understand why you've been so unwilling to do anything about it. I'm ready for it, more than ready and I can't think of anyone I would rather go to the next level with than you."

"Evan, I just don't know how to tell you this, it's been killing me inside for ages and I've been too scared to bring it up, but I guess now I have no choice."

"No choice about what?" I replied, my heart beating in overdrive. Then came the bombshell.

"I already have a boyfriend. We've been together for five years actually, and recently things have not been going so well. The night we first met, I was intending to leave him and had decided to just go out with some friends and have some fun. It felt so good to be out as if I was a single guy, and when I saw you I simply couldn't take my eyes off you. Since then, my boyfriend has been making so much effort with me as he wants it to work, and I have been torn between my feelings for him and you. I simply felt too guilty to take advantage of you, knowing that you were looking for your first 'someone special', while I was in fact having an affair with you. I just don't think I can handle it any more." And with that, he started to cry.

I sat there speechless. Had I heard this correctly? Tom, the wonderful guy I had been thinking of non-stop for the last couple of months or so, already had a boyfriend and had been using me as some kind of escape from a rocky relationship... I prayed that this wasn't actually happening! Had I completely misunderstood him? What had I done to deserve this? It was as if my world had suddenly shattered around me. Was I being punished because I was Jewish and not supposed to be with another guy? Damn the world! This was all too much. I wanted to try and comfort Tom as he sat there with his face in his hands, but then thought what was the point? It could never work with him, that much was clear to me now. I felt like my heart had been ripped out and had no idea what I could possibly say anyway. Feeling numb, angry and betrayed all at once, I stood up and simply walked away, towards the underground station. I thought I may as well just go home, alone to bed. Alone, as I always had been. Despite my best efforts, alone is clearly what God had intended for me after all. How naive of me to think I could be allowed to lead a gay life while still having a relationship with Him. Had my very thoughts of sex with another man sealed my fate? Why did Nathan seem to be so happy then, why wasn't God punishing him? I simply could not understand the injustice of it all. I had to find my way somehow, and factoring God into the equation no longer felt like a viable option.

After the shock of Tom's confession, I started to become further detached from things around me. Nothing much seemed to matter; my studies were just something I was putting myself through mostly because my parents had insisted I had some form of higher education. My friendships also seemed to somehow appear hollow. As much as I loved spending time with Nathan, Toby and Mandy, I realised that it was mostly based on going out into Soho and hitting bars and clubs with them offering me drugs that I had no interest in. What was the real meaning of it all? I thought I had found some meaning with Tom but that was clearly a sham. I blamed God for everything and for apparently allowing me to think I could find some happiness, then destroying it all in one fell swoop. Why was He doing this to me?

In anger, I stopped going to the synagogue altogether with my family on Saturday mornings, much to my parents' disappointment. Instead, I would stay in my room thinking about what I could do to truly make myself happy without being reliant on anyone else's approval. It was time to finally lose my virginity for a start.

I was still not entirely comfortable with going to a bar and picking someone up so I had to think of another way. If I responded to an advert in the lonely hearts columns, I felt it would mean I was looking for a relationship, which at this point, I was too scared of getting into after the fallout from Tom. What other options did I have for meeting someone for sex who you could trust and be comfortable with and maybe still stay friendly with afterwards?

In all the gay magazines that I had been reading of late, there were several adverts for 'rent boys', and I had often wondered what it would be like to pay for someone to fulfil all your desires in bed. The idea of paying for sex was alien to me, and surely not the natural way to be intimate with someone that actually has no feelings for you at all or may not even like you in any way, yet would do it just for money. It seemed so transactional and soulless. But with my hormones raging and feeling as low as it was possible to feel, I decided to play with fire and tempt fate. I found an advert in a paper I had kept hidden in my room, with a picture of a guy looking moodily towards the distance, his firm torso rippling and skimpy briefs revealing the shape of a rather large manhood. If I was going to go down this route, I may as well get the best!

Before I had time to doubt myself further and hesitate, I called the number in the advert. A friendly voice answered and after a couple of minutes of chatting, we had arranged that I would meet him at his apartment in Covent Garden. Nervously, and with my heart beating like a Duracell bunny, I made my way there, thinking that at last I would experience true physical pleasure, on my own terms. I had managed to negotiate a student's rate, down from forty pounds to twenty-five. As far as I was concerned, if I had to do it this way, I would at least get what I wanted out of it. I arrived at the apartment and rang the buzzer. The guy that answered the door was of average height, with a clearly defined body that I could see through his tight-fitting t-shirt. He had short dark hair and blue eyes, altogether a most acceptable package and even better in real life than the photo, which was a definite plus.

After I had told him I was a virgin, he took care to reassure me about everything that was happening and asked me if I was okay several times. Although I found this very considerate of him, a large part of me just wanted this to be an animalistic carefree experience. We ended up doing all manner of things that I had for so long only dreamed about. The feeling of having his body intertwined with mine was overwhelming and brought sheer joy to me. When we were both finished, I lay there exhausted but elated. I was truly fulfilled now and could not keep the smile from my face. I paid and quickly left the apartment and wandered around the streets for a while feeling like I was floating on air. This was what I had been missing. It was everything I had imagined it to be and more. I no longer cared that my first real time had not been with someone special, and that in fact it had been with a prostitute! I also did not care if the heavens opened right then and a large thunderbolt struck me down. I now had a true taste of what it would be like to be with another man and any doubts I may have had on the sexual front were now gone. Remembering how guilty and scared I felt after having barely kissed a man in the park in Israel, I realised how much I had moved on from then, and how I could not let anything hold me back from doing what I needed to.

The next thing I told myself I would do was to finally come out to Simon. Although we were not as close as we had been in the past, I still considered Simon to be one of my dearest friends and thought that I should now put our friendship to the test by telling him the truth. In the worst case scenario if he completely abandoned me after telling him, at least I would know what I was dealing with. I was used to feeling alone and was prepared to take whatever was coming my way as I intended to be the master of my own destiny from now on.

The next evening at home ensconced in my room, I called Simon. I was intending to simply come out with it and not have to see the look on his face, which is why I had chosen to do this over the phone. After some small talk, I told him I had something I wanted to say to him.

"Wait, Evan," interrupted Simon. "There's actually something I need to tell you too, and I've been wanting to for a couple of weeks now."

"Oh, what is it?" I answered, thinking it was probably that he had bought some amazing new designer item or something.

"Well, I was out one night in town and er... well I kissed a man."

"What?" I replied, not quite believing what I was hearing.

"I kissed a man," repeated Simon, his voice trembling slightly. "It was this guy I had met whilst out with a couple of friends from our course... we were just chatting and we ended up kissing."

"Well what does that mean? Are you gay?"

"Well I don't know, I think so."

"Wow, I can't believe it! That's amazing!" I exclaimed.

"What? You mean you don't mind?"

"Of course not! You will never believe what I was about to tell you. I'm gay too!"

"You what? Really? This is insane! Let's get together and discuss this properly. I can't believe it!"

After arranging to meet up the next day, I hung up. My mind was in a whirl. My oldest friend Simon was actually gay too. Nothing could have prepared me for hearing him say that, but it was probably the best thing I had heard in ages! It meant I would not have to keep my life secret from him any more, or make up excuses for being with my gay friends. Suddenly there was a whole host of new opportunities for us to rekindle our friendship.

It meant I could introduce him to Nathan and go out with him and his friends all together in Soho. Things could not have turned out better!

When we got together the following day, we took the opportunity to catch up on everything we had been up to over the last couple of months, as we had not spent much time together. Simon told me that his new group of friends were apparently really cool and very much into music and fashion. I knew a couple of them from our course but there were one or two others that were studying fashion design and who Simon was learning a lot about trendy new looks from.

He then decided to tell me about his gay kiss. He explained that he had been to a party recently in town where one of the guys there tried to come onto him, and although he had rebuffed his attentions at first, he secretly had wished he could explore things further. The guy had continued persevering with Simon and he had then decided to go with it. It was such a great experience that it had apparently confirmed in his mind that he really was gay even though he had been fooling himself that maybe he was bisexual until that point. He had been so relieved and surprised to hear that I was gay too because despite not having been that close recently, he still felt that I was one of the only people he could tell this to.

I then updated Simon on everything I had been through that I had not shared with him, and told him about Alan and the hideous experience in Hampstead Heath as well as meeting Nathan, the situation with Tom and having paid for my first sexual encounter. Simon could hardly believe that I had already done all those things and listened with fascination. We agreed that we would start going out together in Soho and having fun at the various bars and clubs. Simon had only been to Soho a few times, and so explaining that I had been out on the scene for a couple of months now, I almost felt like a veteran. What a strange, small world it was. Finally being able to share all aspects of my life with my friend was surely going to be the best thing ever!

At the next available opportunity, I introduced Simon to Nathan, Toby and Mandy and he in turn introduced me to his friends. We started to hang out more together, experiencing everything the scene had to offer. Simon lapped it all up like an excitable child. However, his tendency to judge people on their physical attributes was still very much in evidence and this was slightly tiresome. It meant that several people who came to talk to us and expressed an interest in Simon, were often dismissed with a derisory glance and bitchy comments behind their backs. This kind of behaviour did not appeal to me, especially as it began to extend to anybody that I was also interested in. I started to feel that I was somehow being judged for the kind of people I told Simon I found attractive. Nathan told me on one occasion that he did not in fact like Simon very much and found him too shallow and false, although he appreciated that he was my friend and so put up with him on that basis. This was a shame, as I had built up an ideal in my mind where we would all become one happy family.

Over the next few weeks, Simon's behaviour became so bad that Nathan ended up telling me that I should go out alone with Simon if I really wanted to and that should I want to hang out with the others, he was not welcome. This created a very difficult situation for me, which I was not sure how to handle. Since Simon had come out to me, I had actually noticed that he was quite a different person from the one I used to know. But somehow I felt a kind of responsibility towards him, maybe based on the longevity of our friendship or maybe because he was still relying on me to accompany him on the gay scene. In any event, I realised I would need to have a chat with him.

One day in between lectures at university, I sat down with Simon ready to broach the tricky subject. I had started to explain that the other people we spent time with found him to be a bit too judgemental and that we were all just quite relaxed and wanting to have a good time with no complications.

"I think your other friends are not really good enough for you to be honest," was Simon's reply. "They seem to have no real taste and that Nathan guy looks at you longingly all the time, or haven't you noticed? Not that he would ever stand a chance, have you seen the hideous clothes he always wears?"

"Simon, Nathan's a really good friend of mine actually. In fact, I have him to thank for easing me into the gay scene. It is comments like that which are causing the problem. Why does it matter what someone looks like or what they choose to wear?"

"Oh come on!" snorted Simon. "If someone has good taste in clothes it means they will have good taste in other areas of life and will have high standards. This makes them more suitable friends or partners."

"I don't agree at all. I don't wear designer labels so what do you have to say about me?"

"Well, that's true but I'm intending to help you out in that area actually. Besides, you are above average looking, so that will always go in your favour."

It was the first time I had heard any kind of compliment about my looks from Simon and it was strange for me to hear this coming from his usually critical lips.

"Actually," he continued, "there was something I wanted to speak to you about. You probably know that since I came out to you, I haven't had any real sexual experiences, except a couple of guys I've kissed. I really need to know what it's like for the first time."

"I agree," I responded, "and you have many options. If you just relaxed a bit, there are plenty of guys you could meet on the scene, or even do what I did and hire someone. Once you've had sex, it makes you much more confident to go and meet other guys, believe me."

"Erm, well, I was wondering about something actually. I am far too scared to try and do any of those things yet and I read in an article in a gay magazine that there have been many friends who have decided to experiment with each other first. You know, to get comfortable with it all with someone they trust. I was wondering if we could do that together."

I was taken aback by this. Sure, I had also heard of situations where friends experimented together, but Simon was almost like my brother! I could never imagine for a second doing anything sexual with him, as well as the fact that he was not remotely attractive to me in that sense. This was certainly something unexpected.

"Look, Simon," I replied. "To me, you are like a member of my family somehow. We've known each other for so many years now and it would seem like incest to me to do something like that with you. Please don't be offended but I just couldn't ever do that. Why don't we just try and find you some guys and I'm sure it will all be okay."

"I see, if that's how you feel," replied Simon in a slightly derisory tone. "I just thought it made the most sense actually, but I'm sure there are other ways to do it. Don't worry about it," and with that he stood up and walked off in a huff.

It was simply impossible for me to consider becoming sexual with Simon. I hoped he would understand and would still allow me to help him meet other guys. After all, I was still prepared to hang out with him alone and give up evenings with Nathan and the others to do so. I decided to allow him as much time as he needed to think about our conversation and talk to me again when he was ready. This had certainly turned out to be an eye-opening few weeks for me and I was ready to take on whatever life had to throw my way.

# Chapter 10

After I had had the awkward chat with Simon about sexual experimentation together, things really seemed to change. He became less interested in wanting to spend time with me and started to go out more with his other friends. From time to time, we would catch up and he would almost too proudly, tell me about great nights out he had been on and the numerous different men he had chatted up, flirted with or fooled around with. It felt as if he was trying to somehow make me jealous, as if to say that because I had turned him down, I was now missing out on some really exciting experiences. The truth was however, that I did not really care that much. Simon had developed into someone that I was starting to like less and less. Although underneath, I still had great affection for him from all the years we had known each other, his way of going about things now and his altered character did not appeal to me at all. It did not bother me in the slightest whether or not he had been invited to some exclusive party or that through his fashion designer friends he had met some trumped up celebrity personalities. I was more than happy spending time with Nathan and his friends, and meeting a number of new people myself.

I generally went out with Nathan about three times a week and every bar or club we went to, presented a new opportunity for me to meet someone. It certainly did appear that I was quite attractive to people, something I still found hard to believe. But the proof was there; men eying me up in bars and coming to chat to me hoping to give me their numbers; other men at clubs dancing with me and whispering things of a sexual nature in my ear. I was having so much fun, and with the carefree attitude that I had developed ever since the experience with Tom, I felt that the world was my oyster.

One Saturday night I went to GAY with Nathan and the others. Whilst standing in the queue to get in, I noticed a guy chatting to a friend ahead of me. He was extremely attractive, quite tall with dark brown hair and beautiful full lips. He looked like he could be Hispanic or Latin, which only attracted me further as this was the type of person I realised was my physical ideal. Once inside the club, I made it my business to search him out. It was not that easy though as the club was quite full and regularly attracted at least a thousand people at weekends. I excused myself from dancing with the others every so often and wandered around, avidly looking for signs of the guy from the queue. I finally spotted him at one of the bar areas with the friend he was with. As I studied him, he looked even more attractive and I began to think of the best way to approach him without being too obvious. I was not actually used to making the first move as so far, other guys had come up to me and initiated things. I did not have to think about this for long though, as soon enough his friend left him alone, presumably to go to the toilet or something. Slightly nervous but fully intending doing what I set out to do, I strode up to the bar. Standing next to him, I ordered a drink and then pretended to look around me. As I hoped, my eye caught his at one point, and I held the stare and smiled. He smiled right back. Great! This was at least a positive sign. I then decided to break the ice properly.

"Hey, good music tonight, isn't it?" I ventured.

"Yes, I really like it here," he replied, in what was clearly a foreign accent. So I had been right to assume he was probably Hispanic.

"So where are you from then? You sound maybe Spanish or something?" I asked.

"Well, I am actually from Venezuela. I am studying English here."

"That's great! You speak very well, I'm impressed. My name is Evan, by the way."

"I am Juan. I am here with my friend Marco. We came to the UK together to study."

So, at least I didn't have to ask if the other guy was his boyfriend. In any case, what I wanted more than anything was to try and get more intimate with Juan somehow. He was extremely attractive and right now, that was all I cared about.

"So, Juan, can I buy you a drink maybe?"

"That is very kind of you, okay I will have a vodka and coke please," he replied, his beaming smile and sexy accent really giving me tingles.

I ordered his drink and then we sat down on a couple of bean bags in the corner of the bar area.

"So, where has your friend gone?" I asked, hoping he would not be back too soon.

"He went to dance for a bit, he loves dancing and in fact he will probably be there for a while. I was just happy to stay here."

"Well, I came here with some friends of mine too and they are all dancing away. I would much rather stay and talk to you anyway if you want to."

"Sure, I would like that very much," replied Juan, who was showing definite signs of interest. I was certainly happy with where this was going.

We sat and talked and drank for several minutes. When I thought I could not contain myself any further, I took Juan's hand and started to stroke it. Without flinching, he put his other hand over mine and looking me directly in the eyes, said:

"You are very nice, I like you. Do you want to go to the toilets together?"

I had not quite expected Juan to come out with that; the toilets were not really the sort of place I had imagined getting sexual with someone and goodness knows what the state of them would be. I wanted to decline, but realising that we did not have many options, I knew it would be there or not at all.

"Sure, why not," I replied, my heart starting to beat really fast at my spontaneous decision. We then made our way to the toilet area. We found an empty cubicle and quickly went in and locked the door behind us. The toilets in gay clubs were actually often used for things other than the call of nature. People would use cubicles for taking drugs, having sex and any other manner of activities where they wanted an element of privacy in a club.

Before I knew it, Juan was kissing me. We then could not stop from making as much as we could of each other and the situation, knowing that we were in a club in a toilet cubicle and that we could get caught at any time by anyone. The fact that this kind of thing was generally forbidden, made it all the more exciting. However after we had finished I felt quite dirty and realised that this may not have been a very good idea after all. I wondered if Juan did this regularly, because as far as I was concerned it was an exciting encounter at the time but no good for your self-respect; I certainly did not intend to make a habit out of it. Once we had left the toilets, Juan said goodbye and then simply wandered off into the crowds.

I thought just how random and uncomplicated this experience had been, but although it was pleasurable I definitely intended my next time to be somewhere more respectable and civilised and ideally with someone I knew better. I definitely felt that being with someone you cared about would make sex more meaningful. It was simply a question of being able to find someone suitable in a sea of people who mainly did not look beyond their next hook up. That was certainly a challenge in itself but I thought that surely there were at least a few others like myself out on the gay scene that had a deeper side to them. At the end of the day, my aim was to settle down with someone in a respectable relationship and live just like heterosexual people did rather than have no focus and continue meeting random guys who I had nothing in common with.

For now however, I had no other options and my sexual needs had to be fulfilled. I decided not to pressurise myself to meet the right guy and that I really should just enjoy any opportunities along the way, as long as I felt I was in control of what I was doing. At least with casual encounters there were no emotional complications involved. With a smile of contentment on my face, I went back down to the dance floor and after a few minutes searching, found Nathan, Toby and Mandy bopping away with abandon.

"You've been gone for ages!" exclaimed Toby with a knowing wink.

"Er, yeah sorry about that. I just kind of met someone at the bar," I replied sheepishly.

"Really! Well tell us all about it then!" piped up Nathan with an excited and expectant expression on his face.

After I had recounted the details of my gratifying tryst, the others laughed and told me how lucky I was. Thinking about it, I realised that Nathan did not get many people approaching him and he rarely seemed to be involved in sexual encounters with anyone else. He had told me previously that he had never been in a serious relationship and that he was quite happy to just enjoy himself and have fun with his friends. As for Toby, he was quite picky about who he got together with and had certain strict criteria for any guy he considered on a sexual level. Mandy was a whole different story. She had had a girlfriend about a year previously which had been her first proper experience of being in love, and after finding out that her girlfriend was cheating on her, was hurt very deeply and decided that life was too short to worry about relationships and so now focused her energies on having fun with her friends until she could meet someone she trusted.

I realised that I really did have a good group of friends, in general, very uncomplicated and just happy to accept whatever life threw at them. It was just a shame that they seemed quite into taking drugs when we went out, something that continued to disturb me but which I knew was simply a factor of the gay scene. However the more laid back approach to things in general was definitely my new attitude and I could not have been happier with my current situation. Somehow, leading a double life as I was doing did not seem to be a real problem. My parents just accepted that I was now going out a lot and probably presumed it was with girls. My siblings did not seem to care less, and it was easy to just fabricate things whenever I met up with Alex and the group. All in all, I decided that discovering the gay world was the best thing I had experienced in a long time.

At university, my relationship with Simon became weirder over the next few weeks. He seemed to be intent on trying to compete with me on some level, either by showing me up somehow in front of others, or continuing to boast about things that he had done or experienced to make me envious of him. I was not sure why he felt the need to do this, was it simply because I had turned him down sexually? That was a couple of months ago now and surely he would have gotten over it and managed to develop experiences with guys all by himself? I had thought it was the best thing ever that we were both gay and Jewish and could therefore enjoy what life had to offer together. Unfortunately the opposite turned out to be the case. I decided that I really did not want to play Simon's game, although it was hard not to feel affected by what he was doing. Although I thought my confidence had grown remarkably since having thrust myself into my new world, my underlying issues and self-doubt were still very much in evidence; I had simply managed to keep these feelings at bay for a while. Simon however, seemed to be able to find my weak spots and exploit them. If it was not my lack of fashion sense as he called it, then there would be other things like my skin not looking great, or my hair looking out of control again, or even that I was clearly just happy to throw myself onto any man that came onto me because I had no real standards.

I realised that from a certain point of view my recent bout of sexual activity came across as loose behaviour, but I simply wanted to enjoy every opportunity that came my way, I did not think it was because I was desperate. Somehow Simon's words made me think about what I was actually doing and if I thought about it all in more detail, I realised that it was my lack of self confidence that drove me to act in the way I did. If anyone showed me attention or paid me a compliment, I was so surprised that I did not want to lose the opportunity to feel wanted. I still did not like my own appearance and found it hard to see what others seemed to see in me. On rare occasions, I would glimpse in the mirror and just for a moment, would see something quite striking looking back at me. Was it this image that most people saw when they looked at me? Most of the time, that was not at all what I saw, and I only noticed a skinny, acne-ridden young man with bushy hair. Why was it that Simon had even wanted to experiment with me? Surely he could find someone far better? Maybe it was the trust thing as opposed to anything physical after all. Not that there had ever been any chance of it happening, it really would have been like incest for me. Why could he not see that too?

Over the weeks and months that followed I started to feel very alone again. Simon was obviously having a great time without me; Nathan, Toby and Mandy were fun to be with but I could not relate to their drug taking and our friendship did not seem to be based on any more than the frivolity of the gay scene. I realised that they did not in fact ask me much about my life or my background. It was as if just being there with them was enough. Did they actually care about how I may be feeling or what my thoughts were on things that really mattered? Then there was my family. Although living at home was fine, I was not really involved in things that were going on and did not even know what my siblings were doing or what their lives were like. They and my parents simply represented the Jewish world and I saw them all as stereotypes in the way they acted and spoke about things happening in the local community or in Israel, as if nothing in the wider world was of any importance whatsoever. None of them would understand the real me for a second, of that I was certain. Even God Himself, who I had felt I had such a close relationship with until recently, was now off my radar. I had been trying to punish Him for having let me down so much and causing me pain with the whole Tom situation. So who was there left to speak to when it came down to it? At the end of the day, I felt I had nobody to rely on but myself.

One evening, whilst in my room I suddenly felt the overwhelming urge to pray. Considering that I had been distancing myself from God, it was strange to have such a strong desire. I had not in fact had this feeling for quite a while and certainly the thought of it normally would have not occurred to me. But despite my issues with my Creator and my religion, I felt the need to connect with a higher source and ask some questions. I closed my eyes and imagined my soul connecting to the heavens.

Questions I had asked myself on several occasions sprung up into my mind and spilled out of my mouth:

Lord of the Heavens and the Earth, Creator of everything – I know I was born as I am. So if I was created as a gay person, why does the Jewish religion condemn my lifestyle in the strongest terms leading to certain persecution if I come out, when none of this is my fault?

Why am I not able to be open about myself within my family just because they are Jewish and do not comprehend things outside of our culture?

If I deserve to have love in my life as everyone does, why have all my efforts been thwarted?

Why do I continue to suffer horrible skin imperfections that nearly everyone else I know does not have to worry about? Isn't my sexuality enough of an issue to contend with?

Why have you decided that my oldest friend should be gay as well and rather than allow us to become a mutually supportive team, use our biggest thing in common to destroy our friendship?

The answers to these questions and others remained a mystery to me. Maybe some of these issues were not down to God anyway and were self-made, but I felt in a way that the path I had been taken down so far was being mapped out for me. I knew that one day I would need to find out the answers but as long as God knew what was in my heart, I had done as much as I could for now. I just hoped that I would receive some kind of sign that somehow things would work out for me.

I also knew that there would only be a certain amount of time that physical pleasure alone would fulfil me. What I really needed was someone to be there for me on a much deeper level, someone who would return my affections and be available to do so. Was I really thinking about having a serious relationship at this time in my life? I was nearly nineteen, but still young and some would say, still with so much to do before needing to settle down. Not that I would be able to have a real relationship with anyone while I was still living with my parents and keeping my gay life secret. So what was the answer? Continue to just have chance encounters? Try and make more effort to find someone special even if it meant having a covert relationship, or take the massive plunge and tell my family about me? It was something I simply did not feel ready to deal with. It was tough having nobody to be able to discuss these issues with properly. I realised that what would actually be best for me would be to at least let God back into my life because after all, whether I was gay or not He was still there watching over me. I decided that I should start to pray again on a daily basis and hope that He would understand me and make everything work out somehow. It was all I had to go on, and it was worth a shot.

After allowing myself to reconnect to my higher source, certain things came into perspective for me. I believed that it was still possible to feel close to God without the need to live in accordance with all the rules and regulations of my religion. Although there was probably no authority that would agree with this point of view, it made sense to me. I figured that God would never want any of His creations to live in pain or unhappiness and so would never have said that gay people were forbidden from living their lives like anybody else. It must have been some kind of misinterpretation in the Bible. I blamed the rabbis for having distorted the original meanings of Judaism over the centuries, to suit their own notions of acceptability and this meant that I felt perfectly within my rights to separate out my spiritual connection with God to my need to fulfil the practical laws of the religious institution. I had therefore been wrong in trying to cut God out of my life altogether, and would now continue on this new path which at least for me, was the perfect middle ground.

Unfortunately, my new way of thinking did not sit well with my parents who, as I became more lax in fulfilling religious practical observance, became more and more vocal in their disapproval. It had started with me no longer attending the synagogue, which I now just saw as a place where everyone was the same, with a narrow-minded view on the world. My mother would attempt to make me feel guilty for my lack of attendance and my father would try to assert his authority through bursts of rage when I declined to accompany him. However this did not make me feel any more inclined to go. I had also stopped wearing my skull cap, or 'Kippa', which was a universal symbol of Jewish attire that I had continued to wear until that point, except when going out into Soho. This was also a big no-no, for which I received murmurings of disapproval or a comment from my parents when I entered the room without it. However, these things simply no longer meant anything to me and I did not believe in living as a hypocrite. One thing was for sure, I had certainly become a wilful young man and stood firmly by the things I believed in, or not as the case may be. Little did I know that any apparent issues this caused with my family were nothing compared to what was about to come...

# Chapter 11

It was 1993. My first year at university seemed to pass by rather quickly, and that summer my nineteenth birthday came and went without too much fuss. I did not wish to do anything major to celebrate really, so just went out for dinner with a few of my friends. I had invited Alex and the rest of the old gang, as well as Simon who I felt I could not get away with ignoring. I had pondered over whether to invite Nathan, Toby and Mandy as well but worried that they may give my sexuality away. Mandy especially, was a rather obvious lesbian and so this alone would have raised eyebrows amongst the others. In the end, I played it safe and went out separately with them.

Thinking about the past year, I realised that so much had happened. I had officially joined the gay scene, made new friends and finally experienced sex, as well as discovering my oldest and closest friend was also gay. There was no going back now and in any case I would not have had it any other way. Things were becoming more awkward at home for me however, as my nocturnal lifestyle was prompting comments from my mother about what I might be getting up to. She would often say to me that she sincerely hoped I was not drinking too much, smoking anything or taking drugs as this would not be tolerated, and that it might also be nice for me to invite some of my friends over so she could meet them. I knew that she had said this so she would have the chance to give my friends the once over and decide if she approved or not. In any case, the very thought of bringing anyone over was unthinkable. As for smoking and drugs, I certainly had no desire to go down that road despite having had the opportunity several times, as neither appealed to me in the slightest. I was just quite happy drinking the odd alcopop and dancing the night away, whilst flirting with as many guys as possible.

I also felt that I would be having far more sex than I had been able to until now if I lived away from home, maybe in a shared flat or something where my space was private. The fact that I had no money ruled out that option straight away however. Most of the people I met had invited me to go back to their place but the thought of staying the night and then having to explain myself to my parents the next day was just too much of a hassle to bother with. I felt that I was really outgrowing my family and that they were still just stuck in their ways while I was exploring new things and learning about a different and more fulfilling way of life.

One night, while out with Nathan, Toby and Mandy on the town, I met an Italian guy who I had ended up getting frisky with in Soho Square after leaving the others at the bar we were in. I had not brought a coat with me that night thinking it was not too cold, but after a while, I started to feel it and began to shiver. Matteo, the Italian, was very considerate and offered me his jacket. When I left him to go home, I realised that I still had his jacket on and now would not know how to find him again. I therefore went home with it and as it was late, simply threw it over the stair rail without thinking and went up to bed.

The next day, my mother told me that she wanted to talk to me. At first I thought it may just be about her current issues with my lack of religious observance. However she then produced the jacket and with a suspicious expression on her face, asked me where I had got it as it was clear that it was not mine.

"Um, well a friend of mine lent it to me last night that's all, as I didn't have one and it was cold," came my swift reply.

"I would like to know what kind of friend would be carrying these around with him," continued my mother, evidently trying to stay calm but her face giving away her disappointment. She had produced a small clear plastic bag with pills inside, which as far as my knowledge of drugs went, was probably ecstasy.

"I, er, I don't know. I didn't even realise they were in there. I can't control what my friends do but I definitely have never taken anything like that," I said, attempting to defend myself.

"Evan, I think we need to have a chat about what you're actually getting up to when you go out to your bars and clubs. Although I don't approve of it, I have always tried to keep out of your business, but quite frankly I think it's time you told me what you do when you are out."

"Why do you care? I'm nineteen now and it's my life so I can do what I want!" I asserted, starting to feel decidedly uncomfortable now.

"Who are these friends of yours? I'm certain that Alex and Simon would not be getting into this kind of environment. Are you mixing with unsuitable people or non-Jewish girls, Evan?"

"I have lots of different friends now, not just Alex and Simon. People I meet at university."

"I'm concerned for you," continued my mother, refusing to let up. "You've changed somewhat over the last few months. You come home at all hours, stinking of smoke. You no longer go to synagogue or wear your kippa, which is something that worries me and your father greatly. Are you sexually active with girls?"

"No, I promise you, I am not having sex with any girls at all," came my totally honest reply.

"Are you telling me the truth, Evan? I can no longer be sure what you are doing, and it seems to me that you are getting yourself involved with the wrong kinds of people. Can you imagine if you decided to have sex with some girl, and even worse, a non-Jewish girl and got her pregnant?" My mother's eyes looked directly into mine, her accusing tone boring into me and making me feel very nervous indeed.

"Mum, I can assure you, I am not doing anything with girls at all and it would not be possible for me to get anyone pregnant, so just leave me alone and let me live my life!" I shouted resentfully, and with that snatched the jacket out of my mother's hands and ran up to my room.

I could not believe what had happened. My mother had never questioned me about my life in that way before. Damn that jacket with the incriminatory pills! I should have checked the pockets before coming home but I simply had not thought about it. At least I had avoided the subject of my sexuality. If my mother was as angry and upset as she appeared to be over some drugs and the possibility of me sleeping with non-Jewish girls, what on earth would be her reaction if she knew I was gay? As I stewed over the confrontation with my mother, my youngest brother Jonathan came into my room. He was now eleven years old and was in his first year at high school.

"Hey, I heard you shouting at Mum before. What's that all about?"

"Don't worry," I replied. "It's nothing you would understand anyway so just go away."

"I understand more than you think. Are you having sex with someone?" he asked, quickly followed by a giggle. "Don't worry you can tell me, I don't care."

I suddenly realised that if I was going to tell anyone in my family about me, I may as well start with Jonathan. He was still young enough hopefully not to have developed any ingrained prejudices and if I swore him to secrecy, then he would not tell anyone else, yet be able to grow up feeling more comfortable with having a gay brother. It may have been an ill-conceived thought, but it seemed to make the most sense to me at that moment.

"Jonathan, do you think you are too young to really understand things about sex?" I asked, testing the waters first.

"No way! I know what a blow job is, and what sex is all about. So what? I am more mature than you think, you know. I've almost gone all the way with a girl before, but don't tell Mum! It's my friend's sister, she's really nice and we messed around in her room once. So you see, I am more grown up than you think!"

Jonathan's confession came as a shock to me. Clearly people were starting out younger these days, but my own youngest brother? When I was eleven, I could never have imagined becoming sexually active on any level with anyone. However, as I was about to tell him something shocking about me, I thought I should force myself to get over this crazy news and try to act nonchalantly about it all and then process it later.

"Okay. Well, Mum's been asking me if I'm having sex with girls and I told her I wasn't."

"So what?" Jonathan replied, trying to come across as maturely as he could. "I don't care if you really are and you were lying to her. So, are you?" His expectant and quite excited face relished any juicy detail I would care to divulge.

"Well, the truth is, I am having sex, but it's with boys, not girls."

"Really? What do you mean? Are you gay then?"

"Yes I am. But nobody else knows, especially not in this family. And if you dare tell anyone, I will kill you."

"Don't worry, I won't. I think that's weird, why would you want to have sex with another boy?"

"Well, I was made like this, and there are a lot of people who are the same. We just like boys instead of girls, that's all. It's no big deal."

"So that jacket you've got there, did one of your boyfriends give it to you?" asked Jonathan, not seeming to be shocked at all, just rather intrigued and somewhat amused.

"Well, I wouldn't say he was my boyfriend, but yes, a guy I met gave this to me. Anyway, remember what I said, if you tell anyone I will kill you and also tell Mum about you and that girl."

"Yeah yeah, I understand. But that's so weird, liking boys like that!" And with that, he left the room.

I sat there for a while, thinking about what I had just done. I had come out to my brother! For some unexplainable reason, it had just made perfect sense to do so. His mainly calm reaction was a surprise though, but I suppose I did not know what I should be expecting from an eleven year old. I also trusted him somehow not to tell our mum about it. In any case, he had divulged something about himself which I could now use against him if need be, so it made me feel more comfortable. I actually felt a great sense of relief that at least someone else knew about me within my family. As for the rest of them, I feared that it would be a different story. As it happened, I did not have long to wait to find out.

The next day when nobody else was around, my mother approached me again, a general air of seriousness clouding her face.

"Evan, I've been thinking about our chat yesterday and I need to ask you something," she began, in a certain tone that made me feel decidedly on edge, as if impending doom was imminent.

"What do you want to ask?" came my guarded reply.

"When I was speaking to you about girls and the possible repercussions of having sex, you seemed to be completely certain that there were no girls in the frame."

"So? I was telling you the truth."

"Yes, I think you probably were but you see, I have this intuitive feeling that you have become sexually active. So when you said that it was impossible for you to have got a girl pregnant, was that because you in fact are having sex with boys?"

I stood there, shell-shocked. I had no idea what to say.

"Well?" continued my mother, intent on finding out what she wanted to know. "I asked you a question and I need to know the answer."

There was no point in hiding it any more and I could not bear the thought of lying in front of my mother, who in any case would see right through me for sure.

"Yes, Mum. I am having sex with boys. I'm gay you see."

For a second, a look of pain crossed my mother's face followed by a concerted attempt to remain composed.

"I see," she managed to continue, clearly choking back what was probably a mix of emotions. I realised that I now had to explain myself further, to somehow put things into context.

"Look, Mum, I er, I haven't just decided to be gay or something. I've always been this way ever since I can remember. In the last year or so I have just decided to do something about it because I'm an adult now and need to experience things that are important to me."

"Experience things?" spat my mother, now clearly unable to hold back her emotions. "The kinds of things you are picking up from people at university no doubt?"

"It's nothing to do with university!" I shouted back, trying to defend myself. "I already knew I was gay, even when I was at school and meeting different kinds of people at university just gave me the opportunity to finally do something about it. I would have been gay regardless, don't you see? I was born this way and I know this is who I am!"

"Don't be ridiculous!" my mother shot back. "Nobody is born this way. Things in life make you become perverted. I just don't understand it. What have your father and I done to make you this way? All you children were brought up the same, maybe we did something without realising, that affected you in a different way. I know your father wasn't around much when you were younger, as he was quite ill before we discovered his condition and he used to work a lot instead of spending time with you kids. Maybe it was the lack of fatherly influence or something. But why this?"

"Mum, it has nothing to do with Dad. I am just how I am because I was made this way. It's not true that things in life make you gay. Do you think I would have chosen to be like this? Do you realise the kind of torment I have been through all during my school years, knowing I was gay, feeling different from everyone else and not being able to do anything about it? Seeing other boys at school taunting and bullying others that seemed a bit effeminate and knowing that all the time, I was the one that was truly gay and could have received that treatment? It was hell! I am just who I am, it's still me, I am no different from how you have always known me. I am just attracted to men instead of women, that's all."

"Well that is unacceptable!" continued my mother, tears of pure anguish now streaming down her face. "I can't talk about this any more right now. You realise I need to tell your father, don't you? I can only imagine what he will think. Right now I can't even look at you!" And with that, my mother stormed from the room.

I simply stood there, completely numb. I had no idea what to think, what to do. How could I ever explain myself to my parents? Why would they even try to understand anyway? They were stuck in a totally different world. I had tried to explain as best I could, but seeing the grief on my mother's face made it almost impossible for me to think rationally. How could I be the cause of so much pain? Was there even any solution? One thing was for sure though, I was who I was and regardless of anything else, I simply could not go back, or pretend to be something else. I had to stand up for myself, it was my only option. Clearly nobody was going to do that for me.

My mind filled with all manner of thoughts and I left the house and took a long walk along the local streets to try and clear my head a bit.

As I walked along, oblivious to anything going on around me, I was startled from my thoughts by a slap on the arm. It was my sister Eva.

"Hey, I was calling you a couple of times from across the road and you ignored me. Are you deaf or something?"

"Oh, no, sorry, I was just in my own world for a moment."

"Well guess what? I'm going on a date tonight with a guy who seems really nice. I met him at my friend's party and we chatted for a few minutes but he had to leave early and then gave me his number. How cool is that!"

"Yeah, really cool I guess. Hope you enjoy yourself and it works out this time," I replied, managing to sound somewhat enthused for her.

"I hope so too! I'm going home to tell Mum and then get ready," she continued excitedly.

"Great, see you later."

Clearly my sister had no idea what had just happened and the revelation I had made about my life. I wondered how she would react when she found out. I certainly was not in the mood to bring that up now, and left her to stroll home to tell our mother who was currently beside herself, that she had a date. At least that would help things somewhat, surely?

At twenty-one, my sister was extremely pretty. She was also firmly entrenched in the local Jewish community and its associated social set up. Many of her friends were by now dating guys on a regular basis, some of them more seriously and my sister was one of the only few still not to have met anyone special, which was something that she felt pressurised to change, although would never admit it. My parents were also actively encouraging her to meet suitable men because in the Jewish culture, meeting and settling down with someone was very common before the age of twenty five. My sister had dated a few different people over the last couple of years but was incredibly fussy in fact, and would often find fault in the smallest of things, physical or otherwise which caused her to lose all interest in whichever poor guy displayed a particular fault. In any case, each time she managed to meet someone, my parents would hold their breath and pray that this would be the right one for her. In the Jewish world, time stood still for nobody and each year that went by without being married, was a year of wasted opportunity. I pitied my sister from that point of view, as girls always had it harder than the boys did.

As I continued walking, I thought to myself that it would be very difficult to go home right now. As soon as my father returned from work, he would find out about me, and probably all my siblings would be told too. Even though Jonathan already knew, it was the others I was more concerned about anyway. What would I be facing then, the next time I was there amongst them? With that in mind, I went to the underground station and caught the train into town, where I made my way into one of the Soho bars. Soho had become such a comfortable place for me now. I felt at home here somehow, and the familiar surroundings and friendly people enabled me to feel at ease. As I nursed an orange juice, I continued to analyse the confrontation with my mother. If she could not come to terms with who I was and the rest of my family felt the same way, how could I possibly carry on living at home? I had another year left at university in London before I had an opportunity to live in either France or Italy for a year as part of my degree. How would I manage for another whole year amongst my family? I certainly did not have enough money to move out. It was something that now made me feel very uncomfortable. Would I be thrown out of the family home anyway, thereby not being given any choice? What on earth were my options? I felt extremely unnerved and unsure about what was in store for me.

Eventually, I decided that I should go home and face the music, because I could not actually stop the train of events that were now taking place. At least in a worst case scenario, my whole family would know the truth and if I was disowned, it would be with a clear conscience and the knowledge that finally I had nothing left to hide from anyone.

# Chapter 12

When I arrived home, the house seemed rather quiet. I was unsure what that meant, but it was evening and normally at this time my family would be preparing to sit down to dinner, the TV on in the dining area and some drama series or other blaring out on high volume. Instead, I saw my mother standing alone in the kitchen. She had her back turned and appeared to be preparing some food. However her slightly hunched frame gave away the fact that something was not quite right.

"Mum," I called out, not sure what I would actually say next.

My mother turned around. She had clearly been crying quite a lot as her face was tear-stained and she looked devastated.

"Evan, your father and I need to talk to you." Her voice seemed broken, as if someone had died and she was struggling with the grieving process.

"Sure, okay. Where are the others?" I managed.

"I told them to go to their rooms and stay there for a while. They don't yet know anything but obviously they can tell there's something very wrong. Your father is in the living room." And with that, my mother went with me into the next room where she sat by my father and asked me to sit opposite them. My father had a strange expression on his face. It was almost stony, emotionless, and quite stern.

"Evan," continued my mother, "your father and I have been discussing your revelation and we are finding it extremely difficult to accept or understand. As you know, our family is everything to us and we have worked all our lives to raise you children in the best way we know how, with strong Jewish values. Your behaviour recently, of apparent disregard for everything we hold dear and lack of observance of our culture has been painful enough but now, with this... this latest blow we simply cannot come to terms with it."

I sat there, words failing me completely. I looked at my father.

"Yes Evan," he chimed in. "We simply cannot understand it at all and we are hurt very deeply." He seemed at a loss as to what else to say. In any case, it had always been my mother that had the main speaking role in my family.

"Your father and I feel that you have been mixing with unsuitable types recently and this has filled your mind with all sorts of things that are alien to our culture and values. We simply cannot believe that you are homosexual, but that you have become confused and are now going down a very dangerous path which if you do not change soon, will end up overtaking you and we cannot sit by and allow that to happen."

At that point, I snapped.

"Have you not listened to me at all?" I shouted, no longer being able to contain myself. "I already told you that I knew I was gay way before university, in fact while I was still at school, surrounded by orthodox Jews and Rabbis. What possible influence could I have had there to make me gay? I was born this way, that's all there is to it! You have no right to make out as if I have chosen to be like this and that I am doing something almost on purpose! That's ridiculous. Anyone would think I killed someone! Don't you even care if I am happy or not in my life?"

"You are still a young man, Evan," continued my mother. "You think everything you feel right now is completely right and that you know best. We have a whole lot more life experience than you and we know what truly matters. It's possible that somehow we didn't give you the best guidance or education when you were younger, and for that we will always be regretful. We are only human after all. But at the end of the day, the homosexual lifestyle is completely unacceptable and against everything we and our religion hold dear. We expect all of our children to lead happy, contented and fulfilled lives, in stable marriages and each one with children of their own. It is unfeasible that you should live a lifestyle that goes against the grain in this way and can only be considered perverse."

"Nothing about me is perverse, Mum," I countered. "You are trying to make out that there is only one way of doing things and that everybody must only have one path in life. That is probably due to you having been indoctrinated by this religion, but believe me, the reality is that God has created people in many different ways and everything is for a reason. I have never felt so happy and so fulfilled in my life since I knew who I was and started to live how I wanted. What on earth is wrong with loving someone just because they are the same sex as you? Look around you at the world. Wars, hatred, people judging each other for no reason. All I want to do is be able to meet someone and love them, and have a happy life just like anyone else. What should it matter that the person will be male instead of female? As for the children thing, well what if I was heterosexual and met a woman who was infertile? What difference would there be then?"

"Evan," interjected my father, "you were born into the Jewish faith and the Jewish way of life is the only acceptable way. Clearly if you met a woman and could not have children, that would be very unfortunate indeed but there are still options in that respect. I am very aware, maybe more than your mother, of different kinds of people in this world and things that drive people to do what they do. Maybe this is some kind of test from God? We have many tests in life that God sets us, and sometimes we need to see the truth of how we are supposed to live and overcome any obstacles to achieving what is set out for us. Choosing to go along a different path, however tempting it may seem, will only lead to damage in the long run. We simply cannot watch that happen to you."

"That's right," added my mother, "there are all sorts of helpful resources out there which we can look at for you, to get you back onto the right path again. You owe it to yourself and your heritage, and to us as your parents."

"I owe nobody any such thing!" I shot back, now full of frustration that my parents were simply not interested in my side of things at all, and my father's words having prompted a flashback to the fateful conversation I had had at the seminary in Israel with Rabbi Levine.

"I don't care what you say, I have not been tempted by this way of life and I chose to act on my natural inclinations, which is the way God made me. Don't you understand? Can't you see beyond your little closed worlds? That's why I can't bear to follow this stupid religion, because it has no relevance to anyone that doesn't fit the mould. What's the point in even talking to you both?" And with that, I ran out and up to my room where I lay on my bed and promptly burst into tears.

What on earth was I supposed to do? My parents seemed to be ganging up on me and for no reason other than they couldn't accept who I was. Goodness knew how my siblings would treat me after they found out. I could just imagine my sister especially, not being able to look at me in the eye out of pure embarrassment. I lay on my bed just thinking about what was happening to my life. The unfairness of everything! I had not actually done anything other than just be me. Why was I being punished for something I had no control over? Again, I looked to God and wondered how a supposedly all-loving Supreme Being would ever be able to do this to one of His creations.

After a while, there was a knock on the door and my father entered the room. I wondered what he might have to tell me, but in fact he just asked if I wanted to go for a drive with him. Unsure what he really wanted aside from possibly giving me another lecture, I decided to go out of curiosity if nothing else. My father had never really asked to spend time with me alone specifically before, so I was a little intrigued. We drove around for about five minutes before my father stopped the car next to a park several streets away.

"I wanted to talk to you alone, just the two of us," he began. "I know you think it's sometimes difficult to have your mother and I both talking to you together and I know that she is quite an emotional woman."

"That's okay," I replied, feeling actually quite grateful that my father had realised the difficulty of trying to get through to my mother and wanting a more civilised conversation. Maybe as the more rational and practical parent, I could make him understand things better?

"There's something I just need to ask you and I need you to be very honest with me," my father continued. "Is all of this, you telling us about your sexuality, just a way for you to rebel against us somehow, to punish us for something you think we've done to you?"

"Oh, no! No Dad, it isn't. I promise you. I would never do that to you. I told you because it's just who I am and it's just how it is. That's what I am trying to make you understand. I would never do such a thing just to rebel, which would be a horrible thing to do. Can't you just accept it's who I am?"

As I looked at my father, he started to cry. I had never seen my father display any real emotions before, let alone cry. It surprised me greatly and I was not sure what to do.

"You aren't dealing with this very well, are you," I managed, putting my hand on his shoulder.

"No, no I'm not," he replied, choking back the tears. "Evan, we have only ever wanted what's best for you, for all our children and with this, well we feel that somehow we must have let you down in a terrible way."

"No, not at all!" I replied, trying to reassure him as best I could. "Why can't you understand that it's nothing to do with you? I was simply made this way that's all. I had no choice about it and nobody has let me down at all. It's just a different life from the one you had planned for me I guess. I just want to be happy."

"You know, as I said before, I am quite aware of things that go in the world. Unlike your mother, I went to university and came across many different types of people. I just never expected anything like this with you. You know that you have always been the closest to your mother, the only one that really talks to her properly. That's why she is so upset. She wanted so much for you to live a full and happy life and make us proud. As for me, I just cannot accept this lifestyle; it's against everything our religion stands for."

"I know, you've told me that already but you just aren't getting it. It's irrelevant whether or not you think it's against our religion, because it was God that created me this way and so clearly He wanted it like this."

"Well I don't believe that. I believe somehow you have been influenced and that maybe you are just being led down a certain path that seems too tempting right now but will only lead to pain later on. I know that with the right help you will be able to overcome this."

"What do you mean help?" I asked, fearing my father was talking about psychiatric treatment or something.

"I mean there are certain groups you could join, certain people you could speak to who would understand things or who have been affected by this sort of problem and could help you find your way."

"Nothing like that will help at all!" I responded defiantly. "I am not the one who is confused or lost. I know who I am and I don't need clarification about anything! Maybe you and Mum should speak to someone? After all, it's both of you that need to come to terms with it all, not me that has to change."

"I'm afraid that's just not the way it is, Evan," said my father shaking his head sorrowfully, and with that, he started the car and drove us back home.

Although I had appreciated my father taking me aside to talk one-on-one, clearly nothing had actually changed although I had seen him display real emotion for the first time which obviously meant he was taking it all very badly. It was obvious that my parents were now set on trying to sort me out somehow and find me some kind of a 'cure'. I despaired over this and their surely futile attempts to come. Was my life now going to be one long battle against my own family, just to be able to be myself? How ludicrous was that? Did I really have nobody at all to turn to? Despite my attempts to connect to God recently, even that had proved fruitless as no sign had arrived that somehow there could be hope and I could be accepted. Could it actually be that in fact I was misguided somehow and despite believing I was born gay, it was not really the case? I doubted it very much but if so, who on earth was I in the end? Nothing could be worse for me, my own very existence the cause of pure anguish for the people closest to me. I thought for a second that death may be a preferable option to living through this hellish situation, but I could never have considered suicide as it just was not in my nature.

I longed for the possibility of being able to just run away somewhere, far away where nobody knew me at all and I could start again and just be me with nobody questioning me. But in reality that was impossible and in any case I had no real means of my own to do anything. My only option then, would be to soldier on and simply live through the hell of what I was sure was coming. I would survive it all somehow, with or without my family or religious ties intact. In the end, I still had myself to rely on and I knew that I somehow possessed an inner strength to be able to see me through.

# Chapter 13

Over the following weeks, the atmosphere at home was extremely strained. My parents had sat all my siblings down one day while I was not around, and had told them, presumably as best as they could manage, that I was gay. The effect of this news on each of them varied somewhat. My youngest brother Jonathan, who I had already told, continued to seem amused by it all somehow. My brother Daniel, having just turned fourteen years old, had asked me at dinner on one occasion whether I really felt happy being gay bearing in mind that it was so unnatural and against the Jewish religion. I did not know how to best respond to that and just replied that I was who I was and if the religion didn't like it then too bad. He shrugged his shoulders and mumbled something about not wanting to tell any of his friends as it would be too embarrassing.

My other brother Lewis, who had recently turned seventeen, was probably the most religious of my brothers. He was rather a moody person and since puberty, had shown increasing signs of social awkwardness. He had not spoken to me directly since he had found out, and refused to look at me in the eye.

Then there was my sister, Eva. She clearly found the whole thing far too awkward and uncomfortable to deal with, and it was clear that she had no idea how to handle it at all. She was twenty-one years old, her entire social circle was made up of orthodox Jews whose main aims in life were to find Mr or Ms Right, settle down and have children, whilst living a good and wholesome existence in accordance with our culture. Something like this would simply be too big a blight on her landscape and certainly none of her friends would understand or accept that she had a gay brother. I had always had an interesting relationship with my sister. During childhood I had emulated her, although she had only shown me disdain. Through adolescence our relationship had changed and we had become much closer, despite sometimes bickering and fighting which is something that most siblings endure, but ultimately we had always got on extremely well and I had a deep love for her. Watching her clearly very uncomfortable with the frequent scenes amongst the family, and with the situation with me in general, I felt a sense of sadness that in some way I had let her down. She had quite simple aims in life and just wanted to fit in with her friends and her environment. I would now always be the one black spot stopping her from being proud of the family she came from.

One Saturday, as we were all sitting down to a Sabbath lunch, the subject of my sexuality arose, due to Jonathan deciding to crack some kind of joke about it. Lewis had then suddenly burst out that it was the most disgusting thing ever and that he would rather die than have to associate himself with a gay person. My response to this was to shout back that he should just die then, because I was here and it was too bad. This subsequently launched a shouting match between everyone at the table and ended up with me standing up and saying to the rest of the family that if they couldn't accept who I was then they could all go to hell and I would leave home and happily never speak to any of them again, followed by storming up to my room.

There were several occasions when things of this nature occurred and almost always ended in my mother starting to cry. It was honestly as if I had committed mass murder or something, rather than just be me as I always had been, but gay. It confounded me entirely why being who I was caused such a strong and extreme reaction within my family. I put it down to the inherent narrow-minded nature of my culture, and scenes like this only served to make me want to distance myself further from any association with it.

Nevertheless, I felt that despite not being able to change who I was, I was letting my whole family down. My parents wanted nothing more than for all of us to continue a heritage that was so very precious to them and had also been to their parents before them and for the family line to be continued in as much abundance as possible. Aside from the religious and cultural aspects of life, children and family were the only things that drove my parents, and especially my mother. For one of their children to go so much against the grain must have been extremely difficult for them to handle.

When I stopped to think about all this, my heart broke with sadness. I knew it was an impossible situation. I simply could not be someone else than the real me, yet by being so, I caused devastation. What a wicked, cruel twist of fate. I had no explanation whatsoever as to why God would want to do this to me and my family who after all, were just innocent people put on this earth, trying to make the best of everything around them. I had never felt so alone or despondent in my whole life.

Because of the situation at home, each day became a struggle just to keep my head above water. My second year at university had started and I thought that I should at least get stuck into something instead of dwelling on what was going on around me. I had not really done much socialising through the summer break, having just seen my friends a few times and found a job working at a kosher burger bar to earn some pocket money. Simon had apparently gone to Israel for the last couple of weeks of the summer and seemed to be much more relaxed and warm towards me again when we met up at the start of the new term, recounting everything he had gotten up to with relish.

One day, we decided to have lunch together. I thought I should tell Simon what had happened to me with my family, as I really needed to talk to someone and had not been able to bring myself to tell anyone else about it yet.

"Oh my gosh, are you serious?" exclaimed Simon in horror once I had finished telling him about everything. "I could never imagine telling my parents, in fact nobody else knows yet about me and I keep everything really hush-hush. I'm just not ready to face something so terrible with anyone."

"Well, I was kind of given no choice really and in the end it all just had to come out. Although it's been awful so far, I actually don't regret it because at last my family knows the truth about me and I don't have to hide."

"Well, maybe, but I intend to have left home and be far enough away before anyone in my family finds out. By the way, can we just forget about all that weirdness between us a few months ago and try to just relax and have some fun?"

"I would like nothing better than to forget about it actually," I replied. "What a relief! I really wasn't sure what was going to happen to our friendship."

"Well, that's cool, I was just new to everything and thought it made sense but since then I've done loads of things with different guys. Anyway, on another note I was thinking that we need to start deciding what to do about our third year, because we're supposed to be going to either France or Italy to study and I would rather go with you so we can study together and at least have each other for company."

"Yes, sure that would be great," I responded, thinking that it would indeed make sense to do that. The truth was I had not actually given the third year much thought yet, especially in light of recent events but now that Simon had brought it up, I realised it was the best thing I had to look forward to as it meant I would create some real distance between myself and my family.

"So, where do you prefer to go?" I asked, starting to get quite excited. "I've been to France a few times actually and have never been to Italy so I guess I would prefer to go there."

"Cool, I would love to as well! We can start thinking of the best place and then look at the options over the next few weeks. I think we need to have decided by January."

"Great, that sounds a plan. And in the meantime, I intend to continue having as much fun as possible, even if my family are on my back."

"Well, I certainly want to do that too," replied Simon animatedly. "Do you still hang out with that frumpy Jewish guy, the other ginger one and the fat lesbian girl? You should try hanging out more with some of my other friends, they are far cooler and more interesting."

So, Simon had not really changed fundamentally at all, but at least I knew what I was dealing with.

"Sure, we can all go out one night, should be fun," I responded and with that we left to attend one of our lectures.

For the next few weeks, I concentrated hard on my studies, which in the second year included French and Italian literature and history. I found both quite interesting subjects, especially literature and the way different French and Italian authors throughout the ages had described things and told stories that continued to fascinate people to the present day. I was faced with the mammoth task of interpreting the works of Diderot, Voltaire and Camus as well as Pirandello and Calvino. Each author had completely different styles and getting under the skin of what they were trying to say was extremely challenging. I also continued spending as many evenings as I could out of the house, and in Soho where the never ending bar and club culture took my mind off my troubles for a few hours. If I was not out with Nathan, Toby and Mandy then I would spend time with Simon and his friends. To be honest, I did not care for any of Simon's clan at all as they were too pretentious and their main topics of conversation continued to revolve around fashion labels and where to buy the next expensive item. These things simply did not appeal to me. I also noticed that on several occasions, some of Simon's friends would look me up and down as if to size up my credentials. I felt like I was constantly being judged by them and it did not make me feel comfortable.

Sometimes, I would go into Soho alone and end up at a bar chatting to one of several guys who would express an interest. I certainly seemed to be popular and the attention I was getting was exactly what I needed for my self-esteem. However what now started to become a pattern was that if someone offered to take me out, I nearly always took them up on the offer even if I was not remotely interested in them, if only to be able to spend time with someone that seemed to want to be with me for who I was and without wanting to judge me or change me. Unfortunately, my date would often then assume that I wanted to see them again or possibly consider something more serious, but this was rarely the case and I would end up often disappointing them and ultimately, myself. Were these random dates and fleeting connections actually fulfilling me? I knew they weren't but my need to be accepted and wanted had become an overriding need in my life. I had no idea where any of it would lead but felt that the alternative of not having anyone to focus on me was too depressing to consider.

One day, I went out for coffee with Alex, who I had not spent much time with alone for a while now. We were talking about life in general and she had updated me on all her latest news which included a guy that she had become really interested in. She then turned to me.

"So, surely by now you have sorted yourself out and are seeing someone?"

"Well, actually I am not seeing anyone but I am going out a lot and meeting new people."

"Well, I know from Simon that you have made some new friends which is cool. Maybe I will get to meet them one day?"

At that point I decided to stop pussyfooting around and just tell Alex what was going on. After all, if my family knew, then surely this would be a walk in the park by comparison?

"Actually Alex," I replied, taking the bull by the horns "These new friends of mine are gay and so am I."

A small grin spread across her face. "I think I've guessed that for a while now, Evan," she said, taking my hand. "Call it women's intuition, but somehow I am just not surprised at all. I know people see it as wrong and everything, but at the end of the day, you are what you are I guess. Not that the others in our community would think the same way unfortunately but you can't help how you are, can you?"

"Are you serious?" I exclaimed, quite surprised. I was not sure what to expect from her as a reaction, but such a supportive response was definitely not it.

"Why wouldn't I be?" Alex replied, with a wink. "Look, I know it doesn't sit well within our religion so I suppose you're going to have to keep it all under wraps but what you do in your private life is nobody's business, is it?"

"But don't you see," I said, suddenly feeling exasperated, "I don't want to keep anything under wraps. I want to be me and live my life openly without having to hide anything. That's the problem!"

"Well let's get serious now," replied Alex. "You don't surely think that it's possible to be gay and live openly in the Jewish community, do you? I may not really care but I know that pretty much everyone else will have something to say about it and surely for your own sake you should just keep everything hidden. You weren't thinking of telling anyone else, were you?"

"Actually, I have told my whole family. They aren't dealing with it at all well but I'm just happy that I don't have to lie to them any more."

"Well," said Alex with a serious look on her face. "I'm not surprised that your family are finding it hard to deal with. As far as I am concerned, I am glad you told me, honestly I am. But you are just going to have to keep it secret if we are ever out with the others. That's my advice anyway."

"If that's the case then I would rather not hang out with the others any more!" I said defiantly, now feeling that my initial positivity was fast disappearing. I was almost hoping Alex may act as some kind of messenger for me, telling the others in the group about me and making sure they were alright about it somehow. But she was simply reinforcing the fact that just being who I was, was not acceptable and should remain some kind of dirty secret.

"Don't take things out of hand, Evan," Alex continued. "You know what Jewish society is like, especially in our community. It's for your own good. I just happen to be very open-minded, but the others simply aren't and you need to understand that."

"Well that no longer works for me," I said, feeling an overwhelming sense of sadness. "I am sick of defending myself and sick of feeling that I am somehow an unacceptable deviant that needs to hide my life from others. Why should I choose to spend any time with anyone that will not accept me? There are plenty of others who will."

"I guess you will do what you want in the end," replied Alex, "and I will always be here if you need to talk or anything but if I were you I would not burn my bridges."

"Well, that's just a choice I will have to make, isn't it. I have a life to lead and I intend to lead it without being judged by anyone."

I realised that although it may help my cause, telling Alex about Simon would not be a good move, as I knew he was extremely paranoid about being found out and would probably want to tell Alex or anyone else, in his own time.

After saying goodbye, I thought about the conversation I had had with Alex. She was a strong young woman and had a lot of influence within our group of friends. She could have stood up for me if she wanted to but somehow even she believed my lifestyle was something that needed to be kept hidden. Despite her personal support, I still felt I was back at square one. Unless we met up together separately, I would now not feel happy hanging out with her when the others were around, it was as simple as that. What would that do to our friendship, which was already nowhere near as close as it had once been? I knew more than ever that I needed to now forge my own way, alone, and continue to build a new world around me with people who did not make me feel inadequate in any way for who I was. It was now or never.

# Chapter 14

For the remainder of my second year at university, I concentrated on trying to get the best grades I could on my assignments. The studying was becoming quite hard, and especially with everything else I had to contend with at home, it was a job to keep myself focused. Simon always seemed to get better grades than me without working any harder than I did. It had been like that for as long as I could remember however and I had put it down to the fact that he was simply more intelligent. Nevertheless, it was starting to annoy me now, as I began to compare myself to him in terms of academic achievement and mostly found myself wanting. On top of this, despite having become closer with Simon again, he continued to be very judgemental about people and especially me, commenting on my appearance and trying to turn me into one of his clones. My skin was still troubled and it was affecting me and the way I saw myself, along with constantly unruly hair that still would never quite do what I wanted it to. Whereas I would buy my clothes from cheap high street stores, Simon would always be turned out in designer labels galore and continue to look at me pityingly for my apparent lack of style. It was something that I always found highly infuriating where Simon was concerned. How did he get to be more intelligent, or at least more academically gifted than me, never suffer from a single spot, have the money somehow to kit himself out in Ralph Lauren and lead a seemingly more carefree life than mine, which was currently fraught with tension? Did Simon see me as some kind of project now, someone to focus his pompous sense of false pride on? I was not really sure but I certainly did not like it.

I began to resent my life and my lot, feeling as I often had before, that I did not truly belong anywhere or fit in with anyone. Even Nathan, Toby and Mandy were starting to bore me somehow, continuing to be mainly obsessed with gay scene culture as a be all and end all in life and appearing completely uninterested in things I had to say that were not related to gay issues. Although I spent a lot of my time on the scene and enjoyed it immensely, I still ultimately saw it as a means to an end, hoping that at some point I would be able to meet someone special and settle down, not having to rely on Soho bars and clubs to fulfil my interests. My time spent with Tom had made me realise that having a steady boyfriend would be exactly what I needed and it was this that I craved. Despite everything, I also still felt a strong connection to God and although my relationship with Him was up and down I still firmly believed that He was the ultimate controller of the universe. I had nobody I could relate my deeper, spiritual feelings and thoughts to within the gay scene as nobody had any kind of interest in it and if I ever brought up the slightest reference to God in any conversation, I would get some very strange and pitying looks. Even where Simon was concerned, his spiritual side had completely taken a back seat. Was there really no place on earth that I could go where both my spirituality and sexuality could live together in harmony?

I continued to spend as much time as possible away from the house and would go out alone more and more, often meeting random men in bars, where I sometimes ended up going back to their place to have sex with them and sometimes just made them think I would as long as I was made to feel wanted. It was enough to keep me going for the moment, even though it did not really fulfil me. At least I was spending time in an environment just being myself, where I was considered normal and I had no need explain myself to anyone.

My mother had started to ask me if I would sit down and speak to one of the rabbis who taught at my high school to see if they could be of any help to me. I knew that this would be a fruitless exercise, especially after having tried to speak to Rabbi Levine in Israel. Nevertheless, just to show that I was trying to be co-operative, I accepted. One day when I came home from my lectures at university, I arrived to find Rabbi Katz, one of my high school Rabbis, at home. It took me quite by surprise, as I had not seen him since having left after my higher exams. Rabbi Katz had always been one of my preferred teachers at school, which did not mean much considering what they were mostly like. However I had found his Jewish Studies lessons somewhat interesting and he did have a more humanlike manner about him compared to the rest. I remembered that I had sometimes mentioned him to my parents as one of the only decent teachers at school who was capable of holding my interest. He was sitting in our kitchen, chatting away to my mother who I immediately realised had invited him over for the specific reason of talking to me.

"Hello dear," called out my mother as I walked into the room, and trying to sound as bright as possible. "You remember Rabbi Katz, don't you?"

"Hello Evan," said the rabbi warmly, as he stood and held out his hand to shake mine. "And how are things going for you at university?"

"Everything is fine, thank you," I replied, deciding I would play along with this game for the time being and see where it led.

"Evan," continued my mother, "Rabbi Katz has been asking about your welfare. As you know, he is now teaching both Daniel and Jonathan and says they are doing very well at school, so he thought he would find out how things are with you."

"Well that's nice of you Rabbi Katz but I'm not sure why you wanted to come to my home to find out?" I asked suspiciously.

"I just thought it would be a great opportunity for us to catch up and have a nice little chat," he said, trying to come across as innocently as possible, which was a manner I had never seen him behave in whilst at school. This alone was a complete give-away.

"Evan, why don't you take the rabbi into the living room so you aren't disturbed and I will bring in some tea for you both."

"As you wish, Mum," I replied, knowing immediately what this was all about. The cheek of my mother, trying to bring my old Rabbi back to somehow counsel me out of my 'condition', or some other such nonsensical plan!

We sat down in the living room and once my mother had brought in a tray of tea and some biscuits and closed the door behind her, the rabbi's face suddenly changed and became quite serious. I was immediately taken back to my experience at the seminary in Israel with Rabbi Levine, only this time, I knew exactly what Rabbi Katz would say and I was fully prepared.

"Evan," he began. "Your mother spoke to me with some concern over the way you are leading your life at the moment, and she mentioned a serious problem with your sexuality. Would you like to tell me more about this? I thought it would be good for me to hear you directly and try to find the best way to help you."

"Really," I replied nonchalantly, "I don't have any problem at all with my sexuality. If you are referring to the fact that I am gay, then yes that is the case, but the only problem with it seems to be from my parents' point of view so it might help you more to talk to them."

"I am aware of some considerable strain that has been caused between you and your family over this matter and believe me, there are many explanations as to why you think your sexuality is as it is. Explanations that we can certainly find solutions to, I'm sure."

"Okay, Rabbi Katz. If you can answer me a very basic and fundamental question to my satisfaction, then I will happily listen to any possible solution you may have to make things better."

"What is the question, Evan? I will certainly do my best to answer you."

"Why did God create homosexual people and then apparently dictate in the Bible that homosexual activity is an abomination, punishable by death, leading to the needless persecution and suffering of innocent gay people throughout history?"

"Well, that is in fact quite simple to answer," replied the rabbi, a slightly smug look on his face. "You see, God did not in fact create people as homosexuals.

Homosexuality is a chosen path, often the result of misguided influences from one's environment during the formative years. It can also be considered one of life's many tests that need to be overcome to reach your true potential..."

"I'm sorry," I interrupted, not feeling sorry at all. "Please do not continue with an answer of this nature. I haven't told my parents this yet, but when I went to seminary in Israel a couple of summers ago, I had a similar conversation with a Rabbi there who tried to tell me the same thing, that being gay is not part of creation but that it is just some kind of obstacle in life to overcome, almost like the desire to steal or something. The Rabbi there tried to tell me that it was just a sex-obsessed perversion of some sort and clearly didn't understand me or the real issue at hand at all, and it seems neither do you. I didn't ask you to try and patronise me, I asked you a proper question and I would like a proper answer. There is no doubt whatsoever that I was created as I am as many others are in the world. Would anyone in their right minds actually choose to be gay, knowing the severe problems this can cause in society and to their families? My sexuality is not an obstacle in life to overcome. I just want to know why God would allow such a paradox by creating people in a certain way who are then forbidden to live as they are, especially when all they want to do is love someone at the end of the day. Unless it isn't God's will at all and the difficulties gay people face are due to religious community leaders twisting everything? Please, clarify this question for me or else we have nothing more to speak about."

"I'm sorry you feel so strongly about this, Evan," continued Rabbi Katz. "Despite what you may think, homosexuality is not a natural state of being and does not form part of God's plan for the world. You may find this hard to believe, possibly because you cannot see things objectively, but there are ways of rectifying many issues that seem insurmountable. I actually know of a Rabbi that lives in Manchester who specialises in this area and has done a lot of research into the homosexual lifestyle and possible cures. It would be very prudent of you to contact him and go to see him. I will happily give you or your mother his details."

"How kind of you, Rabbi Katz. You may as well give it to my mother, as I have no need for it. I actually thought I respected you more than the others at high school but now, after this, I feel nothing but disappointment. My mum can see you out." And with that, I left the room and went upstairs.

Later that evening, my mother came to speak to me.

"Evan, I think it was very good of Rabbi Katz to come and see you especially. He told me that you were a very intelligent boy and clearly passionate about what you thought about things, although he mentioned that you came across as quite stubborn and hot-headed. You do know he was just trying to help you, don't you? He gave me the number of another Rabbi in Manchester that I think it would be really worthwhile talking to."

"Mum, please just leave me alone. It was a complete waste of time seeing Rabbi Katz and having gone along with your little scheme this time, I have no intention of doing so again. Nothing will change what I am; it is people's attitudes that need to change. As for seeing someone else, I think it is you that needs to get help with all this, not me. Can't you see that?"

At that point, my mother started to cry. I had no idea what I could do, she was obviously at the end of her tether and desperate to somehow overcome what she saw as a terrible situation. But why did I have to be sacrificed just to placate her?

"Evan," managed my mother through her tears, "we are doing all we can for you and desperately want to just get the best possible help. The least you can do is respect our wishes. We love you very much, we always have and always will, I want you to know that, but your continued refusal to change your ways will only damage our goodwill towards you."

"Excuse me?" I snapped. "What do you mean by damaging your goodwill?"

"I mean that as much as we love you, we cannot continue to support you or watch you do what you are doing to yourself. Your homosexual lifestyle, as well as your lack of religious observance, is against everything we stand for and we cannot have such disrespect while you are under our roof."

"I see," I replied. "So you would rather have me out of the house than see me live my life and be happy. Believe me, if I had the money I would have left already! I only have about six months until I go to Italy anyway so you will be well rid of me for a year in any case. In the meantime, just say the word and I will find somewhere to stay even if it's at my friends or on the streets if I have to. As long as I am with people who aren't narrow-minded bigots! Now leave me alone!"

My mother turned and left my room, in floods of tears. Despite my aggressive stance towards her, my heart broke inside. I was damaging my family, it was as simple as that. But I could not allow myself to be compromised just because others did not understand me. It was a hopeless situation.

Things continued to get even worse at home after that. My mother now seemed constantly broken, the slightest thing causing her to start crying. I feared she was actually having some kind of breakdown. None of my siblings could look at me in the eye and my father simply appeared sullen and serious. Sometimes my mother would wave a bible at me, quoting passages that referred to what would happen to people who did not follow God's will. She continued to try and suggest different forms of 'treatment' that I should try, including on one occasion a form of electric shock therapy, which I found a startling suggestion. We would often argue, heated tearful disputes that shook the whole house. Somehow, despite my mother's previous caution that she could not allow me to stay under her roof while living as I was, she could never bring herself to do anything about it. My life at home consisted of defending myself on a daily basis and feeling the need to justify my existence. It took all of my inner strength to keep up the fight but I had nobody at all on my side, so what choice did I have? As I continued my struggle to stand against my home-grown persecution, my self-esteem was knocked for six. I would look at myself in the mirror and see nothing but an ugly, pointless person who was destroying his family and who was not good enough to anyone as he was.

I thought back to some important occasions in my life where the whole world around me seemed to be happy such as my Bar Mitzvah, an event so full of joy and hope where everyone thought that I would grow up to be a man worthy of praise. Instead, look at what I had become now.

I had also reached a point where I was becoming deluded with all parts of my life. The Jewish culture had for a long time been the cause of serious doubts for me, and as for the Gay lifestyle, the more I spent time on the scene the more I realised just how shallow and two dimensional it was. It was about either physical enjoyment or political lobbying, and nothing deeper seemed to matter. The most important issues for the gay community at the time were how to lower the age of consent for gay sex to sixteen to be equal to heterosexuals, and various other equal rights challenges such as adoption and the banning of a law then in existence called 'Section 28', that prohibited discussing or teaching students in school about homosexuality. I knew that some of these concerns were very worthy as it was important to ensure equality in society, but I was never really very politically motivated and felt that the more militant types were doing an adequate job of fighting for gay people's needs. Beyond that, nothing else had much value and it was this that I felt disappointed with. My friends consisted of either Jews who did not understand or accept homosexuality or gay people who did not have any time for anything vaguely spiritual. My only two Jewish gay friends, Simon and Nathan, should have fit perfectly in the middle but seemed devoid of any real depth themselves, having become complete slaves to the hedonistic gay world. So where did that leave me?

As my second year at university came to a close, I thought about what the year had been like so far. I had come out to my parents, pulled my family apart and continued to increase my experience on the gay scene. Nothing that would really make you feel a sense of pride or achievement. I had submitted some decent assignments for my course and was now trying to revise for the end of year exams.

Simon and I had decided that we would go to Florence in Italy for our third year, because it was supposed to be beautiful and the centre of culture with a rich and vibrant history. We had tried to do some research on the kind of gay life in existence there and had read in the gay guide 'Spartacus', that there were indeed a number of bars and a couple of clubs that we would be able to go to regularly, so at least everything was available. Florence also had a very large main synagogue which was somewhat of a landmark, and I thought it would therefore be interesting to meet some of the local Jewish community while we were there. It was all quite exciting to think we would be able to have this experience and for me especially, to be far away from home. Despite all this, I had a nagging doubt about Simon, considering the way he was now, and hoped that sharing a place with him for all that time would not end up driving me mad. But I was willing to give it a shot as neither of us knew Florence at all and we would at least be able to discover everything together and have each other for moral support in a foreign country.

I also realised that in a couple of months, I would turn twenty years old. It was the end of my teenage years and the end of a long period of deep discomfort with myself and my surroundings. If the Jewish religion considered you an adult at thirteen, then so far my adult life had been a shambles. Could I somehow turn things around and make the next decade more meaningful and fulfilled? Would I finally be able to find the answers to questions that had been eating me up inside for so long? I did not know what I would be able to achieve but thought about how I could at least start with things I had more control over. The first thing I wanted to do desperately before going away was to at least try to make some kind of amends with my family. I intended to continue living a gay life but I thought that maybe if I tried to be a better Jew, if only for my parents' sake, then they may be able to take the bitter with the sweet more easily. This thought alone made me feel hopeful and ready to face the next stage of my life.

# Chapter 15

It was now halfway through 1994. I was scheduled to go to Florence with Simon at the end of September, and so after my second year exams at university were over, I spent the summer break working in a bakery to earn some extra cash to use as spending money. My parents were paying for all accommodation and major expenses for the year. I also had several conversations with my parents who, despite the ongoing issues we had, still wanted us to maintain a close relationship. The constant look of strain and raw emotion on my mother's face was always difficult to deal with but now that we were talking properly again, we could at least maintain a more civilised environment at home.

I had received from university, a list of several families based in Florence that were willing to take in students for short periods, which sounded ideal whilst Simon and I looked for some kind of apartment of our own. On looking through the list, I noticed a family with a Jewish name. My parents were extremely happy about this as it at least meant that I would have the opportunity to remain in an acceptable environment whilst away from home. When I told Simon, he did not seem overly interested one way or another and in fact said that he would prefer to stay in a non-religious place as it meant we could be freer to do what we wanted. In any case, I ended up making the decision for us and decided to keep my parents happy by choosing the Jewish family. Once arrangements were made for us to go there on arrival I felt much better that things were now taking shape.

I continued to go out with Nathan, Toby and Mandy on most weekends who all said they would really miss me while I was away and that we must make sure we kept in touch. I certainly intended to do so, and in the meantime just concentrated on enjoying myself in their company. Simon had invited me to a couple of parties that his friends were throwing in his honour and I went with him. They were as I expected, most of the people discussing fashion or celebrity culture and obviously sizing each other up for judging purposes. I was happy to be there to support Simon although became very bored and found an opportunity to leave when I saw that Simon was happily ensconced with his other friends and would barely even notice.

A couple of weeks before leaving for Italy, I went to a club in Soho with Nathan as I would often do. Whilst I was there, an extremely handsome guy approached me who I learned was Italian and was called Giancarlo. We hit it off and ended up talking for most of the night. It was great to practice my Italian with him and I actually found him very interesting company. We ended up swapping numbers at the end of the night and I called him the next day. Giancarlo lived in a small studio apartment in Kensington, one of the most affluent neighbourhoods in London, and invited me there that afternoon. On arrival, I found that he actually shared the studio with two others, and that he barely had any room there for his own things. He had come to London to improve his English and was currently working at an Italian restaurant but had no real money to speak of, hence being forced to live as he was for the time being. This did not bother me in the slightest however as I found him quite fascinating and soon was enraptured by stories of his life and travels so far. He was also very much into literature which I had in common with him and we spent a while discussing Italian authors and playwrights that I was also studying at university.

After a while, we went to a café and continued chatting away and before I knew it, it was quite late. I was happy to have met Giancarlo and it was refreshing to spend time with someone simply getting to know them without any attempt to become physical straight away. Over the next week or so, we saw each other almost daily and soon became very close. I had told Giancarlo that I was about to go to Italy for a year's study and he said that he would be happy to make the most of whatever time we had together beforehand. The only thing was that I was by now already getting quite attached to him. It was stupid really, with nowhere for us to go what was the point? But this charming, attractive and passionate man was doing his best to steal my heart and I seemed unable to do much about it. The two weeks we spent together were an incredibly intense time and also very romantic; we would have picnics in the park on our days off, hang out in cafes or bars in the evenings just talking and spend whatever time we could at his apartment when the others were not there, to connect sexually. I felt I was in a whirlwind romance and indeed, that is what it turned out to be.

The day before I left for Italy, we said goodbye. We told each other we would keep in touch but I realised that in reality, I would be gone for a long time and did not expect either him or myself to wait for the other, much as

I would have liked us to; I certainly was not ready to try and handle a long distance relationship. Giancarlo had been the perfect antidote to my troubles at home and had made me forget what was happening in my world for a short while. I did not regret a second of our time together. I also knew that any feelings I had developed for him would fade away soon, with no continued momentum to keep them going and so although sad to leave him behind, I was ready to go on my way. After all, I now had a whole new experience to look forward to!

The following day, after having said final goodbyes on the phone to my friends, my parents took me to the airport. Simon's parents were also with him and after we had checked in, we both bid them farewell. My mother was in tears as usual and as she hugged me, she whispered that she hoped I would manage to remember the things that mattered in life and that I would try to be a good Jew. I whispered back that I would do my best, and with that, turned and went through the departure gate.

"Wow, that was a bit emotional," said Simon, as we made our way through security.

"Yes I know," I replied. "I'm glad we are going though as I really did need a break from everything I've been through with my family recently. My mum has really not been coping with me being gay at all and it's been hard to deal with."

"Well, I simply could not imagine telling my family, maybe I will if I find a boyfriend but until then I am quite happy keeping it all secret. At least now we will have Florence to discover! I hear that the men are so stylish and sexy. All those great boutiques to visit and guys dressed like fashion models. That's what I call sex appeal!"

"If you say so, Simon. As long as you have something to keep you occupied, that's the main thing."

"Oh, by the way," Simon chirped up, suddenly looking very animated. "I forgot to tell you! A couple of nights ago I was out in town and I met this really great guy called Dean. He has an Aston Martin can you believe! We ended up going back to his place to have sex and spent most of yesterday together too. He told me to write to him from Florence and said that maybe he will take a trip out to see me at some point. How cool is that!"

"Wow, yes, that sounds great. I didn't tell you that I also met a guy a couple of weeks ago, a really lovely Italian guy in fact. We've been spending a lot of time together and I'm sad I had to leave him, but what can you do?"

"Oh really? That's a shame," said Simon in an indifferent tone of voice. "I wonder if Dean really will come and visit. I'm definitely going to write to him though. He told me he would take me shopping at all the best stores in Florence and go out to fabulous expensive restaurants. What a classy guy! I can just imagine me trying on all these great outfits in front of him and watching him smile with appreciation at my natural style and flair…"

At that point I zoned out of listening to Simon's ramblings. Sometimes he really did bore me. After having cleared security and paraded around the duty free stores for a while trying on various aftershave samples, it was time to board the plane to Florence. As we took our seats, I realised that this really was it – we were finally on our way!

Just over two hours later, we landed. The airport in Florence was pretty small but thankfully very close to the centre of the city. After collecting our luggage, we got a cab from the airport to the address where we were staying. It was a kind of bed and breakfast joint, otherwise known as a 'Pensione', which was located in the centre of town and we were welcomed by a very Jewish looking woman, who warmly ushered us in and up to our room. It was a small room with an en suite bathroom and a window with a view onto the city. The place was pleasant enough and neutrally decorated. We were given a list of 'house rules', and told to pay two week's rent up front. Our intention had been to stay here for the first month and by then to have found an apartment of our own to share. However the house rules were actually quite strict and included things such as not being allowed to come back later than eleven at night, having allotted times for being able to use the kitchen and having a limit on using the telephone as there was only one phone line in the house. In any event, we were told we had to pay for any calls we did make. Despite the landlady being pleasant enough, I wondered if we would actually be able to survive there for a whole month as it did not seem like we would be entirely relaxed and also the restrictions on when our curfew was, seemed rather at odds with our planned social agenda.

On our first full day in Florence, we decided to wander around the city on foot and take in as much as we could. We started by trying to find our university building. In a week's time, we would need to go and register ourselves at the university and sign on for the courses we were taking. One of our main tasks while abroad was also to do a lot of research for a large dissertation on a subject of our choice that we needed to present in our final year, so we would also need to find out where the main library was. The university building when we found it was large and beautiful. It was situated quite centrally and in fact just a few blocks from where we were staying. There were several ornate looking sculptures around the main entrance door and it all seemed quite grand. I wondered what it would be like inside, as it was closed when we got there. Afterwards, we headed to the library which was on the other side of the city followed by trying to get our bearings in general. We had maps with us and used our Italian to ask people for directions. We found everyone extremely happy to help us and on a couple of occasions, we were taken personally to where we wanted to go by warm and very friendly strangers which was something you never found in London.

After having seen a few landmarks and having worked out how to get to them from where we were staying, we stopped at a café for drinks and to talk about what we thought so far. We both agreed that Florence was indeed beautiful and that we had probably made the best choice. We still also had a week to do some proper sightseeing before our courses started, plus there would always be time between lectures and doing research to just experience what the city had to offer. Already, it felt like a world away from home and I personally could not have been happier.

The next day, we continued to look around the city properly. Florence was filled with small winding streets often paved with cobbled stones and elegant shops of all types welcoming you inside. It had a beautiful river running through the centre called the Arno, across which were a few bridges, one of them being the oldest bridge in the city which was littered with expensive jewellery boutiques on both sides. Right in the centre was also an enormous square which housed the main cathedral, or Duomo which stood proudly and majestically for all to see. Florence was truly magnificent and had a very fairy tale like quality to it. It was also famous for its museums and galleries, where you could find famed sculptures such as Michelangelo's David, and the Uffizi Gallery housing an abundance of stunning renaissance artwork. This was going to be a very cultural experience for us aside from anything else and I was very much looking forward to seeing everything.

Over the next few days, Simon and I managed to open a bank account and register as temporary residents in Italy. We also made the best of exploring the city's treasures including the numerous squares, or 'Piazzas', and the fantastic views from villages in the surrounding hills. Every evening we arrived back at the Pensione exhausted and were mostly in bed by ten thirty at night. We still had the nightlife to check out and promised ourselves that we would visit the gay bars and clubs soon. It also became apparent that things were not ideal at all at our current place. The landlady seemed to be casting her eagle eyes over us all the time and her restrictions were actually hard to live with. We decided to therefore start looking for our own place with immediate effect.

We managed to find a couple of estate agents, one in particular that seemed very helpful. A representative then showed us around a few properties. Most of them were quite nice although one in particular stood out for me. It was located about ten minutes walk from the main synagogue in fact and also happened to be very near to the university. On entering the building, there was a long communal hallway which had green carpets and mirrored walls. Statues lined the corridor, making it seem very posh and elegant indeed. There were a couple of apartments off the corridor and at the end was large door with a brass handle, which we found out was the place we were being shown. As we walked in, I could not believe my eyes. It had wooden panelled walls and a very high ceiling, which was decorated with copper vaulting and various emblems portraying different coats of arms. It looked far grander than I could have imagined and put the other places in the shade by comparison. The main living area was large and fully furnished with a pull out sofa bed. There was a small kitchen and bathroom that was decorated in quite a garish fashion, although that was a small issue in relation to the sheer beauty and grandeur of everything else. There was a stone staircase with wooden handrails that led up to the bedroom area. The bedroom was large and divided into two sections, so that Simon and I could have our own private space. There was also a galleried landing from which you could look down on the rest of the apartment below. It really was quite magnificent. Simon was also extremely impressed and we told the representative that we would take it there and then, fearing that we may lose out if we hesitated even for one day. After heading back to the estate agent's office, we read and signed the contract and paid a month's deposit and a month in advance, using the money our parents had given us. We finally had our own place!

When we went back to the Pensione and advised the landlady we were leaving early, she did not seem too bothered and wished us luck, reminding us that although we had paid for two weeks up front, she would not be returning the remaining weeks' rent as she now had nobody else to take our room at such short notice. She also told us that at the main synagogue, there were several youth activities that took place which we may find useful if we wanted to get to know some other Jewish people of our age. That sounded like a great idea to me as this was one of the things I had wanted to do, although Simon's main desire was to look into the gay scene as soon as possible and start to have some fun meeting guys. We then took all our things back to our new apartment and started to settle in.

The next day, we went to the university to register. It was an extremely long process and we had to queue up for quite a while, followed by going to different departments to have our student cards stamped and then get timetables. The place was filled with students of all types, not too dissimilar from what I remembered when first starting my course in London. I wondered what new friends we would make while we were here. It was all very exciting anyway. Once the proceedings were all taken care of and we knew what courses we were on and when the lectures took place, we decided to go for an early dinner followed by finally checking out a bar or two that evening. We had brought a list of the gay venues with us and once we had found them on our map, we decided to tackle them in order from the closest to the furthest from where we lived. Unbelievably, we found that the closest gay bar was almost opposite our new apartment! It was called 'Avanti', and by day it was a regular coffee shop open to anyone but by night it changed completely and a whole section at the back of the venue opened up and became a hive of activity. Various men spilled out of the entrance and as we pushed our way inside, we realised we were being eyed up in quite an obvious way by several guys, a couple of whom dared to pinch our backsides as we went past. Italians were certainly not backwards in coming forwards!

After we had bought drinks, we ventured into the back of the bar, which we noticed was much darker than the front. A film was playing on a screen on one of the walls and as I paid attention to what it was, realised that it was showing rather hard core pornography.

"Simon, look! I can't believe it!" I exclaimed in surprise, pointing at the screen.

"Yes I know! There's nothing like this at all in London! They must be so much more relaxed over here! Shall we stay and watch it?"

"Erm, actually I think I would rather go back to the main area and maybe see if I can chat to some of the guys out there. You stay here if you want to though."

"Are you sure? Okay then, I think I will. This stuff is kind of turning me on! If you can't find me when you want to leave, then I'll see you back at the apartment – it's not like there's long to walk!"

"Yes, sure. Have a good time then."

The truth was that I felt quite uncomfortable sitting watching pornographic films, especially with Simon and I felt far more at ease with just mingling with the other people. I had nothing to lose anyway, nobody knew me and had no basis on which to judge me. It was a good position to start from. As I wandered around and made my way through the crowded bar, I noticed a guy standing near the entrance by a window, looking as equally out of place as I felt I was. For one thing, he was quite blond which was extremely uncommon in Italy. He was also tall, probably about the same height as me and was classically good looking although not in a way that attracted me as far as I was concerned. He was holding a drink in his hand and looked like he was surveying the scene. I wondered where he was from as I was sure he was not Italian, and decided to try and talk to him.

"Hi there," I began, wanting to find out what language he spoke before continuing.

"Hey," came his reply, which sounded quite American to me. "You're not Italian are you?"

"No, I'm from London. My name is Evan and I only arrived a week or so ago with my friend Simon. We're here studying at the university for the year."

"That's so cool!" replied the guy, breaking into a broad smile. "I'm Jonathan. I've also come here to study from the States but I came alone. I'm from Boston."

We continued talking for a while and I found out that Jonathan was taking a lot of the same courses as Simon and I were. He also lived not far from us and was sharing an apartment with two Italian students. We were soon getting along quite well and I thought that we would probably be able to become good friends. Jonathan then asked me if I had been to the main gay club in the city, which was called Tabasco. When I told him I had not yet discovered what the gay scene had to offer beyond this bar, he asked if I wanted to come with him to the club which he had already been to and was definitely worth the visit. The offer sounded very tempting although I knew I would not be able to leave Simon behind as he would not thank me for having been somewhere that he had not yet been. I went back to find him and saw him sitting avidly watching the explicit film on show. Awkwardly I sidled up to him and whispered that I had met an American student who wanted to go to a club and did he fancy coming along? Excitedly, Simon jumped up and said that it sounded like a great idea as he was in the mood to dance for a while. I then took him back to the front of the bar and introduced him to Jonathan who was waiting for us. Jonathan smiled warmly and introduced himself. After a second or two of looking him up and down, Simon then responded in kind and we were then on our way to our first gay club night in Italy.

Tabasco was situated in a small side street off the main square where the Duomo cathedral was situated. You would never have noticed the entrance, as it was simply a black door, which had a slot in it that slid open when you pressed the buzzer. A face appeared at the slot asking how many of us there were. After we had answered them, the door then opened and we were welcomed inside. I found this to be a strange experience as in London all of the bars and clubs were very obvious and welcoming with no illusion of anything being 'behind closed doors'. I assumed that it was because Italy was a Catholic country where overt homosexuality was not really tolerated. In a way I supposed it was similar to how things might be in Israel.

We made our way down some stairs and were then presented with an entirely different scene. Europop music blared out everywhere and the place was filled with mainly men, dancing away or hanging out by the bar and chatting. As we walked through the club, I noticed several people turning to look at me, most of them smiling and some of them winking. It was the kind of response I was now used to getting from men, who on the whole really did seem to find me appealing. Despite this attention, I still felt that it must surely be someone else they were looking at as I continued to find it hard to believe I was that attractive. Being riddled with self-doubt for so long, it was strange to consider myself in a more confident light.

Nevertheless, I looked and smiled back at my admirers, feeling that I should at least give them something in return for their attention. Jonathan continued to show us around and then took us up some stairs at the other end of the club. There was a toilet area there with mirrors positioned just above the urinals, presumably so that others could look at you while you were relieving yourself without being too obvious. I found it extremely tacky and seedy but thought that things must simply work differently over here as there was nothing quite as obvious as this in London. We then went into a large room which Jonathan told us was a chill-out area. It was filled with soft pink lights, giving the room quite an ethereal glow. There was a separate bar there and several men relaxing on various sofas and bean bags. It had quite a nice feel to it actually, and I imagined it to be a good place to come to when you wanted a break from the dancing and loud music downstairs. Finally, we found another room which very obviously acted as the place to go if you had picked someone up and wanted to fool around with them. The room was darkened and there were small loungers dotted around as well as mats on the floor. On one of the walls was a screen which like in the bar we were at beforehand, was playing some kind of pornographic film. Clearly this kind of set up was commonplace in Italy.

After having explored the whole club, we decided to get a drink and then dance for a bit. Simon spent a lot of the time looking around, presumably to check out the kind of talent that this club had to offer. I was happy to just dance with Jonathan and enjoy the somewhat cheesy pop music. It was a new experience after all, and it was good to have met someone else to share it with. During the rest of the night, I managed to find out a lot more about

Jonathan. He was just a few months older than me and was already out to both his parents, who did not seem to mind at all that he was gay. In any case, he did not come from a remotely religious background and it seemed that his parents were quite liberal. He seemed to be a very happy-go-lucky kind of person and had decided to come to Italy alone to study as he wanted to get to know a new culture and to meet new people. When I told him about my experience so far having come out to my own family, he seemed quite shocked and offered various supportive comments. This was the kind of friend I really needed here in Italy. Simon seemed to have his own agenda somewhat and I had a feeling that as soon as he met anyone he found interesting enough, he would probably spend most of his time with them without worrying too much about me. Thankfully, that would not now be a real problem.

At around four in the morning, we all left the club and said goodbye. Simon and I had no lectures at university until the afternoon, so we at least were able to sleep in all morning. As I lay in bed I thought about the great night I had and of the new friend I had made in Jonathan. This was hopefully going to be a very interesting year and I already knew I had a lot to look forward to. Being away from home could not have come at a better time for me that was for certain. The distance between me and my parents would enable them to think about what I meant to them and put my sexuality in context so that when I next saw them, we could develop a real understanding between us. With these thoughts and hopes in my head and heart, I drifted off into a deep sleep.

# Chapter 16

Over the next few weeks, Simon and I settled into our new routines. We would attend university lectures almost daily and as everything was in Italian, we managed to improve our understanding and speaking skills greatly. When we were not at university, we would go to the library and delve into our research for the dissertations we were preparing for. I had chosen to write mine based on the Jewish population in Italy under Mussolini's regime. There was certainly a wealth of material to choose from and I knew that I would be kept very busy with it all.

One thing that I had noticed was that living with Simon was certainly not all it was cracked up to be. He was rather a fussy person and often played around with his food whereas I had a hearty appetite and tended to wolf mine down. Whenever I chose to cook at home, which was always something incredibly simple and foolproof as my cooking skills were not very developed, Simon would simply stare at it and play with it. It drove me insane as I mostly put a great deal of effort into making something as decent as possible. He would also spend an extraordinary amount of time in the bathroom, which frustrated me because by the time he was finished, I would barely have any time for myself before we had to head out somewhere and I felt I needed a lot of work to make myself look human in the mornings. If I wanted to go to bed at a certain time, Simon would decide at that moment to play loud music or try to talk to me about something. Generally he was very lazy and barely ever offered to help with anything or even attempt to clean or do his share of the cooking. It seemed as if we were living by his rules somehow and I was not happy with the situation.

One evening, I decided to broach the subject with him. I was dressed only in my underwear at the time as I had just come out of the shower which had been lukewarm after Simon had been in it beforehand, and had not yet bothered to go upstairs to put anything else on. Simon was sitting on the sofa watching TV.

"Simon, I want to talk to you about something," I began.

"Are you purposely trying to turn me on by any chance?" was his reply, which surprised me somewhat.

"What do you mean by that?"

"Well, with just those tight pants on, it's quite a sexy look but I'm not sure what you are trying to tell me."

"Oh, for goodness sake Simon, don't be ridiculous. In fact, I wanted to talk to you about some things that are annoying me."

"Like what?"

"Like the fact that you don't help enough around here, you don't eat my food properly, you take up all the time in the bathroom and often use up all the hot water with your long showers."

"Well, it's not my fault if I don't like what you make, and I do need to look good you know, it's very important to me. I'm not like you who doesn't seem to care that much about his appearance."

"What's that supposed to mean? I do care about my appearance actually, but if you're referring to the fact that I don't own designer labels then you know very well that I just don't care about that. As for the food, well if you don't like what I make, then try cooking yourself more often. I wouldn't be so rude as to play with it in front of you and not eat it."

"What's got up your nose then?" replied Simon huffily. "I'll eat how I want thank you and if you want to use the bathroom before me then you need to be quicker about it. I came here to have a good time, not to be lectured! And by the way if I were you, I would put something else on because it's slightly distracting watching you like that."

"Whatever Simon, just try to consider me a bit more, that's all," I said as I went upstairs to get dressed. I wasn't entirely sure why Simon was making such a big deal out of seeing me in my underwear however. It felt quite natural in a way, almost as if I was at home in front of one of my brothers or something.

I realised I probably was not accomplishing anything much and that at the end of the day, Simon would still do as he wanted. He was basically becoming a right pain and not making our experience in Italy as good as it should be. I felt like I was expected to make sure he was happy or that I should keep him occupied when he was bored. In fact, I would have preferred it if he found some of his own friends and just went off with them. Whenever we hung out with Jonathan, Simon would only just complain about things or moan that we were not doing what he wanted somehow. He was sucking the enjoyment out of everything and it was starting to get me down.

As I slept that night, I had a weird dream. It was almost as if it was real, although I was too deeply asleep to wake up and find out for sure. In my dream, I was lying helpless on my bed and a pair of hands was roaming my body, almost examining every crevice and poking and prodding me in the most sensitive and secret places. It was not actually a sexual dream in terms of being the least bit arousing but rather it was quite disturbing and uncomfortable. When I awoke in the morning, I had a strange feeling that something was not quite right, but put it down to the vividness of the dream. Simon was already downstairs watching TV and eating some toast, so I went to take my shower and then got dressed and made myself some tea and cereal which I ate while watching Madonna's new video on a music channel.

"She's just so cool, always changing her style and always looking fabulous," remarked Simon as he sat bopping along to the beat of the song.

"Yes, I guess so. I really like her music but she's not the best singer really, is she?" I chimed in, trying to sound like I cared.

"Well, style makes up for everything in my book and this woman certainly has style!"

"If you say so. By the way I had a really strange dream last night, I felt like someone was molesting me. I must have a lot on my mind."

"Oh, really? It was just a dream, don't worry about it," replied Simon, who then quickly got up, put his plate in the kitchen and told me he was off to the library to do some more research. Before I knew it, he was out of the door.

I decided that I could not be bothered to do any research that morning and as there was only one lecture to attend in the afternoon, I went out and walked to Jonathan's apartment to see if he was around. Luckily he was at home and as he did not have any lectures that morning either, we decided to wander around the city for a bit. I felt very comfortable with Jonathan, it was almost like we had known each other for years instead of just weeks. He had a very relaxed style and always seemed genuinely happy to see me and spend time with me without appearing to want anything in return, similar to the kind of relationship I had with Nathan, Toby and Mandy in London. It was an incredibly comforting feeling. I somehow knew that I could go to Jonathan with anything and he would always try to help me out, which was no longer the way I felt about Simon who had truly turned into a self-obsessed diva.

That evening, there was a youth event at the synagogue which was the first time an event of this nature had taken place since we had arrived. It was not so much an event in fact, than a social gathering where various young Jewish people could mingle and get to know each other. When I told Simon about it, he told me he would rather go to a bar and see if there were any hot guys to chat to, but I managed to convince him that he should at least try to attend this with me to meet some other Jews and that we could go to a bar on any other evening. Simon eventually agreed and we headed to the synagogue where I was looking forward to seeing who else would be there.

The social gathering was taking place in the synagogue's function hall at the back of the building, which in itself was a grand and beautiful structure with pointed dome-like sections of roof, giving it a slightly eastern look and feel. As we entered the hall, we saw that there were already several people there and that there were some tables laid out with food and soft drinks. Although slightly hesitant at first, I went over to the table and started to pour myself some cola. At that point, a girl of around my age came up next to me and smiled. She had brown curly hair that was quite short and wore baggy jeans and what seemed to be a man's shirt.

"Hey," she said, holding an empty cup next to me so that I would pour her some cola too. "I'm Caroline, nice to meet you."

"Hi there, I'm Evan. Are you American?"

"Yeah, from New York. I guess my accent gives me away. I'm here studying Italian and Business for a year. How about you?"

"I'm from London and I am studying Italian literature and history. Do you know any of these other people? I came here with my friend Simon over there," I said pointing to Simon who was standing in the corner looking around and not seeming to be impressed by what he saw.

"Well that's cool. Why don't you introduce him to me? I know a couple of others here who I met on my course but that's it really. I would definitely love to meet some new friends though."

With that, we went up to Simon who looked rather nonplussed by the whole situation.

"Simon, this is Caroline," I said enthusiastically. "She's American and she's at our university but on a different course."

"Hi there," said Simon, barely looking her in the eye. He then leaned over and whispered loudly and not very discreetly "She looks like a lesbian to me. Just look at what she's wearing!"

"Actually," replied Caroline, who had clearly overheard Simon's comment, "I AM a lesbian. Is that a problem?"

"Oh, no not at all," I quickly interjected. "In fact, Simon and I are gay too, although we're just friends. Coincidence, huh?"

"Oh really?" replied Caroline eagerly. "I never thought I would get to meet any gay Jews over here. That's pretty cool!"

"Yes it is!" I exclaimed. "What's it like being gay and Jewish in the States then?"

"Well, it's no big deal for me as I am not in the least bit religious but there are several gay Jewish communities that exist within synagogues that cater for minority groups."

"Wow, I can't believe it! It sounds like things are far more relaxed over there then. In London, nothing like that exists as far as I know and I am from a religious environment where it's not tolerated at all."

"Oh that sucks," said Caroline sympathetically. "I would hate to live in an environment like that. Anyway, it would be nice to hang out with you and get to know you more while we are here."

"Absolutely! I can introduce you to my friend Jonathan as well, he's from Boston. We can all get together and do stuff, it would be really great."

"Okay, you're on! How cool to have met you, I wasn't sure if I would meet many people who I would be able to hang out with and have fun with here."

For the rest of the evening we chatted further and I also got to meet some other people including a flame-haired girl called Bonnie who was another American and a hippy looking guy called Eduardo who was from Pisa but studying law in Florence. It was certainly a melting pot of different kinds of people and I enjoyed getting to know them. They were quite a mixed bunch of more religious and also liberal types. I wondered if that was a reflection on the general community here in Florence and decided that if it was, it was definitely more varied than the North West London Jewish community that I had been brought up in.

Throughout the evening, Simon did not say much and only made the smallest of efforts to speak to anyone. I felt slightly ashamed as I was doing my best to introduce him to people and thought that they would just find him rude and somehow tarnish me with the same brush. When we got back to our apartment, Simon complained that it had been a boring evening and a waste when he could have been at a bar having a good time. I did not bother to get into an argument with him and simply got ready for bed.

That night as I slept, I had the distinct feeling that I was being groped again. It was such a vivid dream like the time before, and yet I could not bring myself to wake up properly. Those hands were back, they were everywhere and I seemed to be rigid with fear and unable to even move. My body was being violated and somehow I could not do anything about it. In the morning, I decided to simply try to ignore the feelings of discomfort that were still with me and carry on as usual.

"I had a great dream last night," said Simon as we ate breakfast. "I was in bed with this guy and I was feeling him all over, he was so hot and his body felt great. It made me feel really randy. I am definitely going to a bar tonight to pick someone up."

"That's nice for you. Hope you manage to find someone," I replied, my cereal sticking in my throat as a bolt of horror ripped through me. Could what I dreamed last night and the time before possibly be what I thought it was? Surely not! I decided to suppress my thoughts and try and forget all about it. Surely it was just a dream after all and Simon's own dream had nothing to do with mine? I was certain that this must be the case.

At university that day, Jonathan found Simon and I and introduced us to a gay Italian student he had made friends with through one of his lectures. His name was Luca, and he was quite a short guy with rather black bushy eyebrows, an aquiline nose and a cheeky smile. I also noticed that he had extraordinarily long eyelashes, something most women would probably die for. We chatted for a while and then all went to a café to continue getting to know Luca better. He was the same age as the rest of us and still lived at home with his family, as was often the case with students in Italy. He had a twin brother and was not yet out about himself to his family, who were quite strict Catholics. I found this quite interesting and wanted to know how he felt about his situation. As far as he was concerned, he was in no rush to tell his family anything and was happy with the way things were. He certainly feared what his father and brother may think if he told them, as both of them were by all accounts very chauvinistic with very traditional views on sexuality. Surprisingly, he and Simon seemed to hit it off rather well and there seemed to be a physical attraction between them too. This was something I was quite happy to see as it meant that hopefully Simon would become more occupied and may calm down somewhat if things went anywhere.

After we left the café, I managed to catch up with Jonathan separately. We discussed Luca and the fact he seemed to be a really nice person who I was looking forward to spending more time with. I then asked Jonathan what he really thought about Simon.

"Well, he seems friendly enough and all," replied Jonathan, appearing to want to be diplomatic. "I guess he has an edge to him though, like he looks at others and judges them a lot. I noticed he did that with me when we first met. He also likes to complain, doesn't he?"

"Yes, he can be quite like that I guess. I just wasn't sure what you really thought as he can sometimes be rude and hard to deal with."

"I can see that actually, but I'm cool about it and happy to just hang out and have a good time as long as he doesn't direct anything against me."

"Well that's good then," I said, happy that at least Simon hadn't got to anyone else too badly yet.

I was feeling more and more uncomfortable living with Simon in fact and after only a couple of months into the year, I dreaded to think how I would cope with the rest of our time here. There was also the nagging feeling I had in the back of my head that something was going on at night while I slept which I could not bear to try and think about too much.

Over the next few days, I managed to be quite productive. I did a lot of research at the library, introduced my new friend Caroline to Jonathan and Luca and spent more time with them going out at night. Simon continued to get on well with Luca and soon they were inseparable. When they came out with the rest of us, they simply spent most of the time kissing each other or whispering in each others' ears. Other times, they would just do their own thing separately. I felt that Luca was a very genuine and sensitive kind of person and was slightly worried that Simon may end up hurting him somehow once the initial flurry of excitement was over. Simon normally only bothered with anyone that could give him something he wanted, or made him look good somehow and I wondered what it was that he wanted from Luca. Time would tell however.

One morning, our doorbell rang and when Simon went to answer the door, a small group of four female students that I recognised from our course back in London, entered our apartment. I was surprised at first as I did not realise that anyone else from London was in Florence, but it was actually quite comforting somehow to see some familiar faces. I had not really had anything to do with them before now and found out that they were all sharing an apartment together and had contacted the university in London to find out if there was anyone else in Florence, which led them to finding us. Once students had found somewhere to stay for the year, it was their responsibility to send their addresses to the faculty department in London so the university could keep track of everyone on a list. This then enabled them to provide contact details of all the students for anyone who needed to know.

The girls introduced themselves as Gemma, Miranda, Kate and Anyesa. Gemma and Miranda were apparently close friends already and had asked the other two to share an apartment with them in Florence when they found out they were also going to be here. Gemma was quite a loud girl who seemed to dominate the whole group. She had a habit of playing with her long curly hair as she spoke, almost like a little child would. Miranda seemed to be Gemma's 'yes' girl, agreeing with whatever she said. She was quite pretty in a subtle way and incredibly slim. Kate was a typical English rose. She had what you would call a 'peaches and cream' complexion and straight blonde hair. She seemed quite open and friendly and someone you could always rely on to make you laugh, although she appeared to be somewhat independent from the others. Finally there was Anyesa, easily the quietest girl in the group but who I immediately felt the strongest connection to. She told us that she was half Italian herself, on her father's side which explained her name. She had long straight black hair, and a very full figure. Some would say she was overweight but for me, her slightly mumsy appearance in fact gave her a very warm and friendly aura.

As we continued to talk, it became clear that Gemma and Miranda were definitely more Simon's type. They enjoyed talking about others and making judgements on appearances, whilst being almost as obsessed with designer labels as Simon was. Kate stood out in her own right as someone who was just happy to go with the flow and do her own thing. Anyesa was clearly quite shy and I could tell that she probably needed to have a close friend who was happy to spend time with her and who she could look after somehow.

It had been good to meet these new people and I felt that my year in Italy would probably be very rewarding and more importantly, would also help to give me a real sense of belonging somewhere while I was here.

Later that day, I spent some time calling home. I spoke to my mother who asked how I was getting on. I decided not to bring anything up about my foray into the Florence gay scene and instead concentrated on talking about the friends I had met and how my research was going. The conversation was somewhat strained however and I could tell that my mother was still trying to come to terms with things while at the same time, missing me a lot. For my part, I felt I really was a world away from home and not having had my family on top of me for a while felt quite liberating. As my mother continued to ask me questions about what I was getting up to, I became more closed and vague, not liking the feeling of being interrogated. The truth was that although I was involving myself to some extent with the local Jewish community, I was not leading a religious lifestyle in the least, which was something my parents had expected me to try and do. I was also clearly enjoying my gay life and so if I were to tell my mother everything I was doing, it would not paint a very pretty picture for her. After I hung up eventually, I felt a sense of relief that the conversation was over. There was clearly still much to be resolved between me and my family.

I also spent a couple of hours writing various letters to my friends in London: Alex, Nathan, Toby and Mandy. I considered writing to Giancarlo as well, but in the end decided against it as, although he was a special person who had given me a great experience just before leaving for Italy, I realised I could not picture things working out for us in the future.

That night, after having been to a couple of bars with Jonathan and Caroline, I lay in bed and thought about my experience in Italy so far. The first couple of months had flown by and I had met some great new people. Being away from home was the best thing for me at this time as well, and allowed me to feel I could be independent from my family, which is what I needed. I sincerely hoped that things would turn out alright in the end as I really wanted nothing more than to be close with my family again and for them all to accept me properly for who I was but I realised that would still take some time. My thoughts then turned to Simon. Somehow our friendship just wasn't the same as it used to be. In fact, it had deteriorated somewhat and I no longer felt I really understood him or even liked him that much. It was a real shame, and I could only trace it back to when he told me he was gay. Somehow, living as a gay man brought out the worst in him, all the worst characteristics often associated with the gay community. I felt a sense of discomfort about this as it was so far removed from my own approach and yet I felt I may be associated with him by default by everyone we met. I really was not sure what to do about the state of our friendship. As these thoughts buzzed around in my head, I drifted off to sleep.

At some point during the night, I had my dream again. Exactly the same as the previous times although this time I could almost feel someone on top of me. It was a terrifying dream, and as before, I seemed to be frozen in my sleep, rigid with fear and unable to do anything. I felt the hands again, this time more urgently probing me and pulling at my groin area. I was certain that someone was straddling me and it felt like they were trying to insert something inside me, between my legs. The whole thing had a very bad feeling about it. After what seemed like an eternity of torture and with a concerted effort, I dragged myself out of my sleep and with a jolt, sat up and shoved my molester as hard as I could so that he fell off my bed and onto the floor. When I focused my eyes, my worst nightmare became reality. It was Simon. With a surprised and scared look on his face, he immediately jumped up and ran from the room.

My head started racing. Simon! Why? Why are you doing this to me? What have I done to deserve being molested in my sleep by someone I am supposed to call my friend? I wanted to run after him and make him explain himself but I simply could not move. I felt sick to the core, and completely violated. My world crumbled before my eyes.

# Chapter 17

Life after discovering Simon had been molesting me in my sleep was not the same. The night I had caught him in the act, I had not been able to bring myself to move or go and speak to him. However the following morning, I saw him trying to leave the apartment without me noticing and had stopped him, made him sit down and talk. He had refused to admit anything at first other than he must have been having a dream and somehow acted it out, almost like when someone sleepwalks. I did not believe him and forced him to stay until he told me the truth, becoming quite aggressive towards him. Then suddenly he snapped and began a tirade which took me aback somewhat.

"You really think you are something special, don't you!" he spat venomously. "You think just because people always seem to like you that you can look down on me or something. I know you don't approve of how I do things but I choose to be how I am and I love my life. Your little attempt to try and lecture me a couple of weeks ago really showed how you think you are better than everyone. You may be far better looking than me but I have style and taste, more than you could ever dream of. The only reason I still hang around with you is out of pity! Ever since you thought you were too good to experiment with me when I asked you a year ago, things have changed between us. Please don't think you were doing me any favours back then, it was simply a convenient option as far as I was concerned. I also see how you try and put me in the shadows whenever we go anywhere. You always demand people's attention; you barely ever let me get a look in! But you're not better than me, you're nothing! What I've been doing to you was all about power. It meant I could do what I wanted and you didn't have any choice. It made me feel great. I certainly don't need people like you to judge me and how I am, and you needed to learn a lesson!"

"You twisted, disgusting monster!" I shouted. "You're no friend of mine, you're sick! I have never looked down on you at all, in fact for most of our friendship I've looked up to you and envied you, but now I can't imagine what I was thinking. You had better keep your distance from now on; I want nothing more to do with you!"

With that, Simon got up and left the apartment, slamming the door behind him. I really did not know what to think, but all I knew was that I no longer saw Simon as the friend I had always had. He had changed beyond recognition and his behaviour of late had been deplorable even aside from what he had been doing to me physically. He had betrayed our friendship in a way that I could never have expected. How could I continue living with him here and how could I bear to even look at him again? I thought about trying to get my own place, but it was not exactly feasible as I would not be able to afford it and I did not like the idea of sharing with some complete strangers. We would just have to ensure we kept out of each others' way although it would be difficult. I wondered if I should go to the police and report him, as it was surely a criminal activity to molest someone against their will. It's what he deserved after all. However the thought of this getting out anywhere and anyone else knowing about it was something I could not bear. I knew Simon would not think for a second of telling anyone and bringing shame on himself in the process. I just did not want this to spill outside into the wider world, or for any of my friends to know what had happened. I realised that it would now be very hard to carry on as normal, as if nothing had happened especially as long as I was at such close quarters with Simon for the rest of my time in Florence.

Feeling devastated and somehow blaming myself for having made this happen, I started to pray again and ask God some questions, something I had not bothered to do much since arriving in Italy. Why had this happened to me? Why Simon? What did it all mean? Did he really hate me that much and if so, was there anything I could have done differently? Why on earth had our friendship come to this? I needed God to give me some answers. Suddenly, even despite having met my new friends, I felt lonelier than ever. Maybe everything was indeed my fault. Maybe the pain I had caused my family was coming back to haunt me. Maybe being gay was so very sinful that the only result of my lifestyle could be this kind of trauma. I did not know what do think, what to do. I just knew I could barely face anyone for the time being.

Outside of university lectures and trying to continue my research, I pretty much stayed at home, not feeling sociable at all and ignoring calls from people. I knew that Jonathan would certainly wonder where I had got to but I simply could not face anything. I would see Simon going about his business, never saying a word to me and sometimes defiantly bringing Luca back to have sex, mostly as loudly as possible knowing I was around. I just felt sick.

One day, when I was alone at the apartment watching music videos, the doorbell rang. I contemplated not answering the intercom but after a few rings, I decided I may as well see who it was. It was Jonathan, who had been worried about me and come to see what was wrong. I realised that I could not hide forever and decided to let him in.

"Evan, are you okay? I haven't seen you for about two weeks!"

"Sorry, I've just not been well and not felt like going out anywhere."

"I tried to call you several times but you didn't answer. Are you sure everything is alright?"

"I would really rather not talk about it if that's okay with you. It's just been a difficult time for me, that's all."

"Is it about your family or something? You know I'm here if you need a friend, right? Caroline has also been asking about you and Luca told me he has seen you when he comes over with Simon but you almost ignore him each time."

"I'm so sorry, it's nothing to do with him at all or even my family, really it isn't. Honestly can we just talk about something else?"

"Why sure, that's cool. Let's go out for a coffee, come on it's been ages and I really wanted to spend some time with you. We don't have to stay out long, promise."

Eventually I agreed and Jonathan and I went to a local cafe where he managed to cheer me up somewhat with tales of guys he had met at bars recently. I knew that I would have to snap out of my state of depression otherwise people would really start to worry and when I thought about it, I could not bear the thought of Simon thinking he had succeeded in crushing me. With supreme effort I brought myself back into the land of the living. After all, I was in a truly magical place, experiencing something that many people only dreamed of and I needed to make the most of it and treasure each day. I arranged with Jonathan that we would go out that night and also spoke to Caroline who was relieved that I was alright and said she could not wait to see me.

The evening did me a world of good. We went for pizza at one of Florence's many 'Trattorias', followed by drinking at a few bars and then ending up at Tabasco nightclub. It was a great night and I was so glad I had kick started my life back into action.

It was almost Christmas time before I knew it, and most of the foreign students decided to go back home to spend the festive period with their families. Being Jewish, I had no real reason to go back and felt I would definitely rather stay in Italy anyway. Unfortunately, Simon felt the same way but at least Jonathan had also decided to stay. A week before everyone left to go home, Gemma, Miranda, Kate and Anyesa decided to have a pre-Christmas party at their place to mark the occasion. I asked them if I was able to bring a couple of friends and they said of course, it would be great to meet anyone I wanted to bring along. The party was a really nice experience. I introduced Jonathan and Caroline to the others and we spent the evening drinking, eating snacks and dancing to current European chart hits. Simon had come, apparently alone which was strange as I expected he would have brought Luca. But he spent most of the time sticking closely to Gemma and Miranda allowing me to conveniently ignore him. I spent a lot of the evening getting to know Anyesa far better and felt that she was someone I really could see myself being friends with after this whole experience was over. Her natural warmth made me feel really comfortable and somehow I knew that she valued my company as much as I was beginning to value hers.

Christmas itself came and went and was rather quiet. In Italy, everybody went back to their families as it was considered an extremely sacred day, more so than in the UK where somehow it just appeared to be a highly commercialised event. Thankfully, I managed to stay away from Simon and had gone to Jonathan's apartment for dinner on Christmas day. On New Year's Eve, Jonathan and I went to a nearby city called Bologna which was also extremely pretty, as there was a big party taking place for the gay community at a rather famous nightclub called Depot. We spent the night having fun and both managed to meet interesting guys to chat to, who we kissed as the clock struck twelve. It was the perfect way to see 1994 come to an end.

When the new term started at university in January, I managed to catch up with Luca who I had not seen for a while by that point. I explained that I had not been feeling well for a couple of weeks before Christmas and that I had not intentionally ignored him when he had been round to my place with Simon. I also said that it was a shame Simon had not brought him to the Christmas party we had all gone to. Luca then told me he was no longer seeing Simon. When I asked what had happened, Luca explained that Simon had suddenly gone cold on him and told him he had gotten bored. He had not offered any other explanation and Luca had been quite upset and somewhat hurt by the sudden rejection. This did not surprise me however, knowing that Simon had lost any sense of morality or humanness about him. It meant at least, that I could continue being friends with Luca without worrying about Simon being around. I no longer cared what Simon did or where he went at all, I was simply happy with my group of friends who were all genuine and caring people.

The next time I spoke to my parents, my mother informed me that she was going to be coming out to Florence to visit me for a few days and that she intended to stay with me at the apartment. Although usually this would have been a great thing and of course perfectly normal, I was not psychologically prepared for it, and thought that it would be an awkward environment especially as I still lived with Simon. On top of this, she would soon see that I was not leading a religious lifestyle and may find this hard to deal with. But I could not prevent her coming as after all, she and my father were paying for me to be here and so I simply had to prepare for the visit the best way I could. I felt a mixture of emotions about my mother's forthcoming visit. On one hand, surely it would be a good thing for her to see that I was capable of living my life independently, and meeting some of my friends. That is what any student in my position would be happy about. But of course, I was in a very different situation. The life I was leading was simply not the life my parents wanted for me, and more than that, it was causing them real anguish. So I was not in the privileged position of being able to proudly show my mother what my life was like, because it was my lifestyle that was the issue. On top of this, my home life in Florence had crumbled after the situation with Simon and so my mother would immediately notice that we were not on speaking terms. I loved my mother more than I could ever describe, but at this time, being in her company made me feel like I was evil. I was the one that caused misery and pain and I was the one that had disappointed my family in such a big way. In truth, I simply hated myself and so could hardly provide a relaxed and welcoming environment for her.

Two weeks later, my mother arrived. She had brought some clothes for me and some basic kosher food items. When we arrived at the apartment from the airport, Simon was not there, which was a relief, but I had left a note on the table a week beforehand to warn him of my mother's impending arrival, not caring whether or not he was happy with the arrangement. My mother looked around appreciatively and after sitting down with a hot drink, we went out for a long stroll around the city centre where I showed her most of the main monuments and places of interest. I was slightly wary that she would begin to question what I had been up to and try to find out how I had been living, but I decided that hiding anything would simply not work and so should anything come to light, I would just be upfront and honest about it. In fact, the first couple of days seemed to go by without too many issues, which included an occasion when Simon stayed to have a chat with my mother. I noticed with amusement that Simon immediately attempted to come across as he used to, making reference to things of a Jewish nature and even mentioning girls at one point to keep my mother off the scent of anything. Clearly he did not want a whiff of any suspicion getting to his own parents.

One evening, when I was having dinner with my mother at home, she decided to bring up the subject of my sexuality again.

"Evan, your father and I have been having a terrible time with this whole thing, and think that it would really be a good idea if when you came home, we all went to see someone together."

"What do you mean 'someone'? Are you referring to a counsellor or a shrink?"

"Well, yes I mean someone that can help us all get back to where we were before somehow. My emotional health has suffered lately and both your father and I still feel quite devastated, not to mention your sister and brothers who are suffering in their own way. We just need to find a way to get the family back to normal."

"But Mum, don't you understand? The only way things can go back to normal is if you and Dad accept me for who I am. Is that what you are saying you would like to try and do?"

"No, Evan. I simply cannot accept how you are and still think there's something terribly wrong. I need you to try and see what you are doing to your life and make the necessary, if painful, adjustments so that you can be brought back to the true path. It's the only way."

"I am already on the best path I have experienced so far in my life and have never been happier than since I have started to be true to my sexuality. Why isn't my happiness good enough for you?"

"Of course we want you to be happy," continued my mother, now getting quite emotional. "You are just surrounding yourself with the wrong types of people, people who are making you think that their lifestyle is acceptable. It may be for them, but it certainly isn't for you as far as we are concerned. Look at Simon. I'm so glad you are at least living with him as he seems to be the only good influence around you at the moment."

I tried as hard as I could to bite my tongue. Simon, a good influence? If only my mother knew the terrible truth.

I realised that there was simply no hope and that my parents were just not ready yet to accept me. I was so happy that I still had a few months left in Italy and did not have to go home yet because what was waiting for me there was clearly the same situation I had to endure before I left, and that was something I could not bear to think about.

A couple of days later, my mother went back home and I heaved a sigh of relief. I felt quite bad that I was relieved she had gone and wished things could have been better, but my relationship with my parents was obviously still very much strained and it was something I was not yet ready to have to deal with again. Also, I knew that my mother was interested to find out about what I got up to and as I had no intention of causing further difficulty, I had to change how I lived for the period that she was there. So of course, it was a relief for me to be able to just get back to my own kind of normality after she left, however right or wrong that was.

After my mother had left, I concentrated on doing further research for my dissertation and continued to spend time with Jonathan, Caroline, Luca and Anyesa who had become my new close group of friends. I did not tell anybody else at all about the situation with Simon and what had happened and somehow managed to put it to the back of my mind a lot of the time. Simon and I had essentially stopped speaking to each other or even acknowledging each other and although we continued to live together, our lives became completely separate. Jonathan sometimes tried to include Simon in our activities, not knowing there was a real problem but soon realised that Simon seemed to prefer to do other things and so left him to his own devices. I sometimes saw

Simon at bars or clubs that we visited but I always managed to avoid getting anywhere near him.

I also continued to attend Jewish social events with Caroline at the synagogue, and although none of these occasions offered anything of real spiritual value it was at least good to spend some time with people I could relate to on a cultural level. My own relationship with God continued to hover between active interest and near indifference, depending on my state of mind. I still saw God as the source of everything in the universe, although I was still suffering greatly inside from what I saw as His desire to punish me for things I had no control over. This especially included the situation with my family that always broke my heart when I thought about it, and Simon's terrible betrayal of my trust and apparent contempt for me that I truly believed I did not deserve.

I was more and more certain that being gay was absolutely inherent in my make-up and every day that I lived as a gay person only cemented this feeling further. Therefore, being forced to deal with what I was going through apparently at God's hands seemed all the more unfair and was something I simply could not make sense of. It also did not help me that the only other gay Jews around me apparently had no interest in the religious side of things. Caroline was not spiritual at all and did not care to discuss God in any context and as for Simon, that was clearly no longer an option, although I had already noticed the extent to which he had divorced himself from his culture in order to embrace everything frivolous that the Gay lifestyle stood for. I knew that as always I was alone in the end, happy to have the friends I had around me but knowing that my internal struggle was still mine alone to deal with and work out.

# Chapter 18

As my year in Italy went on, I began visiting other cities with my friends. We went on a few trips and discovered the wonders of Rome with all of its grand architecture and fantastic monuments sitting alongside the manic lifestyle of its inhabitants. We went to Venice, Naples, Siena and Milan, all with completely different atmospheres and paces of life but each with its own distinct history and character. Italy really was breathtaking and I had certainly not appreciated the true wealth of culture and history that existed there before now. Drinking real Italian coffee or world renowned rich hot chocolate at various cafés and feasting on cheap but delicious and hearty foods of all kinds at the many Trattorias, gave me a truly enhanced appreciation of what Italy had to offer and I loved each and every experience. It was all the more enjoyable because I got to share these experiences with my new friends. It was just a terrible shame that I could no longer count Simon as one of them any more.

I also had another visit from both my mother and father, who stayed at my apartment. It was thankfully uneventful and I somehow felt slightly more relaxed about them being there than I did when my mother had come alone. Simon had once again, miraculously changed character while they were there and pretended to act like a regular, respectable human being for their benefit. At least my parents had brought some nice kosher food with them, which I realised I had missed eating.

At this point it is important to note that despite barely observing the practices of my religion, I still found that when it came to food, I could not quite bring myself to eat non-kosher meat. Everywhere I went with my friends, I always ordered vegetarian food, or something with fish, even though we were in restaurants or cafes that had fantastic sounding things on the menu that my friends were able to indulge in. At the end of the day, these places had no consideration at all for kosher needs, although of course, they had no reason to. I suppose I felt it was just a step too far to eat meat that was not kosher and I felt I owed it to God to maintain any remnant of religiousness that I could muster however upset, angry and bewildered I was with the way He was treating me.

One Friday evening, I went to a party with the others that one of Luca's friends was throwing for their birthday. It was at their apartment on the outskirts of Florence, in the hills with a fantastic view of the city where you could see the collage of red roofed buildings and the dome of the Duomo standing proudly at the centre. As we entered the apartment, I noticed that most of the people there were in full swing already, drinking, chatting and dancing to music. There were tables laid out with snacks and alcohol and after introducing ourselves to the clearly quite drunk host, a skinny short guy called Paolo with slicked back dark hair and bright blue eyes, we made our way to the tables to get some drinks while admiring the sumptuous view of Florence in the sunset through the large living room windows.

During the evening, I noticed that one of the guys in the room was looking at me quite intently. I ignored it at first, but continued to feel his eyes burning in the back of my head and each time I turned around, he was still there staring at me. As I was having quite an enjoyable time chatting to my friends, I did not feel inclined to start a conversation with this person, although he did seem quite attractive being rather tall with short dark hair, olive skin and a powerful glint in his eyes. At one point, Anyesa whispered to me that someone was clearly infatuated with me, as she had noticed he had not kept his eyes off me for some time. I, of course, knew exactly who she was referring to, but decided to continue ignoring him. I thought that if he really did want to speak to me, he could make the effort and come over to me himself. After having had quite a few drinks and dancing for a while we realised that it was almost midnight. We decided at that point to leave the party and go to one of the nicer bars in the city centre. In Italy, most bars stayed open until the early hours unlike in London where everything was pretty much closed at eleven o'clock, meaning the only alternatives were more expensive nightclubs. As it was now the weekend, we decided it was not a problem to continue drinking as we were having a great time together and simply wanted a carefree night out.

We managed to get a taxi back down to the city centre and then made our way to a bar called 'Segue', which was probably the most popular place to go on a Friday night. On entering the bar, I saw that it was rather busy which was always a good sign. This particular venue had a chill out area at the back with sofas and tables, which was good if you wanted to escape the throng of the crowds in the main part of the bar. After standing around for a while with the others, I started to feel quite tired and so I decided to go and sit in the chill out area and told them where I would be if they wanted to join me later. Luckily I found an empty sofa and sat down with my drink of vodka and orange juice. Almost immediately, someone came and sat right next to me. When I turned to see who it was I realised that it was the guy from the party who had been staring at me all evening. He looked at me and smiled broadly, exposing white, even teeth.

"Hello," I said in Italian, not quite sure what he really wanted.

"Hi," he replied, still smiling. "My name is Lorenzo. I saw you earlier at the party and after you left I wanted to try and find you. I have not seen anyone as attractive as you for a very long time."

"Well thanks, that's a nice thing to say. I am Evan," I replied. In reality, I could not believe he really meant what he had said, after all I was in a country where the average looking person was still leagues above anyone in the UK as far as I was concerned and I still considered myself to be far from attractive most of the time.

"You have a very intriguing look and something about you is compelling me. I am so happy that I found you again here. I thought you might go to a bar and guessed that it would be this one as it is the nicest gay bar in Florence. Do you mind if I smoke?"

"Actually, I hate smoking but I can't stop you if you want to," I replied, thinking that this person had purposely come here to follow me, which was both flattering and slightly worrying at the same time.

"You hate smoking? Does that mean you would not kiss someone that smoked?"

"Well, I just don't like the taste or smell really, it's not exactly attractive for me that's all, but as I said, you can go ahead if you want to."

Suddenly Lorenzo took his packet of cigarettes and threw them across the floor in a dramatic fashion.

"From this moment, I no longer smoke at all! It's no problem for me to give up, I just haven't had a good reason to until now."

"Please don't do anything on my account," I quickly remarked, wondering why he was trying to please me when he did not even know me. "What is it you actually want anyway?"

"Well, for a start, I would love to just talk to you and get to know you more. You really have something very appealing about you and I like it a lot. Then from there, well, we can see what happens can't we?"

"Well, I don't mind talking to you, I guess," I replied, feeling that Lorenzo was certainly very confident and was assuming I found him as interesting as he apparently found me. Nevertheless, receiving this kind of attention was something that made me feel good and right now after what I had been through recently I really needed to feel as wanted as possible.

We chatted away for a while until my friends found me. Anyesa and Caroline wanted to go home as they were tired and had had enough so I quickly introduced them to Lorenzo and then kissed them both goodbye. Jonathan and Luca had wanted to hang out a bit more with me, but seeing me chatting to Lorenzo and realising that it was probably best not to intrude, they decided to go home as well. Once I was left alone again, I decided that although it had been interesting to meet Lorenzo and speak to him, I really would rather go to bed myself and stood up to leave. Lorenzo immediately insisted on accompanying me for the walk home and after initially trying to persuade him I would be fine alone, I eventually gave in and so we left the bar together and walked through the by now empty streets of Florence where we continued to chat until I arrived outside my front door. I thanked Lorenzo for walking with me and was about to turn and go inside when he put a hand on my arm.

"Would it be alright if I kissed you goodnight, Evan? It's been really wonderful to meet you."

"Well, okay then, why not," I answered after hesitating a few seconds, thinking that Lorenzo's gentle persistence and confidence was becoming more and more attractive to me.

Lorenzo leaned towards me and planted his full soft lips onto mine, while at the same time placing a piece of paper into my hand, which I assumed must be his number. The tenderness of his kiss was quite unexpected as I had somehow thought he would try and grasp me and attempt a hard passionate embrace. I was certainly pleasantly surprised.

"Goodnight, beautiful Evan," said Lorenzo, looking directly into my eyes. "I am very much looking forward to seeing you again," and with that, he simply turned and walked away.

As I lay in bed, I thought about how random the evening had been. A guy who saw me at a party and who was apparently captivated by me then tried to follow my movements and managed to find me at a bar where he ended up walking me home and kissing me. I simply could not believe that I could provoke such an interest in someone. It all seemed like quite a romantic situation, something that only happened to other people. I was certain that at some point the bubble would burst and that he would see me again in the light of day and realise what a mistake he had made. In any case I had kept his number scrawled on the piece of paper and decided that I would call him in the next couple of days. What did I have to lose after all?

The following day, I woke up quite late and heard some kind of drama downstairs. I went and looked over the banister of the galleried landing where I saw Simon with Gemma and Miranda. Simon appeared to be quite upset and rather anxious and the girls were attempting to calm him down. I had no idea what the problem could be but did not really care, thinking that he deserved whatever had happened to him. Gemma then suddenly looked up and noticed me watching them.

"Evan, for goodness sake come down here and help comfort Simon. Poor thing has had a terrible shock. He called us over especially as he was feeling so bad."

Not feeling inclined to do anything to support Simon, I went downstairs anyway, more out of curiosity than anything else. After all, the girls had no idea what had happened between Simon and me and assumed I would surely want to help my friend in times of distress.

"What is it?" I asked nonchalantly.

"Simon, tell him about the letter, go on!" Miranda piped up, appearing to want the drama to unfold even more for her own entertainment.

Simon looked at me, an awkward expression on his face coupled with sheer embarrassment. He knew I could no longer stand being in his company and for good reason, although I was certain he thought that showing up our serious problems in front of the others would only cause further issues which he would want to avoid. Instead, he just came out with it.

"About two weeks ago, I wrote a couple of letters to send to London. Normally I write out the envelopes first and the letters afterwards and just stick them inside to post when I'm finished. One was for my parents and the other was for that guy Dean I met just before we came out here. We have written to each other a few times already. Anyway, clearly the letter I wrote to Dean was very different from my parents' one and for some reason, I must have put the letters in the wrong envelopes, so that Dean got the one for them and they got his. This morning I received a letter from my parents and it's so terrible, I just don't know what to do. I have basically just come out to them without wanting to! They said they are shocked to the core and cannot believe I would go down such a dark road and that no son of theirs can show them up in this way. And you should have seen some of the things I had written to Dean about my memories of when we had sex! I just want to die..." and with that he burst into tears.

I stood there, not quite believing what was happening. Simon had always greatly feared his parents finding out about him and had done his utmost to keep his life a secret from them, which he had managed quite well until now, it seemed. I could not bring myself to offer any words of comfort at all despite Gemma and Miranda's expectant glares. This was the perfect retribution! Could it be that God had listened to my prayers and acknowledged my pain over the last few weeks? So my suffering had not been in vain after all and Simon's abhorrent crime had now come back to rest on his shoulders. I felt the need to laugh at the situation, but managed to stifle it. Instead I just told the others that I needed to go to the toilet and left them there, Simon in tears and the girls continuing to try and comfort him. I locked myself in the bathroom, and before I knew it I was overcome with laughter which I was unable to control. Laughter that came from deep within, a kind of sheer relief coupled with satisfaction at the justice in the universe. I had to cover my mouth to stop myself laughing too loudly and remained there for a few minutes until I could calm down. I then had a quick shower and when I came out, they were gone. I assumed Simon would have needed some air or something but in any case just not having him around was good enough. He at least had his friends with him to provide comfort and whether right or wrong, I simply could not pretend I was one of his friends any more.

I then got dressed and had some tea and cereal whilst watching TV. After breakfast I also decided to pray as I felt that God had been good to me and I wanted to show my gratitude. It was not so much that I had malicious thoughts about Simon and wished him ill; it was rather that having been through what I had experienced at his hands and the devastating effect it subsequently had on my self esteem, I felt that God really did punish crimes and was somehow showing me that despite being gay, I still did not deserve what had happened to me. After I had reconnected to God, I felt much more positive about things, more so than I had really felt for a good while. Maybe there was a reason for some of the things that I had been through over the last few years; maybe I needed to experience certain situations in order to grow up somehow or become stronger and appreciate things better. I felt more certain that I could maintain a successful relationship with God even if I was not actively part of a religious community, and that as long as I kept turning to Him, my prayers would be answered one way or another.

The rest of the day was spent grocery shopping, meeting Anyesa for a delicious hot chocolate followed by late lunch and generally hanging out, walking along the bustling streets, looking at the passers-by and sitting along the beautiful river chatting about all manner of things. Anyesa was so easy to talk to and so interested in what I had to say; I really did feel very lucky to have met her. She asked me what had happened with Lorenzo after she had left with Caroline the night before and I filled her in on his insistence to accompany me home, his flattering words and his soft goodnight kiss. She asked me if I was intending to contact him and said that he did seem to be a very interesting person although slightly intense looking from what she remembered. I said I would probably call him the following day and maybe go out somewhere to get to know him better, but that I was not entirely sure if he really liked me for who I was or if he had said all those things to me just to try and get me into bed. Anyesa told me there was only one way to find out for sure, and I realised she was right. He definitely gave me butterflies in my stomach and so it was worth a shot if nothing else. Sometimes I just needed to hear someone else's opinion. With a renewed sense of anticipation, I spent the remainder of the day imagining what might lay in store for us and after meeting the others for a quick dinner I went home where there was thankfully still no sign of Simon and so I went to bed where I drifted into a blissful sleep.

# Chapter 19

It was now the start of a glorious springtime in Florence, when the temperature began suddenly rising and a presence of mosquitoes from the river Arno began to make itself known. As it was situated at the bottom of surrounding hills, Florence had a valley-like environment that seemed to trap heat and humidity which meant that wearing anything more than a single layer during the day would cause sweating and discomfort after a while. Over the following weeks, I saw less and less of Simon except while at university lectures, and soon learned from Anyesa that he was spending almost all his spare time with Gemma and Miranda, seeming to practically have moved in with them. I knew that not having showed him the slightest sympathy or comfort regarding the situation with his parents had made him feel there was no point being under the same roof as me if he could help it. In actual fact, being alone to do as I pleased in the apartment most of the time was a great benefit.

Having made further contact with Lorenzo after that first night, we had begun spending more and more time together. I found out that he was very intelligent and knowledgeable about many things including culture, literature, politics and art. After I had told him I was Jewish, he had said that he was interested in my religion as it had after all been the basis of the Catholic religion and he was fascinated by the similarities between the two. He would lap up any information I would share with him about my culture and its teachings. It felt strange at first to have someone listening intently to you talking about religion, and certainly I had not experienced this before but it was rather refreshing to have such a captive audience because it allowed me to somehow reconnect with my heritage simply by talking more about it. I felt that without the pressurised and stifling environment of the Jewish community back in London, I actually felt much more positive about being Jewish in general. Not living a practicing religious lifestyle did not seem to matter, as I felt it was all about how I was contributing to the world around me and my personal relationship to God as opposed to a barrage of rules and infringements that were imposed on me. It was based on these rules and expectations that I was judged at every turn by my family and wider community, and the fact was that I did not even relate to it all on any real level.

Lorenzo was also quite mature and passionate at the same time. It gave me a feeling that he really took things seriously and that he would not try to play any kind of game with me, which heartened me greatly. After having spent some time with my friends, Lorenzo told me that he really liked them all and that he could see how well we fitted together. I was happy to hear this as it was important for me that someone I was essentially dating, approved of my friends. Something they all told me about Lorenzo however, was that they noticed an intensity about him that somehow made them feel uneasy, although none of them could put their finger on it. As far as I was concerned there was nothing dubious about him at all, and any intensity he emanated, was in fact something I found appealing. It was not long before I started to develop real feelings for Lorenzo as I felt so comfortable with him. I thought he was someone I could learn from, who I could in turn educate about things that were important to me. We had developed a kind of intimacy on every level and I was looking forward to seeing where it would lead us. I had no idea what would happen when I had to go back to London but just being here and being able to spend time with someone I liked this much was all I needed for now.

One evening, I was invited round to Lorenzo's apartment for dinner. He lived on the other side of the city to me, in quite a suburban tree-lined street that had a lovely little square situated at the end of the road. I had not actually been to Lorenzo's apartment before, as we had spent most of our time together either at my place which was centrally located, or hanging out at various restaurants and bars. I knew that this invite was probably for a special reason of some sort and I felt an air of anticipation as I buzzed his apartment and went up to the first floor where he lived. Lorenzo answered the door, looking more nervous than I had ever seen him. In fact, he always appeared rather confident to me, so his current state came as something of a surprise. This only added further to the atmosphere and made my heart start beating much faster than usual. As I was ushered onto a large black leather sofa in the open-plan living room area, Lorenzo offered me a drink and then poured himself a healthy slug of whisky which he drank a bit too quickly for my liking, while pacing up and down the room. I thought he really must be nervous, as I had not seen him drink in this way before. It suddenly occurred to me that something may be very wrong and that this could easily be all be about something bad.

"Lorenzo, you seem so nervous, is everything okay?" I asked, getting up and putting a hand on his shoulder.

"Evan, this is such an important evening for me; there are things I really must tell you and I have not been able to do so before now."

I suddenly felt a shiver of fear down my spine. This seemed strangely reminiscent of the fateful conversation I had had with Tom back in London a couple of years previously. Could it be that Lorenzo had someone else tucked away somewhere and that I had not been his only one? I could not bring myself to think about it much more and instead became very impatient.

"Lorenzo, please just tell me what it is! You're making me feel very uncomfortable and I can't bear it. Whatever it is, I'm sure I can handle it."

Lorenzo sat down on the sofa where I sat beside him, looking expectantly into his eyes, trying to suppress any sign of the fear that was now rippling through me. Lorenzo took my hand, and I could feel that he was shaking slightly.

"Evan, I am in love with you. I haven't felt this way for a long time and I knew from the moment I saw you that there was something special about you."

"Oh, thank goodness!" I exclaimed with relief. "I thought it would be something terrible and got really worried for a moment! If you were just nervous about telling me your feelings, please don't worry. I think it's wonderful!"

"No, Evan," replied Lorenzo, a sombre look on his face. "I have not finished. I wanted to tell you how I felt about you because I need you to be there for me whatever happens, to know that I can count on you."

"I don't understand, what do you mean?" I asked, becoming extremely confused, and feeling a sense of impending doom descending on me.

"Evan, I am HIV positive. I am not sure what it's going to mean for my life, but I'm trying to deal with it as best as I can. I'm going to need a lot of love and support and I really hope you can be there for me."

"What? I... I can't believe it..." I managed, in complete shock. I was still relatively naïve about HIV and everything I had heard about it before was terrible, with endless devastating stories about the people who were living with it and others that had not survived when it turned into the AIDS virus. I had never met anyone before with HIV either and had never been confronted with it first-hand. I had had sex with Lorenzo several times and although it was always completely protected, the fact that he had not told me before doing anything intimate with me was in itself something I found extremely hard to deal with.

"Evan," continued Lorenzo, looking concerned that my face had gone white and that I was obviously somewhat horrified, "I need you to understand and to be there for me, it's all I am asking. Please, I need you."

"I just don't know, I'm not sure if I can handle it," I replied, beginning to feel rather sick. "Why are you only telling me this tonight, and why did you allow us to have sex on more than one occasion without me knowing about it? I should at least have known so I could make my own decision. Am I supposed to go and get an HIV test now?"

"It's not like that Evan, please believe me. I didn't tell you before because I knew it might be too much for you if

I told you when we met, and it's not exactly easy for me to talk about. As for sex, I always made sure we were safe but if you want to, feel free to have a test, it might put your mind at rest. You are so important to me, I just need you with me to support me through this."

I could barely bring myself to respond. A wave of nausea came over me and I felt like I may pass out.

"I... I think I need some air or something, please, I need to go out. I need some space," and with that, I stood up and left the apartment where I started walking, my head filled with any and every thought.

At the time, HIV was still considered by many to be a death sentence and the drugs available were nowhere near as developed and effective as they are today. What was I supposed to do? I had no idea how to cope with someone that had such a serious disease and emotionally I did not consider myself mature enough either. I was going through so many of my own issues and dealing with this was just something I could not factor in, regardless of how much I liked Lorenzo. On top of which, the thought of getting tested for HIV scared me to the core. Was there any chance at all I could have been at risk? I simply could not deal with the situation. Why did my life seem to take such turns like this? I seemed to live on a roller coaster of terrible things happening followed by apparent respite, only for something else even worse to hit me afterwards. Was God continuing to punish me after all? Why was I suffering in this way? Did it really all relate to me being gay and was my lifestyle so very wrong that I deserved only heartache? I looked to the heavens and begged God for an answer. I could no longer live this way, every time I thought I had found some meaning and some sense of belonging, I was knocked for six. Did I not deserve to meet someone decent and nice who I could really connect with, that would not hit me with some bombshell unexpectedly? I had thought Tom was that person and that had ended in disappointment. I had also lost my best friend in the worst possible way and now this was happening with Lorenzo. I felt numb, devastated and terrified all at once. Staying with Lorenzo was simply impossible; I could not give him what he wanted and could not cope with it all. I was also very angry that I could have been put at risk of HIV and was not given the choice about whether or not to have sex with him based on knowledge of his condition.

I decided I would have to simply harden myself to the situation regardless of how much pain it would cause both myself and Lorenzo, and distance myself from him. It was the only way I could handle things right now, even if it seemed harsh. With these thoughts running through my mind, I continued walking without looking back and somehow found my way home eventually where I saw Simon sitting on the sofa watching TV. Ignoring him completely, I went straight up to my bed and lay there plagued by my thoughts and unable to sleep.

At some point during the night, the buzzer started ringing. I had obviously somehow drifted off to sleep and it woke me with a start. I had no idea what time it was but it felt like the early hours of the morning. As the buzzer continued to ring, I forced myself out of bed and downstairs, Simon also appearing and following behind me looking startled.

"Who the hell is that at this time? It's probably some drunk!" he exclaimed, clearly annoyed at having been woken.

I ignored his comments and went to answer the intercom, realising that I knew who would be at the other end but wishing that Simon's guess was right.

"Hello?" I said warily into the intercom.

"Evan, it's Lorenzo. I need to talk to you, please come outside or let me in."

"I can't talk to you now Lorenzo, please just go away. It's the middle of the night!"

"I can't leave you, Evan. I understand that you had a shock earlier and had to go but I need to talk to you. I need you to be there for me."

"Please Lorenzo, I can't deal with this. I don't think I can handle it right now, don't you understand? Please just give me some time."

"I don't have time, Evan. Nothing matters any more, I just need to be with you. I love you."

"I'm sorry, I don't know what to say. I can't cope with this, please just leave and we'll talk tomorrow."

"I will continue to ring this buzzer until you at least come out and talk to me."

Simon then piped up impatiently. "Why the hell are you having a conversation at this time? Tell him to get lost!" he shouted, clearly agitated by the situation. He then suddenly grabbed the intercom from me and hung up. The buzzer started ringing again continually. Simon then picked up the intercom and started barking hysterically down the handset.

"I don't care who you are or why you're here but you have no right to come in the middle of the night and cause a commotion like this. If you don't go away right now I am calling the police!" And with that he hung up again.

"Why don't you just go back to bed, I can handle this," I said trying to stay calm.

"Well, if the pathetic and disturbed guys you obviously hang out with wouldn't ring our buzzer in the middle of the night then I wouldn't need to get out of bed in the first place, would I!" snapped Simon, marching back upstairs.

I felt so confused. Should I go outside and talk to Lorenzo or should I continue to ignore him? After Simon's rant, he may have left now after all. I had never felt so bad before. Lorenzo was obviously in a terrible place and I was just treating him like a piece of dirt simply because I could not deal with his shocking news. However on the other hand, his behaviour just now was rather disturbing and showed me a side I had not seen before, which was slightly obsessive and desperate. In any case, I decided to leave it till the next day and then contact him and just talk about it all properly because right now I was just so very tired and could barely concentrate on anything. Despite my difficulty in taking Lorenzo's situation in, he at least still deserved a proper conversation. With my decision made, I went back up to bed and miraculously managed to fall back to sleep.

# Chapter 20

When I awoke the next day, I looked at my watch and realised it was already midday. After such an eventful night, I was not surprised that I had slept in so long. Suddenly remembering I had a lecture at twelve thirty, I jumped out of bed and ran downstairs into the bathroom to have a quick shower. I did not think I would be able to make it on time as I rushed around trying to get dressed and ready. There was no sign of Simon in the apartment so I assumed he must have left by now. Thinking about the previous evening with Lorenzo and the subsequent drama in the early hours, I knew that I had to try and resolve everything one way or another today. Straight after my lectures, I decided I would call Lorenzo and arrange to meet him.

As I rushed out of the apartment and across the road, I noticed someone sitting on a bench a few yards away. With horror I realised it was Lorenzo, who as soon as he saw me, got up and started to walk towards me. As I was so late for university, I did not feel that talking to him right now would be very productive and so pretended to ignore him and continued walking quickly until I reached the university building where I hurried up to the lecture room with barely a couple of minutes to spare. What was Lorenzo doing waiting for me like that? Had he been there all night? I simply could not believe he would be that intent on catching up with me. Feeling incredibly anxious, I was unable to pay the slightest bit of attention for the duration of my lecture which was based on Dante and his famous work the *Inferno*, and after it was over, I started to make my way out of the building.

"Hey, Evan!" called Jonathan, striding towards me. "Where are you going in such a hurry? I was going to ask if you wanted to grab a coffee or something."

"Hi, Jonathan. I really don't feel that great and was going to just take a walk actually."

"You look pretty tired I guess, weren't you supposed to be seeing Lorenzo last night? Oh, unless you saw him in more ways than one, know what I mean?" said Jonathan with a cheeky grin and a wink.

"I saw Lorenzo alright," I replied with a sigh, "but it was far from a nice experience. Actually, I need to talk to someone about it; maybe we can get that coffee after all."

As we sat in a nearby café munching on delicious panettone cake and sipping strong cappuccinos, I filled Jonathan in on everything that had happened the night before. He sat there looking quite surprised, almost as if he was trying to take it all in.

"So he didn't tell you he had HIV before you slept together? That's serious, I would probably have freaked out too," exclaimed Jonathan when I had finished. "It sounds like he's a bit unbalanced actually, especially with his antics in the middle of the night. I knew there was something about him when I first met him. The others thought so too when you introduced him to us properly, but we didn't want to come across too negative with you because we saw how much you seemed to like him. What did Simon have to say about it all?"

"Apart from having to share the experience with Simon last night, I haven't spoken to him about it. To tell you the truth, we don't exactly get along these days."

"I thought there was something up for sure, you never seem to do anything together any more or even speak when you are in the same room! I just didn't want to pry, but everyone has noticed it," replied Jonathan, looking at me with a concerned expression.

"Well, I would rather not talk about Simon if that's okay. As for Lorenzo, well I haven't told you everything. Earlier as I left to come to the lecture, I saw him sitting on a bench opposite my road and I think he's now following me. I was going to talk to him properly about everything today but I'm starting to feel quite worried as I think you're right that he may be unbalanced and is stalking me. I can't believe he seemed so down to earth and normal all this time!"

"Well, only to you I'm afraid," replied Jonathan sombrely. "Do you think he's still waiting for you outside your apartment?"

"I have no idea, but I just feel so exhausted by everything and I really don't know if I can deal with seeing him now, especially alone. His appearance this morning kind of gave me the creeps."

"Well I'll tell you what," said Jonathan reassuringly, "let me come back to your place with you and if he's there then we can handle him together. I will be right with you, don't worry."

"Really?" I replied gratefully. "That would be a great help. I just feel like I need some kind of moral support."

"You got it," said Jonathan, and after we left the café we walked back together to my apartment.

There was no sign of Lorenzo thankfully and we decided to sit and chat some more and just hang out listening to music. After a while, I felt much better and decided that I would in fact call Lorenzo and just arrange to meet him to deal with this once and for all. I simply did not need this hanging over my head any longer. When I dialled his number there was no reply so I left a brief message on the answer phone. At least he would not be able to accuse me of continuing to ignore him. I then called Anyesa who came over shortly afterwards to join Jonathan and I, and I took the opportunity to fill her in on the story as well. Her reaction was similar to Jonathan's and we sat discussing it all for a while more before deciding to go out and get some early dinner.

As we left the apartment, I was surprised by the sight of Lorenzo again, wandering up and down across the road opposite us. He was clearly waiting for me to come out at some point. I told Jonathan and Anyesa that I would be a couple of minutes and asked them to wait for me while I spoke to him, which they happily agreed to do. Their presence nearby would at least provide me with some comfort and deter Lorenzo from possibly doing anything stupid. As I approached him, I noticed immediately that he had big dark circles under his eyes, almost certainly the result of not having slept at all.

"Lorenzo, we need to talk," I began.

"I have been trying to talk to you since last night but you did not want to listen or speak to me," he spat. "I thought you were different but I see now that you are just like everyone else."

"What do you mean?" I asked, thinking that he had probably been let down by a few people who he had told about his condition before.

"I told you that I loved you and needed you to be there for me. Instead of offering any support you just run away and then get your flatmate to try and scare me off. I want you to know that I get the message. You clearly are not capable or strong enough to be any support to me and I must have made a big mistake believing anything different. I still can't help how I feel about you but I am so disappointed in you. I thought you were special. That's all I wanted to say, and I wanted to tell you to your face. You can go back now with your friends, they are waiting for you."

"I'm so sorry, Lorenzo," I replied feeling like I needed to somehow explain myself further. "You need to understand that I am younger than you and have not had experience of anything like this before. The whole thing scares me so much. I am also angry that you could have put me at risk and that I might need to get an HIV test before I can completely relax again. I have been through quite a few serious things in the last couple of years actually, things I have not yet been able to deal with and this on top of everything else is something I just can't handle. I'm sorry if you think I have let you down, I certainly didn't mean to. It might be best if we just don't see each other any more."

"Yes, I agree. Goodbye Evan and have a nice life," said Lorenzo, who then turned around and walked off shaking his head sorrowfully.

As I rejoined Jonathan and Anyesa, I felt a sense of deep disappointment in what had happened. Things could have been so different for Lorenzo and me. Maybe I could have been there for him if I tried but I had too much going on around me and inside my head. This had turned out to be yet another blow to my self-esteem and I realised that without having my friends to lean on, I may actually have fallen apart.

To try and forget about the latest drama, we spent the evening at a lovely little rustic Trattoria eating pizza, talking about the lucky escape I had probably had and updating each other on our most recent news. I had become so absorbed in my own issues lately that I realised I had not even bothered to find out what was happening with anyone else. Anyesa took the opportunity to announce that she was going to be leaving Italy early and going home in two weeks' time, which came as a surprise. I had a good couple of months still to go before I was due to return and really wanted to spend it with Anyesa around but she said she was really missing her family and after having had a long chat with them on the phone a few days ago, felt it was the right thing to do. We certainly agreed to keep in touch and stay friends during our last year together back in London, which heartened me greatly.

Jonathan said that he was probably going to stay on in Italy throughout the summer and spend more time with Luca having fun and visiting other cities to get the most out of his experience before making the long trip back home to Boston. This made sense as if I had come all the way from the USA to Europe I would also want to stay as long as I could. Jonathan then mentioned that Caroline had met another American girl at a bar one night recently and that they seemed to be getting along very well, which explained why she had not come out with us much in the last couple of weeks. I was happy to hear this, as Caroline was more of a quiet, serious type and I knew that she deserved to meet someone nice that she could feel comfortable with. I just prayed that she would not have to deal with anything like I had been through with Lorenzo. We all decided in any case that we would have a big party before anyone left, so that we could all celebrate our new friendships and our shared experiences in Italy. I was excited about this and knew that I would definitely be keeping in touch with most people one way or another.

Thinking about going home again, I had mixed emotions. On one hand, none of the issues I had with my family had been resolved and I would be returning to an environment where I felt I had to justify myself and my life again, which I had not needed to do while in Italy. I would also have to contend with living back in the religious community I had come to despise with nobody I could really relate to around me. On the other hand, I had received a few letters from my mother since her visit to see me, updating me on family news and almost sounding like life was normal which made me miss them all somewhat. I knew that my relationship with my family would not be sorted out quickly and that it would just have to continue to be a work in progress. I had also received a couple of letters from Nathan since I had been away, whose life seemed not to have changed at all. I felt in some way that I had now outgrown Nathan, Toby and Mandy who, by all accounts, were still completely involved in the London bar and club scene and had nothing more interesting to say other than what was going on in Soho. I realised that I had also almost completely lost touch with Alex, who, aside from one letter I had received and replied to about a month into the year abroad, I had not heard anything from since. It would be interesting to see what life was like again once I returned, but I certainly felt that I had been through so much while in Italy that nothing would be quite the same.

# Chapter 21

The end of my time in Italy seemed to approach more quickly than I expected. The night before Anyesa left to return to London, I had hosted the party we had discussed, at my apartment for all the people I had met whilst there. I was forced to include Simon as we still lived together and he had invited a few people he had apparently met recently, but I managed to steer clear of him throughout the evening. My closest friends were all there and it was the first time I got to meet Caroline's new girlfriend who was called Helen and was quite tall and strikingly pretty with short blonde hair. They definitely seemed to be heavily into each other and I felt happy to see them together. I had bought quite a lot of cheap alcohol for the evening which went down very well and created a relaxed and carefree environment as well as a great opportunity for people to just catch up with each other and get to know each other better. Some people had brought one or two friends with them and soon it appeared that there were about twenty-five guests. I certainly could not have imagined that I would be surrounded by this number of people in my own apartment. It was a great atmosphere with people dancing, drinking and generally enjoying themselves. Feeling more liberated than I could remember being for a long time, I became quite emotional during the evening, realising that once this experience was over and I was back in London, I may not feel this free again. I may have lost my oldest and closest friend whilst here, but I had made amazing new friends and that counted for a lot. Apart from Anyesa who I would be seeing regularly back in London at university, I promised myself that I would stay in touch with Jonathan, Caroline and Luca and try to go and see them whenever possible. It would certainly be a great excuse to visit the USA where I had never been until that point, and of course, to come back to Italy.

After Anyesa left, everything seemed to quieten down somewhat. The weather in Florence had gotten extremely hot and humid and the mosquito problem felt like it was out of control. They were everywhere, including in the apartment and soon I was covered in a constant rash of bites over my arms and legs. Aside from that discomfort, things appeared to be calmer overall. I concentrated on finishing the research for my dissertation which I felt had really taken shape, and also attended the last few lectures at the university. Nearly all my social time was spent with Jonathan, Luca, Caroline and her girlfriend Helen. I heard that after Anyesa left Italy, her flatmates Gemma, Miranda and Kate had also decided to go back home a month early for various reasons. I had been invited to a goodbye dinner with them, although knowing that Simon was also invited, I declined the offer feeling that certainly Gemma and Miranda were more Simon's friends and Kate had always done her own thing anyway and I did not feel especially close to any of them. I wondered what Simon would do in the last month of our stay without his precious cohorts. Not that it mattered to me in any way and I thought that as long as he continued to stay away from me, I would be fine. I still felt a sense of revulsion and betrayal whenever I was forced to think about him or be anywhere near him and I knew I would need to try and come to terms with what had happened properly when I came back to London. I also decided that after the Lorenzo experience, I would brave an HIV test when I returned, just to be sure. I had been through so much over the last year and had been forced to grow up in a way that I had not expected. Somehow I felt that all of my experiences so far, in the year or so before Italy and everything that had happened here since, had made me feel stronger and more able to handle whatever was waiting for me back home.

On the night before I left, I had dinner at Jonathan's place along with Luca, Caroline and Helen who he had also invited. I was presented with a beautiful card signed by everyone and several small gifts that they had bought or made for me. I was extremely touched and knew that these were the kinds of friends I wished I could have around me all the time. It would be hard not to be able to see these people regularly and to only have contact through letters and maybe the odd phone call once I returned. In fact I no longer felt I had much of a base back in London any more, with my family the only people that mattered in any real way. I had come to take the total acceptance and support that I had received while in Italy for granted and realised that I would not have such a support mechanism waiting for me at home. It was a thought that filled me with anxiety.

The following day, having packed everything in sight, I headed to the airport with Simon in a cab. We sat there, neither one speaking to the other, engrossed in our own thoughts. I wondered what he considered his overall experience of Italy to have been like, and I also wondered what had happened with him and his family since they had discovered he was gay. Certainly the way they found out must have been a dreadful shock. For a split second, I felt sorry for him that he was going back home to have to confront whatever difficulties were waiting there; difficulties that I myself had been through and was still going to have to endure. However I immediately remembered why my relationship with Simon had broken down and was again filled with the disgust and sense of betrayal that I had lived with daily ever since the incident had happened. This allowed me to close my heart again to any pain Simon might be going through.

The plane ride was uneventful and after we landed and I had collected my baggage, I made my way out of the airport without saying goodbye to Simon, expecting my parents to be waiting for me. As it happened, a friend of the family was waiting at arrivals and after warmly welcoming me home, explained that my parents were both busy with work and could not make it. Were they really too busy to welcome me home personally after all this time? Maybe they simply could not face seeing me for some reason even though I would very soon be with them again and we would all have to make an effort to accommodate each other somehow. I had hoped that during my time away, my parents would have tried to come to terms with everything. Certainly from the letters I had received while in Italy, no real mention was made of the problems that we had, although this could just have been because my parents didn't want to bring everything up when we were unable to discuss anything face-to-face. I was in any case rather disappointed about not seeing them there to welcome me and wondered if it was a sign of how things were going to be.

My arrival back to the family home was a very strange experience. My parents were not actually there when I walked through the door and I was instead greeted awkwardly by my sister and brothers. Everybody seemed quite different somehow and I noticed that in the space of a few months, my siblings had all matured somewhat, at least physically. My sister Eva, now an extremely pretty young woman of twenty-two years old, politely asked me how my time in Italy had been and then updated me on several things that had happened while I had been away, including showing me the new kitchen that my parents had refurbished recently. I marvelled at Eva's striking looks, wondering why she had still not managed to meet anyone suitable for her, knowing that this was all she really wanted to do. Would we be able to recapture the closeness we had enjoyed before I had come out to my family? She certainly seemed a lot more distant from me now.

My brothers Lewis, Daniel and Jonathan had all definitely grown up somewhat. They were now eighteen, fifteen and thirteen respectively. After a certain amount of wariness from all of them at first, they seemed to warm up slightly as I sat with them and started telling them about Italy and Florence and the things I had seen and done. It was as if I was an unwelcome guest who was trying to gain the trust of my audience who were greeting me with suspicion. As I spoke about my time in Italy, I decided there was no point in referring to anything related to my gay life and certainly no point talking about the serious things I had been through, as they simply would not understand or appreciate anything. I therefore decided to keep to the more generic and cultural aspects of my time abroad.

I really felt like a visitor to my own family, someone that did not belong there but who somehow had been thrust upon the rest of them and who was now trying to find some common ground. What were my siblings thinking as I sat there speaking to them, telling them about beautiful architecture, fantastic food and astonishing scenery? Were any of them actually happy that I had returned? Had life been easier for them without their brother who had brought such pain and turmoil into the family before simply jetting off to another country? I did not have to wait long for some kind of insight.

"You know, you've really screwed up Mum and Dad since you told them you were gay," piped up Lewis after I had finished. "Especially since you've been away, life's been hell for us. Mum cries at the drop of a hat and now pokes her nose into everything we're doing, asking us questions about our lives all the time. Dad's not the same either, he goes into a temper and starts shouting for no reason, over the smallest stupid things. All because of you and your perverted life!"

"I'm really sorry," I replied, upset at Lewis's still hostile attitude to my sexuality and not sure how to really respond. "It's not my fault I am who I am, you need to understand that I did not choose to be gay, believe me. If Mum and Dad are finding it so hard, they should really go and get help or something. What am I supposed to do?"

"It would have been better if you had just kept the whole thing to yourself. If you really are gay, then we don't actually need to know about it," Eva joined in. "You've always been the one that has pushed everything to the limits, refusing to practice our religion and showing no respect for what we believe in. I have been forced to lie whenever any of my friends mentions you or asks about you, just to make you seem normal. It's like a big black cloud is over us now and nothing's the same."

I felt so very let down that none of my siblings were showing any support or understanding for me and that they, like my parents, were finding it difficult to come to terms with something that was beyond my control. I looked at Daniel and Jonathan, my two youngest brothers. They had not really said anything and simply looked down, an awkward and embarrassed expression on both their faces. I somehow had expected Jonathan to say something supportive seeing as he had been the first one I had told about myself. But still being quite young, it seemed that he had no desire to try and contradict what Eva and Lewis were saying and I realised I was all alone.

"I'm sorry I can't live like you all do and fit in neatly with what you want," I retorted, already wishing I was a million miles away again. "You can't just live in a bubble and wish that the whole world was filled with people who are exactly the same as each other! I'm going upstairs. Let me know when Mum and Dad get back from wherever they are."

"They had to go to work but they'll be back soon so you can fill them in on your little adventures then," said Lewis, a sarcastic tone to his voice.

They then all abruptly got up and went into the front room where they simply switched on the TV and sat there watching it as if nothing else mattered. Realising there was nothing more I could do or say to them I went up to my room, which I could tell had been used by someone while I was away but was now prepared for my return. I sat on the bed with my head in my hands and realised that my life was about to take several steps backwards.

# Chapter 22

Life back at home after my time in Italy, was extremely difficult. As I had feared, I felt like I needed to tread on eggshells all the time and that I could not really be as I wanted to be. When my parents had arrived home on the evening of my return, we had exchanged hugs and kisses and during dinner I had updated them on various things I had done in the same way as I had with my siblings earlier. Although a large part of my experience in Florence was based around my further development as a gay man, I felt I could relate none of this to my family and that it would be best to stick to more generic things. Even talking about the new friends I had made was met with relative disinterest by everyone, almost as if by not having a religious Jewish circle, my life was not really approved of or worth paying attention to. Although I had certainly evolved and moved on quite a lot over the last year, it was clear to me that the others were simply stuck in their same old routines, way of life and way of thinking about everything. I felt like an alien in my own home.

Looking at my parents now that I was back in London, I could tell that there was a marked change in both of them, but especially my mother whose very soul seemed to have been ripped out of her body. It was as if someone had died and they had just finished grieving, their emotional strength having been completely wiped out. Both my parents were a shadow of their former selves; exhausted looking, pale and with no spark of any real life. Is this what I had done to them? No wonder my siblings had felt so resentful towards me if this was what they had to live with while I seemingly disappeared off to gallivant around Italy. I knew that there would not be an easy way for us all to recover but I felt that it really was down to my parents to come to terms with my life somehow as I knew I was unable to change for them. Nevertheless, I carried a sense of extreme guilt with me for the apparent devastation I had caused within my family. It is very hard to express how I felt at that time, about myself, my family's situation and the world around me. I was constantly treading water, trying just to breathe to stay alive, but not really living. I had instinctively switched to defence mode in every aspect of my life, believing that anything anyone said to me was an attempt to attack me and take me down. I therefore had an automatic aggressive reaction, especially where my family were concerned. Just being amongst my family made me feel broken, dirty and evil. They all blamed me for destroying their status quo and there was nothing I could do about it.

I felt that I was in a catch-22 situation that I could not possibly break through and so in order to keep myself sane, I decided I had to simply carry on with my life regardless and do what was best for me whilst trying to minimise any pain caused to anyone else by not rubbing their noses in what I was getting up to. The first thing I needed to do was to find a job as I had absolutely no money and refused to allow myself to be beholden to my parents financially. I also had to have an HIV test as the worry of what I might have contracted due to Lorenzo was still hanging over me. My final year at university was not due to start for another three months and so I would have time to try and get my act together. I was also due to turn twenty one very soon. It was actually quite a scary thought, thinking that I was now truly an adult and within my short life so far had already experienced so much.

Over the next few days, I managed to locate a clinic in Soho where you could go and have HIV testing done anonymously. This sounded like the perfect option and although I felt very nervous at the prospect of it all, I made an appointment and went along for my test. As I sat in the waiting area, I looked around me and saw a handful of other men sitting there either with blank expressions, or appearing deep in thought. I wondered how many of them were in my position and who had found themselves in situations where they were unsure if they had caught anything, but needed to be sure. One of the men sitting across the corridor from me appeared to be quite sick, and was extremely gaunt. It suddenly dawned on me that there was the possibility I could one day be like this man, my life probably ruined and my future uncertain. I was struck at that moment by a bolt of fear. This was no game. If I really did have something, what would that mean for my life and for those around me? My family almost certainly would not survive the shock of it on top of everything else.

Finally, I was called into a room and a friendly male nurse sat me down and asked me if I had ever had a test like this before. When I told him that this was my first time being tested for anything, he started to explain in a very relaxed manner what he was going to do and that I just needed to relax. I tried to remain as calm as possible as the nurse injected the syringe into my arm and took a sample of blood, after which he simply put a small plaster on me. He then told me that I should call them back in a couple of weeks' time for the result and that, dependant on what it was, I would have the option of being able to talk to someone for some counselling. The nurse was extremely matter-of-fact throughout and I could tell he had gone through this procedure countless times before. So that was that. My fate now lay in the results of this test and I had two weeks to get through before having to face the truth one way or another. It was going to be an extremely scary and uncertain time.

Deciding that I simply had to try and forget about the test until I got my results, I concentrated on my job search. I noticed that a new Italian restaurant called 'Mamma Amalfi' had opened in my local high street and thought that it may be worth trying my hand at being a waiter. One day I went inside and asked to speak to the manager about possible jobs. I was asked to sit down for a minute and soon was approached by a middle aged, short Italian who asked me about my experience and why I wanted to work there. I somehow managed to concoct a story about my love of Italian cuisine and the fact that having just come back from Italy, I wanted to immerse myself in an Italian environment again and be able to serve customers, which was one of my passions. The manager, who was called Alonzo, seemed impressed with my spiel and with almost no hesitation, told me I had a job as a waiter with a two week try-out period. He said that I should come back the following day to start my first shift where I would be taught the basics of how everything worked, under the supervision of a senior waiter and after a couple of days I would be able to start serving customers myself. I could not believe my luck. This was one of the first places I had gone to and now I had a job for the summer that paid reasonably well and was within striking distance of home.

With my employment now in hand, I started to think about how to approach my social life. Certainly I needed to kick-start things again. The question was, did I want to just fall back into the Soho scene or did I have other options? I definitely intended to spend much more time with Anyesa in any case but first I decided to make contact with my old friends Nathan, Toby and Mandy as I was sure they would be waiting to hear from me, and it would be nice to catch up with them again after all this time. That evening, I dialled Nathan's number and waited expectantly as the phone rang. I was then greeted by a familiar voice.

"Hi Nathan, it's Evan," I replied.

"Evan! Wow, are you back from Italy then? It's been ages! I can't believe it! We simply have to get together and catch up. You must have had such an amazing time out there. I want you to tell me all about everything!"

"Sure, of course," I replied. "Why don't we meet up with Toby and Mandy and make a night of it or something?"

"Huh, well," snorted Nathan in a tone that took me by surprise a bit. "Toby and I no longer talk to Mandy, we had a massive falling out with her. I'll have to tell you all about it but basically she's disappeared off the scene now."

"Goodness!" I exclaimed, hoping that nothing serious had happened "Well, looks like we will be filling each other in on quite a bit then, won't we!"

"Yes indeed! Let's get together tomorrow night, are you around?"

"Actually, I am starting a new job tomorrow at a restaurant and have a training shift so won't be available until after nine. I don't mind coming out after that though if you want?"

"Sure, that's fine with me! Let's meet outside Ku Bar and we can go from there. I'll tell Toby to come too. Can't wait to see you!"

"Me neither. Bye for now then."

"Bye!"

After I had hung up, I felt more positive that at least I had someone who I knew I could rely on to keep my social life going. I had pretty much lost touch with everyone else in London and realised that I would need to start from scratch again to build a network around me that I could relate to. Thank goodness I now had Anyesa. I also really wished Jonathan, Luca and Caroline were here and missed them all already. I knew that I had to try and meet more Jewish gay people too, who at least had some kind of appreciation and knowledge of my background and culture but unfortunately I had no idea how to go about that. I decided that I would make this one of my priorities now as well, as simply ignoring the spiritual side of my life and not having someone to share this with, would leave me feeling unfulfilled.

My shift at the restaurant the following day was very interesting indeed. The waiter that was looking after me was a tall dark man with slicked back greasy hair called Gino. He was apparently the most experienced waiter there. I was shown how the food ordering system worked and was introduced to the rest of the staff on duty that day who all seemed to be a friendly bunch. Many of them were Italian themselves and as soon as I told them I had just come back from Italy, they became excited and started talking to me in Italian. It felt really great to be able to converse with them in their own language and it was also a good way to continue practicing my speaking skills.

At the end of my shift, I rushed home to change and then went into town to meet Nathan and Toby. Although I had not been into Soho since before Italy, not much seemed to have changed. The Ku Bar was one of the places we had always hung out at the most and as I approached it, I spotted Nathan and Toby outside chatting to the host, a tall sequinned drag queen with a curly blonde wig and extraordinarily long eyelashes. When they noticed me their eyes lit up and they both in turn embraced me with a big hug. Afterwards we went inside and ordered drinks whilst settling down at a corner table upstairs.

I updated them on everything I had been through in Italy except the whole situation with Simon, which I still felt too raw about to want to discuss with anyone. I spoke about where I had been, the things I had done and the friends I had met. Nathan seemed mostly interested in what the bars and clubs were like as well as the men. I told them about Lorenzo and how it had ended badly, without discussing the HIV issue and making out that he had just turned nasty towards the end and that I had subsequently gone off him. I was still so nervous about my test results and even mentioning HIV gave me shivers of anxiety.

After I had finished updating them on my escapades, Nathan filled me in on Mandy.

They had apparently all been fine until about two months previously, when Mandy had flushed their cocaine down the toilet. I was surprised to hear that they had moved onto cocaine in the first place as they had only ever taken things like ecstasy and speed as far as I was aware. It transpired that they had found a dealer who could provide cheap cocaine and they had then started to take it regularly. One evening Toby had got hold of their usual stash and he and Nathan had gone to the toilets together to snort it without telling Mandy. Mandy had caught them just about to go into the men's toilet with it and had started a huge argument with them because they intended to leave her out. She had then wrestled the cocaine from Nathan and run into the toilets where she promptly flushed it away to teach them a lesson. The subsequent argument had been so bad that in the end, Mandy told them she never wanted to talk to them again, and as she certainly was quite a stubborn type of person, she had stuck to her word ever since. I sat there astounded. I could not believe that a friendship could be broken up over something like this but more importantly, I was quite shocked that Nathan and Toby were using cocaine regularly. The very thought of this was abhorrent to me as I had always considered drugs to be dangerous and simply did not feel comfortable around them.

The rest of the evening passed reasonably well, except that Nathan and Toby made a couple of 'toilet stops', presumably to snort their new drug of choice as when they came back, they seemed remarkably hyped up. I felt that I had less and less in common with these people whose world really did centre on the gay scene and recreational drug use. I certainly did not want my future to be tied up with people who would now be a bad influence on me. If for some reason my parents ever found out I was hanging around with drug users, my life would be even more difficult than it was at the moment. I therefore made the decision that night to actively seek out new friends as soon as possible.

# Chapter 23

A couple of weeks later, I called the clinic. I had managed to somehow keep the test at the back of my mind, instead focusing on my new job which was certainly quite demanding but enjoyable at the same time. I had also caught up with Anyesa and we had spent a lot of our spare time together which helped me to forget about things somewhat. However now the time had arrived and I was about to find out my fate. As I waited for the phone to answer, I started to tremble with nerves. The thought of a positive result was something I could not begin to imagine.

"Hello, Axis Health Centre?" answered a receptionist at the other end.

"Hi," I replied nervously, my throat becoming suddenly quite dry. "I had an HIV test a couple of weeks ago and I was told to call today for my results."

"Yes, can I take your name please and reference number?"

"My name is Evan Bloom and my reference number is 35637."

"Thank you, hold on while I check your records."

The wait of probably about twenty seconds seemed to last for ages. I felt my hands become extremely clammy and prayed desperately that everything would be okay.

"Yes, thanks for holding, Evan. Your results came back negative, which means that you have no sign of any HIV infection."

"Oh, thank you so much, thank you," I blurted out, an enormous sense of relief sweeping over me. I felt the urge to cry but managed to contain myself. After I hung up, I sat down for a few minutes just taking it all in. So I had not contracted anything and could now finally put the whole experience with Lorenzo completely behind me. With this result, it meant my life could really start afresh. I looked up and thanked God for having spared me this time. It was surely a sign that I could begin again on a clean slate and make sure that I was in control of things going forward.

On reflection, I assessed the way my life was going at this point. I had one year left at university, I had a job that would provide me an income over the summer and allow me to continue practicing my Italian; I had a close friend in Anyesa that I could spend time with and I now had the opportunity to seek new friends and try to meet more Jewish people that I could relate to. I also really did wish I could meet someone special, someone balanced and regular who had no other agenda than just to be with me for who I was and who had no scary baggage or serious health problems. My friendship with Simon was now in the past as far as I was concerned and although I was still dealing with what had happened emotionally and would still have to see him at university, I felt that I could turn a corner. The main obstacle to feeling content about my life was my family. I had no idea how to help them come to terms with me and decided that if I could manage to survive the next year of having to live at home, I would be able to then find a full time job and hopefully move out as soon as possible. I needed to remain strong and prayed to God that I would be given the conviction to stay true to myself whatever happened.

One day, I decided to go out in town alone to look around the Oxford Street shops and hopefully pick up a few new items of clothing. I went into a large menswear store that had some interesting looking gear in the window, and started to browse the various rails. After a while, I noticed a man standing nearby looking at me in what seemed to be quite a scrutinising way. The man appeared to be around forty years old or so and apart from a thick mop of jet black curly hair, almost seemed quite nondescript. Wondering what he wanted and thinking he was probably just attracted to me, I ignored him and moved off to another part of the store. A couple of minutes later, the man approached me and before I could decide what to do he introduced himself.

"I'm so sorry to bother you and I hope I haven't frightened you in any way," he began, in a distinct public schoolboy accent. "My name is Edward Crispin and I work for a modelling agency called Elite Premier. I am in fact a model scout and I could not help noticing that your look is very interesting. Have you ever thought about modelling before?"

"Er, never actually," I replied, wondering what on earth was going on. Was this some kind of joke? Why would any modelling agency be interested in me, a skinny, bushy-haired young man who still suffered from an ongoing acne problem although by now quite mild, and who probably did not dress the part of a model by any stretch of the imagination?

"Well," Edward continued, "your look is definitely of interest to us at Elite Premier and we would like to talk to you further. Here's my card. Please just think about it as we would love to see you at our offices for a chat and see what we can do for you. I understand if you have never considered something like this before but believe me, it can be an extremely lucrative career and something I recommend you to consider. Call me again when you are ready and we will set it up. I am certain you won't regret it."

"Thank you Edward," I replied unsurely. "I just never expected anything like this really but I will certainly think about it."

"Excellent! I look forward to hearing from you then. Goodbye for now," and with that, Edward turned and left leaving me somewhat stunned.

I had never in a million years considered myself remotely attractive enough to be a model, having always struggled with my appearance. I knew that I was attractive to other men as by now it was commonplace for guys to look at me whenever I went into a gay bar or club. However I had always thought models were striking looking with perfect complexions and a great sense of style. As Simon used to always tell me, I had absolutely no fashion sense and although I was definitely tall enough, I did not think I possessed any of the other attributes required. On top of the physical side, I had a very low self-esteem which was the result of everything I had been through in my life so far, and models all seemed to be full of confidence. How very bizarre that someone would consider me suitable to be a model. I looked at the card Edward had given to me and decided I would think more about it over the next couple of days.

That evening at the restaurant, I was due to work a shift alongside a very friendly French waitress called

Carine. We had worked together a couple of times before and had got on quite well. As we set up the restaurant for the evening shift, we started chatting. She was from a village outside of Paris and had come to London to improve her English which was already quite good, and also just to get away from her parents who she seemed to have a somewhat difficult relationship with. As we spoke, I learned that Carine was an only child and that her parents were very traditional and set in their ways whereas she was more of a free spirit and it was this difference between them that appeared to be causing the issues. I decided that I would fill her in on my situation as well, as I certainly was not worried about coming out to her and felt in fact that we may be able to become friends. Carine listened intently as I told her what my relationship with my family was like and told me she could completely relate to me, albeit from a different context. We would have carried on talking for far longer had Alonzo the Manager not told us to get on with our preparations due to the dinner shift starting in ten minutes.

It turned out to be quite a busy evening and pretty tiring but we managed to help each other serve some of the busier tables and received a few remarks from people that we made a really good team. When our shift was over, we decided to go and get a drink somewhere and just continue getting to know each other. We chatted well into the night, leaving the pub we had gone to when it closed and continuing to just wander around the streets. It turned out that we had quite a lot in common, both feeling repressed within our families and that nobody really understood us. The only difference was that Carine had already done something about it by coming to London to start a new life on her own terms. My experience in Italy, although liberating, had still been funded entirely by my parents and I could not wait for a time when I had nobody else I needed to rely on financially. I also decided to tell Carine that I had been approached by a modelling scout and that I was not sure what to do about it. She became very excited about this and told me I must definitely at least go to their offices and see what happened. She said that she certainly found me very attractive and that she could completely understand why I had been approached. This was very flattering to hear and with a new sense of motivation, I decided I would give Edward Crispin a call the following day.

When we finally decided it was time to go home to bed, Carine and I agreed that we would hang out with each other much more from now on. I was happy that I had met someone new that I could relate to and who understood what I might be going through in my life. Feeling buoyed by my new ally, I went to sleep dreaming of the possible new paths that lay ahead and the modelling opportunities that might be available to me.

The next day, I called Anyesa and after chatting for a while, I filled her in on the modelling situation. I was interested to know what she had to say and felt I just wanted a final push before taking the step of contacting Edward. Anyesa was just as positive as Carine had been the night before and said she was not surprised this had happened. Was everyone else seeing something that I wasn't? I still found it hard to believe I had the looks of a potential model, it almost seemed ludicrous. In any case I was now ready to make contact and see what happened.

After calling Edward, who sounded very pleased to hear from me, I made my way to the Elite Premier Modelling Agency which was based in Mayfair. As I sat waiting for Edward, I noticed several young men and women, all strikingly good-looking, sitting around or chatting away confidently, most of them with large portfolios of several different photos that they seemed to be browsing through or talking to others about. I suddenly felt extremely out of place. What on earth was I doing here? This was not me at all and I certainly did not feel confident enough to be one of these people. Before long however, Edward appeared and shook my hand warmly.

"It's great to see you again, Evan. I'm so happy you made the right choice to come and see us. Why don't you come this way?"

I followed Edward to a small office where another man was waiting.

"This is Laurent," said Edward as they both sat down and indicated for me to do the same. "Laurent is a great photographer that we use often and he will help decide what the best approach for you should be."

Laurent was French and quite tall. He was probably around thirty years old and had classically good looks with quite chiselled cheekbones and tousled brown hair. I wondered why he was not actually a model himself as I certainly considered him to be attractive enough.

"Hi Evan," Laurent began, in a soft French accent. "First of all, tell us something about you, what you do in life and your background."

"Well, er, I'm a student at university right now, but as it's the summer break I'm working at a restaurant to earn some cash. I come from a large Jewish family and I am one of five children. That's it really, I'm not sure what else you want to know."

"That's okay," chimed in Edward. "We just wanted to get an idea of what you are like and your personality.

Please don't be nervous, just relax and be yourself. It would actually be good if you could stand up so we can see how you measure up. Would you mind taking off your top?"

Nervously, I stood up. I had not expected this at all. Having never gone to the gym or done any form of disciplined exercise, my body was not very defined, although I was certainly very slim. Trying to appear calm, I took off my top and stood there awkwardly, waiting for some kind of comment as both men across the table began to scrutinise me.

"Hmmm," pondered Laurent. "I think this guy could do with a good gym routine to develop his chest muscles and arms."

"I agree," added Edward. "I think that in about three months' time you will be ready to do something with us, if you make sure that you start an exercise regime of some sort in the meantime to develop your physique. However I still think it would be worth us taking some shots of you now as you do have quite a strong face and I want to see how you come across on camera in different poses. Laurent will arrange this with you directly."

"Erm, will I have to pay for any of this?" I asked, feeling like I was being thrown into something I had no control over.

"No, not at all, these shots will be free," said Laurent. "Come back in a couple of days with a few different changes of clothes, including casual and smart and we will take some pictures! You can leave now, just turn left outside and you will get to reception and the way out."

"Okay then, thanks very much," I said as I shook both their hands and left the room leaving them sitting there probably to discuss me further. I really was extremely unsure about this whole thing. Who was I kidding anyway? I did not even really want to be a model, it seemed to be such a vacuous world. I had also felt very exposed and vulnerable standing there topless in front of those two men who were looking me up and down like a piece of meat. Is this what all models went through? I certainly needed something deeper and more fulfilling than this in my life. In any case, I decided to turn up again to have my pictures taken as it would at least be an experience which I could tell my friends about, and if I was able to keep the pictures then they would be an interesting memento. I was also certain that if somehow Simon ever found out about this, he would be extremely jealous and the thought of that alone helped to strengthen my resolve to go back. Me, a model? Life just kept getting stranger.

# Chapter 24

On my next day off work I decided to stay at home and start trying to find a way to meet other gay Jews which I had been promising myself I would do for a while. My previous attempts at this in the past had brought extremely disappointing results but this time I was certain it would be different. At least if I had some regular Jewish friends then it could also help take the pressure off me with my parents. I began by scouring through the main Jewish newspaper in the UK that my parents always kept copies of, which was called the *Jewish Chronicle*. In the classified section at the back I noticed several help lines for support services of different kinds. To my surprise, one of these was for a 'Jewish Gay and Lesbian Helpline'. I had never seen this before. Was it possible that such a service had sprung up while I had been away in Italy?

Excitedly I called the number straight away. A woman answered and I introduced myself, explaining that I was someone who had already come out as gay but had no real contact with other gay Jews, which I wanted to try and change. I was told that the help line was a new service that mainly operated to help people come to terms with their sexuality issues as opposed to acting as a networking or dating service. However the woman also told me that there was an Orthodox Rabbi who had recently come out to his community and had been subsequently sacked and ostracised. He had then left the community and set up his own Jewish liberal gay group and Sabbath services for people that no longer felt they could attend their own synagogues. This was a revelation! I was told that the rabbi was called Mark Steinberg and was given a contact number for him. If I called him, I would have access to a whole group of like-minded people who had been through exactly the same thing as me! I felt elated at the thought of connecting with Rabbi Steinberg and after hanging up from the help line woman, I dialled his number. I received an answer phone message and tentatively left my details for him to call me back. So that was that. I felt sure my sense of isolation as a gay Jew would be coming to an end and that I may even be able to meet someone special amongst this new group of people. Time would tell.

That evening, I had arranged to go out with Anyesa. I was looking forward to being able to tell her my news and for her to give me some confidence for my photo shoot the next day with Laurent. While having dinner with my family before heading out, the phone rang. My mother answered it and after a few seconds, turned to me looking quite pleased and said that a Rabbi Steinberg was on the phone for me. I jumped up and took the phone from my mother. It was obvious that she did not know about Rabbi Steinberg and his story and probably thought I had taken it upon myself to find someone who could bring me back onto the 'right path'.

"Hello?" I answered tentatively, wondering what a gay Rabbi was actually like.

"Hello Evan, I am Mark Steinberg. Thanks so much for contacting me."

"That's okay. Erm, if you wait a second I will take the phone in another room and we can have a proper chat," I said as I noticed my family looking over at me with intrigued expressions on their faces. I felt far too awkward to hold a conversation with him in front of them. I hung up and went into the living room where I picked up the extension.

"Sorry about that," I continued, "you called in the middle of dinner and my family were all there looking at me and making me uncomfortable. I would much rather talk in private."

"That's perfectly understandable, Evan," replied the rabbi. "So, why is it exactly that you contacted me?"

"Well, I am a gay Jew and my family is quite religious. I've already come out to them all and it's quite a hard time at the moment, but one thing I promised myself I would do is try to meet other gay Jews somehow and try to be part of a community where sexuality doesn't matter. When I was told about you by a help line advisor I thought it sounded unbelievable! Did you really come out to your community and get sacked for it?"

"Yes Evan, all of that is true. I was brought up like you, within an Orthodox community and all I ever wanted to do was to help people come closer to God and share my love of Judaism. When I was fortunate enough to become the rabbi of my community I was so happy, because finally I would have the opportunity to do just that. I also knew that I was homosexual, and despite personal struggles with myself, I knew that I was fulfilling my role in life. Unfortunately, keeping my private life hidden for so long took its toll on me and after being questioned by many people about the lack of a wife and children I decided to just take the bull by the horns so to speak, and tell people the truth in one of my sermons on Sabbath a month or so ago. Unfortunately, the understanding I thought I might receive from the community I held so dear, was sadly lacking and I was told I was no longer suitable to lead them as an Orthodox leader. So I decided to set up my own community of people who still wanted to follow the Jewish way of life but who didn't feel they could comfortably fit within the traditional Orthodox environment. We are still quite small at the moment with a good handful of members, but every new person we find, like yourself, helps us to grow and makes me more certain that what I am doing is for the best."

"Wow, that's amazing," I said thinking that this man was probably the bravest person I had come across recently and feeling that I wanted to meet him as soon as I could. "Can I come to your next group meeting or service?"

"Absolutely!" replied the rabbi. "That's just what I was going to suggest. This weekend I am holding a Sabbath service at a community centre in Hampstead and that evening there will be a party at my home, both of which you are extremely welcome to join. What do you think?"

"That sounds great!" I replied, thinking that finally I would be able to meet people that were in the same situation as me. After taking the details of where the service was going to be held that weekend and heartily thanking Rabbi Steinberg, I hung up and went back to finish my dinner.

My parents looked at me expectantly, hoping I would divulge the details of my conversation with them, probably hoping I would tell them I was now willing to seek counselling or something similar from this Rabbi.

However, not wanting to go into any details at that point and start a whole discussion, I simply said I would tell everyone the following day and that I was heading out for the evening. I then finished eating and promptly left to go and meet Anyesa. I now had something really exciting to look forward to and hopefully a new sense of purpose. I could not wait to find out where it would take me.

The following day at ten thirty in the morning, I selected some of my nicest clothes that I thought would be suitable for my photo shoot, and headed out to meet Laurent at Elite Premier's offices. When I arrived I was told to wait in reception. Looking around me again, I felt more certain than ever that I would never be able to fit into this kind of world. The entire modelling industry was focused on physical appearance and every model was scrutinised for any possible imperfections. This was apparent from overhearing some of the models hanging around the reception area, saying that they were having the biggest nightmare ever because they had discovered a spot somewhere, or they had seen a new grey hair or a wrinkle. I doubted that anything deeper than that ever factored into these people's lives. Before I had time to think much more about it, Laurent appeared, warmly shook my hand and took me along the corridor into a room that had been set up with lights and a white background ready for the shoot. I was told to change into the first of my outfits behind a screen and to then go and stand with a relaxed pose in front of the camera. Doing my best to look interesting, I stood there as Laurent snapped away, encouraging me constantly to put my hand there, tilt my head that way, lean slightly to the left. It felt quite surreal and certainly not very comfortable.

After a couple of changes of clothes, Laurent then took me outside the building for some outdoor shots. I was told to look moody, sexy, coy and ecstatic. Is this really what models did every day? If only I felt comfortable with it all, I would be able to earn quite a lot of money for apparently very little effort. By the time we had finished I was relieved. It was possibly the most unnatural experience I had been through in a while and certainly a world away from taking holiday snapshots. Laurent asked me for my address and said he would be sending a sample of the shots to me. He then told me that if I was serious about a career as a model, I would need to attend the gym regularly and then go back and see them in three months' time as Edward had advised a couple of days previously. I knew I would never be seeing either of them again.

With the photo shoot out of the way, I went back home. That afternoon, I decided to wander around the local shopping centre to while away some time before going to start my shift at the restaurant. As I stood outside a men's clothes shop looking at the window display, someone came up behind me and put their hands over my eyes. When I turned around I was surprised to see Alex standing there. Alex – one of my oldest and dearest friends, who I had not spoken to properly since having gone to Italy. She had put on quite a bit of weight since I had last seen her, but she somehow looked incredibly radiant.

"Alex, oh my goodness!" I exclaimed, as we hugged each other tightly.

"It's been absolutely ages!" squealed Alex in delight. "I'm so happy I caught up with you, I have so much to tell you! Do you have time to sit in a café with me?"

"Of course! I had no real plans for the next couple of hours actually. I have loads to tell you too!"

As we sat in one of the shopping centre cafeterias, we started to catch up on everything since I had gone away to Italy. I told Alex about meeting Jonathan, Caroline, Luca and Anyesa and the things we got up to. Not wanting to go into the situation with Simon, I simply mentioned that we had fallen out whilst over there.

"Well," said Alex, nursing a long glass of café latte in her hands, "you seem to have kept yourself busy! I've already met up with Simon actually and he pretty much said the same thing about you falling out, but hasn't explained why, just like you haven't. Is there something I should know?"

"No," I replied sheepishly, "nothing worth talking about really."

"Hmmm, if you say so. But don't you think it's a bit drastic, not speaking to each other any more over some silly argument or other?"

"Believe me, there are good reasons for it and if it was just a silly argument then there wouldn't be any problems, but I just don't want to go into it if that's alright with you. Can we just talk about something else, like what on earth you've been up to all this time?"

"Okay, okay. Well, to get straight to the point, I'm getting married!"

"What? Goodness, that's amazing!" I shrieked. "Who is it, anyone I know? Tell me everything!"

"Well, his name is Neil and I met him not long before you and Simon went to Italy. Do you remember me talking about someone I was interested in? A friend of my mother's introduced us actually. He's a couple of years older than me and he works as a stockbroker. It was a bit of a whirlwind romance I guess and now we're engaged! Oh, and by the way, I know I was crap at keeping in touch but I was quite preoccupied by everything I suppose. We haven't set the date for the wedding yet but it will be in about a year's time. I'm so excited! I need to really start thinking about everything now."

"That really is amazing Alex, I'm so happy for you!"

"Thanks! So now tell me, how is everything with, you know, you and your family and stuff?"

"If you mean the fact that I'm gay, well that's still problematic. I'm working on it but living with my family after so long being away is really hard."

"I can understand I guess. By the way, I also know about Simon. He told me last week when we met up. He seems to be having a nightmare with his own family too. I feel for you both, really I do. Are you sure there's no way you can try and change things? There are so many beautiful girls out there you know and your life would be so much simpler if you just managed to settle down."

"Thanks Alex, but you need to understand that this is just who I am and I couldn't change my sexuality even if I wanted to. I know that people in our community couldn't possibly get where I'm coming from and won't be able to handle it which is why I don't consider myself a part of it any more. I have my own life to lead and I just want to be happy."

"Well, just be very careful, Evan," warned Alex, taking my hand in hers. "Don't burn all your bridges unnecessarily. I know it's not ideal but I am here for you if you need me, okay?"

"Thanks Alex, that means a lot to me. It really was good to see you again, I thought you had abandoned me actually."

"Me? Never! Life just got in the way I suppose."

"It would be nice to meet up again with the rest of the group, you know, like we used to? I haven't seen them or spoken to them for so long."

"Well, I hate to say this to you," said Alex with a remorseful look on her face, "but they all know about you now, it kind of came out when we were talking one night at my house while you were away. They were discussing everybody's sex life and when it came to you, they said they thought you were gay because you had never had a real girlfriend. So I kind of told them the truth because you had told me you didn't want to have to hide yourself from anyone, and after all, these are meant to be your friends. They were not very nice about it and said some quite nasty things about you actually. I don't think any of them would want to hang out with you socially now, they really aren't mature enough in my opinion. I'm so sorry."

"Well, what a surprise," I managed, actually feeling quite hurt by this revelation. "Looks like my so-called friends never really were my friends after all."

"I'm really sorry Evan. I wouldn't bother with them anyway, what's the point in allowing yourself to be taunted or made fun of? You deserve better than that. Anyway, I really need to dash now I have so many things to sort out! Look after yourself Evan, and just be careful whatever you do. You know where I am if you ever want to talk, I promise I am not going to abandon you."

We then got up, hugged each other again and then turned to go our separate ways. I could not believe that my old friends who I used to spend so much time with, could be so hurtful about me just because they found out I was gay. Could they not still see me as a person, as their friend? This was the first group that I had ever felt remotely comfortable with and I had thanked God for them all and for making me feel like I belonged somewhere. Yet now, knowing that they looked down on me because of my sexuality, I felt like they had never really cared about me as a person at all. Maybe I was only ever just a number in the group, someone to fill a gap or something? Suddenly I hated my community and the people in it. You could only fit in and be accepted if you were like them, that was it. And I would never be like them.

Nevertheless, I was so happy for Alex to have found someone and hoped she would end up living the life she wanted. It seemed so straightforward for heterosexual Jews – they simply met someone suitable and were then encouraged every step of the way with the full support of family, friends and the community. Why couldn't things be the same for gay people? After all, the only difference was the gender of the person we loved. Love was still love, wasn't it? Yet it was impossible to hope for a situation nearly as supportive. I felt a deep sense of despair at that moment and as I wandered back home, I prayed that Rabbi Steinberg's community really could offer a structure that I could feel part of.

# Chapter 25

The following day, I told my parents more about my phone conversation with Rabbi Steinberg. They seemed quite fascinated by the story and were surprised that he was gay and had been brave enough to come out to his community in the way that he had. They did not however, approve of his having decided to set up a separate community for gay people, believing that he should simply have joined another Orthodox synagogue as a regular member, keeping his sexuality private. According to them, his being gay should not have had any bearing on his religious life or practices in any other way. Therefore when I told them I was going to be away that weekend at a gay Sabbath service he was running, my mother told me to be careful not to go down a path of confusion where real Jewish values were being distorted in a community like this which promoted and harboured homosexuality so openly. I realised my parents would never be happy whatever I did as long as it related to my sexuality so I decided to leave it at that instead of getting into an argument. At least I had told them about it and as far as I was concerned I was going to the Sabbath service in any case whether they approved or not.

That night at the restaurant, I told Carine that I had found Rabbi Steinberg and that I was looking forward to seeing what he and his community were like. Carine was very supportive and told me that at the end of the day I needed to do what made me happy, just like she had done. She certainly seemed to have a very liberal attitude about everything and a carefree way of looking at things. I found it incredibly refreshing. As usual, we made a great team serving the customers that night and I actually managed to pick up some decent tips. The down side to my job was that the head waiter, Gino seemed to always be watching us and would frequently come and tell us what we were doing wrong and try to exert his own authority over us. I had put up with Gino's behaviour for a while now and his arrogance and micromanaging ways were starting to get on my nerves quite badly. Unfortunately, the restaurant Manager Alonzo, did not seem to care whenever I brought it up with him and went along with anything that Gino had to say. I sometimes felt that if it were not for Carine, I would not bother sticking around for long although the money was certainly very handy.

Before I knew it, the weekend had arrived. I packed an overnight bag and early on Friday evening said goodbye to my parents and made my way to Hampstead, where Rabbi Steinberg had booked a hostel near a community centre where the services were taking place, for all the guests who wanted to stay overnight. Everyone attending had been asked to pay a nominal amount of money to help cover the food and accommodation as required, which I had been happy to do. After I had checked into the hostel I made my way up the road to the community centre, and started to think about the kinds of people that may be there. I hoped there would be some people my age at least who I could become friends with and possibly someone special there too. I did not really know what to expect, but was extremely eager to see what it was all about.

As soon as I entered the community centre, which was housed in an old building that apparently used to be a library and was squeezed between a couple of apartment blocks, a man of about forty years old came striding towards me with his hand held out. I immediately took this to be Rabbi Steinberg.

"Welcome, welcome! Are you Evan?" asked the rabbi with a warm friendly smile. He was of average height and had a short cropped beard, dark hair and greying temples. I found myself thinking that he was actually quite attractive for a Rabbi, comparing him to nearly every other one I had met before.

"Yes I am," I answered nervously, suddenly feeling quite anxious about the whole thing.

"Please, come this way, most of the others are here already. We're having drinks and snacks in the hall and then we will begin our Friday evening service followed by a lovely dinner. I ordered food in for everyone."

As I entered the small hall which had wood panelled walls and slightly worn pale blue carpeting I saw several people, possibly about twenty of them, mingling and chatting away. Clearly they all knew each other already and I assumed I was the new boy.

"Hi everyone, this is Evan who I am delighted has joined us this weekend," exclaimed the rabbi as he gestured for people to come and greet me.

I was then introduced to people one after the other. The group was quite mixed and included a handful of older men, a few women, a couple of whom looked rather masculine to me and slightly scary, and the remainder were younger men who all appeared to be still in their twenties. There was nobody that seemed to stand out especially, although I would need to get to know them all better to see if I could relate to them and at least become friends. After the initial introductions I went to a table at the side of the hall and grabbed a soft drink and a biscuit. After a few seconds, the group of women approached me. They seemed to be sticking together quite closely in a clique and unsure what on earth I would have to say to them, I started to feel quite uncomfortable. They mainly appeared to be more masculine than the men themselves, and one especially who I learned was called Sharon, did not even look female, having shaved her entire head except for a Mohican quiff down the middle and with several piercings. I wondered why on earth she wanted to try and make herself look so masculine if she was gay and attracted to women. Surely other women would want someone that looked female? Even generally butch lesbians like Mandy still had an air of femininity about them, and my friend Caroline from Italy was certainly quite feminine. It puzzled me but I was too nervous to ask her anything about it. After some meaningless chit chat, I manoeuvred myself away from them and went towards a couple of the older men who seemed very friendly and quite gentle. As we chatted about nothing in particular, I realised that they were rather camp which made me feel slightly uneasy for some reason.

Making my way through the group, I managed to speak to most of the younger men thinking that surely they would be more on my wavelength. They all seemed very nice and down to earth, however I noticed that most of them came across a little strangely as if they were not quite on the same planet as I was. It was hard to pinpoint what it was exactly. It was almost like the struggle of being gay and Jewish had affected their personalities so that they lost any passion or animation in their characters and instead were quite drippy. As far as I was concerned, the fight to maintain my sanity within the environment I had been brought up in had only made me stronger and more determined in character and I was surprised that none of these others seemed in any way to be like me.

A couple of them were especially friendly however. One guy was called Steve and he was twenty-six, quite tall with wavy brown hair and a smattering of freckles across his nose. He was pleasant looking enough and had kindly hazel eyes, although as with the group at large, he seemed to have quite a soft personality that lacked any real edge. He was the type of person who you would find it hard to imagine ever getting angry or even fighting his corner on any issue. The other one was called Josh. He was originally from New Zealand and was twenty-eight, also quite tall and extremely thin with short black hair and brown eyes. He should have been quite attractive but the boniness of his face gave him a look that was altogether too angular. He was an amiable type and seemed to take a certain interest in me that I found comforting at first. If nothing else, I would have Josh and possibly Steve to stick with over the weekend so that was at least something.

Before I knew it, the service commenced. Rabbi Steinberg led the proceedings which followed a traditional Sabbath programme, singing several hymns in Hebrew and reciting prayers communally. He then gave a sermon which was all about how we as Jews should be proud of our heritage and also of our sexuality and not let our issues get in the way of our relationship with God. He emphasised that the culture of mainstream Orthodox Jewish society meant that anything different from the norm of settling down with a partner of the opposite sex and procreating, was looked upon with fear because other Jews felt that homosexuals threatened their way of life. He continued to say that gay Jewish people like us should not feel pressured by this and should take every opportunity to show the wider community how we are just as important to the religion. We all needed to be strong in our faith because despite the treatment and persecution we received from our heterosexual brethren, we could continue to perpetuate God's wishes and Jewish values on earth and set an example to the world. The Rabbi finished by saying how valuable it was to have us all present that weekend and that if we could all make this community grow from strength to strength then we would create an influential movement that made the wider community stand up and take notice of what we stood for so that we could start to lobby the other synagogues and really eradicate homophobia on our own doorstep.

I listened to the sermon intently. It was an impassioned speech of solidarity, with the main message being that we needed to be proud of our sexuality and use it for the greater good somehow despite outside pressures. I wished it were as simple as that when your own family made you feel that you were a complete disappointment and were destroying them and the religion they held so dear. The thing that worried me however was that the rabbi was advocating that gay Jews should stand separately from the rest of Jewish society and become ambassadors for the cause somehow. I was uncomfortable about this as I simply did not want to make my sexuality a separate entity from the rest of me or try to be political or militant in any way. All I had ever wanted was to live like anyone else did within my community, my sexuality being irrelevant.

Considering the rabbi's words, I wondered if nevertheless it was part of my role to try and educate my parents and siblings somehow which I had already tried to do with no luck until now. Did I even have the desire to continue doing so? I thought about the amount of effort my parents were putting into my sister in trying to help her find a suitable partner and wished that they could be as interested in doing the same for me, even if it was a man that they would be helping me to find. But life just did not work that way. As well as this, my family would certainly not be happy about me being part of this group and trying to ram gay messages down their throats. Was this community going to be any real help to me at all? I had just wanted to find somewhere that other gay Jews were so that I could make new connections, rather than join a group with some kind of political vision. I realised then that I would not feel comfortable being part of a community focused on gay people and that I would rather continue to have my own personal relationship with God and make sense of life my way. It was what I was used to doing by now after all. The reality of things rarely ever matched expectations and being introduced to this community now, made me more certain of that as the kind of direction it wanted to go in was not right for me. At least thanks to Rabbi Steinberg's sermon I had come to realise this sooner rather than later.

As we all sat down to eat dinner after the service, the rabbi came up to me.

"So, how's the evening going for you, Evan? Do you feel you got anything out of the sermon?"

"Well," I answered, wondering whether I should just come out and tell him my thoughts or remain diplomatic "It was really interesting to hear what you had to say although it's still a bit of a strange experience for me I suppose," was all I managed.

"Well that's perfectly fine," replied the rabbi, "you will come to realise that being part of this community gives you a new sense of purpose and a new sense of belonging where you can really help to change people's attitudes. We may be small now but we intend to grow and will soon have a strong unified voice that the Orthodox communities will not be able to ignore, isn't that right, Sharon?" he asked the scary mohican-haired woman sitting opposite me.

"Absolutely!" she replied, as she stuffed a large piece of chicken into her mouth. I suddenly felt quite ill at ease. This was definitely not my scene, it almost felt a little cult-like somehow. I wondered what tomorrow would bring and if I would be subjected to a similar kind of gospel. I was here now though, and despite my sense of discomfort, decided I may as well stick it out in the best way I could.

The following day, I woke up and made my way back to the community centre where breakfast was being served for anyone that wanted to come early or who had stayed overnight at the hostel. It appeared that most of the group were there already including Josh who greeted me with a smile and offered me a hot cup of tea. He certainly was very friendly but I did begin to wonder if he had any kind of ulterior motive as his gaze seemed to linger on me a little too long.

The rest of the morning was taken up with the main Sabbath service which included another sermon about passage 18:22 in Leviticus. Ironically, this passage concerned the commandments involving sexual behaviour and included the prohibition "Thou shalt not lie with a man as with a woman; it is an abomination." The Rabbi's take on tackling this was simply to say that at the time the Bible was written, many commandments were put in place for the High Priest to follow during his time in the Holy Temple and that sexual abstinence of many kinds was one of the required prohibitions. However these commandments did not relate to the masses and it was just unfortunate that throughout the ages, people had taken these passages as read for the entire community, hence the difficulty with Orthodox communities accepting gay people. I found this explanation implausible as if it was as simple as that, then all Rabbis would have realised this by now and there would not be any issues anywhere. However I could not find any alternative explanations and with a growing sense of frustration that even within a community like this I would not find any answers, I knew that my ongoing struggle to make sense of everything would probably continue for a while yet.

After a long satisfactory lunch, which consisted of various salads and cold meats followed by fruit and cakes, we were all free to do whatever we wanted until the evening when the rabbi was holding a party at his home. I was wondering whether I should actually take the opportunity to leave, when Josh and Steve approached me and asked if I wanted to walk through the high street with them and look at the shops. Seeing as I had nothing better to do, I decided I may as well take them up on their offer and so we headed out together. On chatting further with them and getting to know them some more, I realised that I found Steve altogether too boring. He was an engineer and designed computer parts. His placid personality simply did not spark anything in me and I found nothing in common with him although he was perfectly harmless. Josh was altogether a different story, although not in a good way. His constant focus on me and his lingering eyes made me uncomfortable. His by now apparent sexual desire for me made me think I needed to stop this going any further, just cut my losses and put this whole weekend down to another experience. After about an hour I told them both I was really tired and was going to lie down for a bit back at the hostel. Before either of them could say anything or stop me, I said goodbye and that I would see them later.

As I lay on the bed in my hostel room, I thought about my experience so far that weekend and knew it was something I was glad to have been part of as otherwise I would never have known what it was like to meet a community of gay Jews, which I thought I had wanted for so long. However it was simply not for me and at least I could put it all behind me now. I recognised that my real need was not to join a gay Jewish community as such; I simply had to make sense of my own life within its own context and get to a point where I felt comfortable with my spirituality and sexuality living side by side. I had my own friends that understood me and I was sure I would make many more throughout my life. My family would hopefully one day accept who I was and in the meantime I would do what I needed to do and try to keep strong. It always came back to this. Me, alone, forging my own way and lucky enough to find people that were happy to accept me and be my friend just for who I was.

# Chapter 26

Having decided not to go to Rabbi Steinberg's party that evening, I waited until nightfall and then made my way back home. I felt it was best to leave without saying goodbye to anyone so as to avoid them trying to change my mind and in any case I did not expect to really see any of them again. I was sure the rabbi would want to speak to me and find out what had happened afterwards and I was prepared to explain my reasons when the time came but the truth was I had nothing in common with any of the people I had met, other than being gay and Jewish. Clearly that was simply not enough despite me thinking it would be, and I had always been the kind of person who acted on instinct.

When I arrived home, my mother asked me what my weekend had been like and I filled her in on everything. I was certain that she was expecting me to say that I finally realised being gay was completely wrong and that I was coming back to normality. Instead, I had told her that I wished the rabbi the best of luck with his community and that I just felt personally that I did not have anything in common with the others but that I was glad there was at least somewhere for gay people to go. I felt that it was necessary to provide a supportive stance about gay Jews when it came to my parents because any sign of doubt about the gay environment would probably cause them to build up all sorts of false hopes. My mother reiterated her view that a specific gay community just was not right and that if only I could appreciate the importance of Jewish values and the true path, I would somehow be able to turn my life around. Anyone would have thought I had committed a series of crimes against society that I needed to go through rehabilitation for, instead of just wanting to be me and find friends with common interests like anyone else.

I then went upstairs and called Anyesa to tell her about my experience, after which she told me I did not need any special community and always had friends like her that would accept me for who I was and loved me regardless. Her supportive words made me feel much better. I also had some post waiting for me and saw that I had received a letter from Jonathan and a postcard from Caroline. Excitedly I lay down on my bed and read them both. Caroline's postcard showed a lovely picture of Florence from above, the red rooftops glistening in the sun and the Duomo standing out like a beacon of architectural brilliance. Caroline had written that she and her girlfriend Helen had moved in together for their last couple of months in Italy and that when they returned to the USA they would be setting up home. They clearly seemed to be very much in love and ready to make such a big commitment even after only a couple of months. I was happy for them and hoped I would get to see them again before too long.

Jonathan's letter was also very interesting. He had spent the last few weeks with Luca, travelling around Italy again and had met a couple of interesting guys along the way. He was currently seeing someone called Fabrizio who he was quite into although realised that there would not be much mileage in it as he would be leaving to go back to Boston the following month and so was just happy having as much fun as he could. Jonathan never seemed to have met anyone particularly suitable while I had been in Italy and so I was glad things had changed for him now. I wished so much that I was still in Florence, spending time with my friends and going everywhere like we used to do. I wondered if I would ever be able to recapture the close-knit group feeling I had enjoyed there and if I would ever feel so unreservedly accepted again.

I then remembered that it was my birthday in a couple of weeks and that I had not planned anything at all for it. The truth was that most of the people who I now considered my friends were not around and mostly lived abroad. Maybe I would just do something low-key with Anyesa and also Carine, who certainly was a lot of fun. It would be a good opportunity to introduce them to each other in fact. I would probably do something separately with Alex too as seeing her again recently had been nice and it would have been a shame not to continue our friendship. I was going to be twenty-one. I could barely believe it. I was a real adult and still had so much to deal with. Time seemed to be flying past and yet in so many ways I was a child inside, still looking for my place and trying to understand the world around me. Would that ever really happen?

When my birthday came around, it passed by without much fuss. I had managed to see everyone I cared about and that was all that mattered. I had gone for dinner with Anyesa and Carine who seemed to get on okay although I could tell that Carine was a little too loud for Anyesa's liking. Alex met me for a few drinks at a bar in town one evening that week, although she seemed quite taken up with her forthcoming wedding plans and spoke of nothing other than her fiancé and what kind of event they would have. My parents took the whole family out for a nice dinner to celebrate at a local gourmet kosher restaurant, which should have been a good experience but most of the evening was spent barely speaking to anybody. My brothers mainly chatted about football to each other and clearly felt too awkward to try and engage with me in any real way. My sister did her best to show me some attention but was preoccupied mostly in trying to analyse why things had not worked out with the latest guy she had dated and despaired of ever meeting someone decent. My mother spent the bulk of the evening trying to convince my sister that she should join a Jewish dating agency run by a friend in the community where all the available men were compared against the women's backgrounds and values so that there would be more likelihood of a suitable match. My sister did not seem very keen on that idea as she wanted to be able to find someone in her own way and on her own terms. My father remained quiet on the whole, and just concentrated on eating his food, chipping in every so often on my brothers' football conversation.

I had sat there all evening feeling entirely out of place. If I had met someone recently that I had wanted to talk about, would I have ever had the opportunity, or would it even have mattered to anyone? I felt so jealous of my sister, who had my mother pushing her all the way to find a suitable man and trying to understand my sister's issues with each man she dated. I was sure I would never have such a luxury. It was as if my whole family had stopped showing any interest in my personal life for fear of finding out something controversial that they were unable to handle. What was the point anyway? I was a blight on the family landscape and although they could not stop loving me as a brother and son, I was now clearly too much of an awkward and uncomfortable subject for them to focus on. Thank goodness for my friends, otherwise I would have gone completely mad by now.

A couple of days after my birthday celebrations, I received a package in the post which contained the photos that Laurent had taken of me at the modelling agency. It was strange to see myself in such obvious poses although I was certainly quite surprised at how good I looked in the photos. For the first time, I really could see what others probably saw when they looked at me. Through his camera lens, Laurent had managed to highlight my strong face, deep eyes and full lips and the pictures really were something. Having these pictures in my hands gave me a real boost of confidence as now I knew what the agency had seen in me. However it did not change my mind about going into the modelling business because I considered the whole environment simply far too shallow and not my thing. I put the photos in a drawer in my bedroom and decided that if ever I needed to feel better about myself, I would always have these pictures to look at.

Back at the restaurant, things were not getting any better. Gino was on a permanent ego trip and continued to treat Carine and me as if we were his skivvies, criticising the way we did anything. After a couple of months of having worked there, Carine asked if I wanted to go to France with her for a break, and to just quit the restaurant. It did not take long for me to decide and I thought it would be a great idea and just the kind of thing I needed before I started my final year at university the following month. I had also managed to save a decent amount of money by then which I felt was doing me no good sitting there in a bank account when it could be used to help me enjoy my life. One day, we approached Alonzo together, and simply told him that we were leaving because we did not like the way we were being treated. Rather than try to work out any issues with us or even to stop us going, Alonzo simply said that people like us were two a penny and that he would easily just be able to hire replacements. We were told we would be given a week's pay and that we would need to work our shifts until the end of the week and could then go. Considering that this was only in three day's time it was no hardship.

When I told my parents I was going to France with a friend of mine from the restaurant, they were not overly impressed. They wanted to know what this friend was like and what exactly I would be doing there. I told them it was a girl who I got on really well with and that we would be staying at her parents' house just outside Paris. The fact that she was not Jewish did not sit well with them either but I still thought I noticed a glimpse of hope in my mother's eyes when she knew it was a girl I would be spending time with rather than a boy. I decided not to try and put her in the picture and to let her think whatever she wanted. I had told my parents I was going away and that was all that I needed to do.

That weekend, I met Carine at the station and we made our way to Waterloo to take the Eurostar to Paris, where her parents who she had prepped for our arrival, would be collecting us. Despite her own family difficulties, she still liked to be able to see her parents once a year and by all accounts they were happy to be receiving us. I was really excited to be going away with Carine as it was the first real opportunity we would have to spend quality time alone together outside of work and bits of time afterwards. Carine had such a carefree and exuberant air and I really felt liberated when I was with her. She was also quite expressive with her sexuality, and despite knowing I was gay, still commented on my apparent attractiveness and sometimes let slip that she actually fancied me. I hoped that she would never actually try anything with me, and just knew that our time in France would be an exciting and different experience. I was certainly not wrong.

For the first few days, Carine and I went out a lot in Paris, sampling the vibrant nightlife including bars and clubs where we would often dance until the early hours. We also spent some time with her parents in the South of France, where we went on a camping trip by the Pyrenees. I soon found out what her relationship was really like with her parents. Her father especially, was extremely strict and set in his ways and would often come to blows with Carine over the smallest things. Her mother was a very prim, traditional type who continually commented on the way Carine dressed and behaved. I was not in the least bit surprised that she had wanted to run away somewhere to be free; her home environment whilst growing up must have been stifling. After a slightly uncomfortable time with her parents, we returned to Paris where we decided to leave her family home and spend our last few days in a cheap hotel in the city centre. It was at this point that my relationship with Carine changed suddenly.

One night after having been out to dinner, we had come back to the hotel to rest before heading out to a club. As I lay down on my bed, Carine decided to come and lie with me.

"You know," she began, "I have been really attracted to you since we met. I know you said you are gay, but surely with a sexy woman like me next to you, I could help to change your mind?"

"What do you mean?" I answered, wondering what on earth she was doing. I did not have to wait long. Her hands started to roam and before I knew it she climbed on top of me.

"I know I can show you a great time, you won't regret it. We are already good friends so surely it will be even better if we can enjoy each other too? Let me show you."

"Er, I don't think that's a good idea Carine. I definitely like men and in any case don't want to risk anything with our friendship."

"Our friendship is just about to get better!" she purred as she unzipped my jeans. For some unexplainable reason, I had become aroused at her attentions. I was not sure why, because in all honesty I was petrified of being touched in this way by Carine. I knew I had absolutely no sexual interest in her or women in general, yet could it be that my very need for acceptance and to feel wanted in general, knew no boundaries? Despite myself I decided to let things run their course. Carine was certainly determined and I felt that if there was any woman I would want to experiment with in this way, it would be her.

Afterwards, we just lay there side by side. I could not believe I had actually had sex with a woman and not just any woman but someone I considered my friend. She had known exactly what she was doing and just the intrigue of the unknown was somehow exciting. I had willingly gone along with it, yet at the same time I felt violated and dirty. My mind was everywhere. Could there actually be a possibility that I was not 100 per cent gay after all? My body had reacted to her attentions in the end, and yet here I was, regretting every second. What did this mean? I still had no doubt that my entire being was attracted to men, both emotionally and physically.

I tried to analyse our encounter to make sense of it all. In fact, the feel of the whole thing just wasn't right. The softness of her body, her womanly curves and large breasts just did not ignite anything inside me. I had closed my eyes for much of the experience and tried to imagine that her hands and tongue were those of a man. The balance was just wrong and the whole experience seemed somehow unnatural to me. If I had not been sure about my sexuality before, I certainly was now. There was simply no way I could do something like that again. The only question was, would this affect my friendship with Carine?

"So, you didn't regret that I hope?" asked Carine tentatively. I was unsure what to say really, I did not want to upset her by saying I had regretted it but knew I would never want to repeat it, so had to make that clear.

"Well," I explained carefully, "it was certainly interesting and now I can say I have at least had sex with a woman."

"Don't bother trying to find guys now Evan, I am here and available for you whenever you want me," said Carine taking my hand in hers.

"I really think our friendship is more important than messing it up with sex though, don't you think? You can have any man you want, you're so attractive and sexual. I really am gay and need a man. You know that already though, right?"

"Well I was kind of hoping you would change your mind," said Carine with a slight tone of disappointment in her voice. "You see, I may be starting to fall in love with you..."

"I think we'd better get ready to go out," I said quickly as I jumped off the bed. I had no intention of getting into any discussion about Carine's sudden declaration of feelings for me, which had caught me off guard. "Come on, let's just go out and have a good time!"

"Well, we will need to talk about this at some point you know," exclaimed Carine as she reluctantly got off the bed and went to have a shower.

I was confused. Surely if Carine had always known I was gay, she would never have allowed herself to develop romantic feelings for me? How on earth could I handle this situation now? I was so happy to have her as my friend, the last thing I wanted was for it all to fall apart. I could have kicked myself for allowing us to have sex together. It had now made things more confusing and I simply did not want to have to deal with that. Damn everything! Why couldn't I have friends who were happy to be just friends? Why would Carine want to change me anyway? I thought she fully supported my sexuality? I suppose she had not intended to fall for me and now that she had, she wanted the possibility for things to happen between us. Unfortunately I would now need to take action and remove any such thoughts from her mind.

Later that night, we went to a trendy and quite glamorous club in Paris called Queen, which was situated on the Champs Elysees and was very well known. It was predominantly a gay club, although attracted people of all sorts who simply wanted to be seen there. Throughout most of the night Carine was all over me, holding onto me as if I were her prize possession and attempting to kiss me at several intervals. I found it incredibly uncomfortable and realised that she was probably doing this to give out a message to any interested men at the club, that I was unavailable. I knew I should never have become intimate with her, it had been a mistake and especially since she had also told me how she felt about me. What could I do?

At one point, I noticed a man looking at me on the dance floor and I smiled at him. He seemed quite attractive, tall and dark haired and had a quirky kind of grin that appealed to me. I told Carine I would go to get us some drinks at the bar and to stay where she was. I then gestured to the man to join me at the bar, where we introduced ourselves to each other. His name was Fabian and he was twenty-six and lived in Paris. I decided that callous as it seemed, I would have to use Fabian as my opportunity to show Carine that there really was no chance for us as a couple.

At several points during the night, I kept leaving Carine to go and continue chatting to Fabian and after a while, we were kissing on the dance floor. Before I knew it, Carine had stormed up to us and pulled me away, shouting angrily at me that I was there with her and should not be spending time with anyone else. I had shouted back that there would never be anything between us except friendship and I could do what I liked. Carine had started to cry and in the end I had to sit down with her and comfort her, explaining that I was really flattered that she felt about me the way she did but that I could not do anything about it and should never have consented to having sex with her.

After several minutes with Carine, I managed to calm her down and she admitted that she had been a fool for letting herself develop feelings in the first place but that I was the nicest and most attractive guy she had met in a long time. This alone made me feel really good about myself and hugging her, I said that I really wanted us to continue being good friends as we had been until now and that we should probably just leave the club and go back to the hotel. Carine then surprised me and said she would very much like to watch me having sex with another man. At first I wondered if she was serious but she reassured me that it would be fun for her and the next best thing to being able to have me again. I knew that Fabian was certainly interested in trying to get me into bed, which I had worked out very quickly, so after thinking about it for a few minutes I decided why not, and went to find him. Thinking he may find the suggestion quite strange, I was surprised that he accepted immediately, saying that the thought of someone watching us was quite exciting to him. So, before I knew it we were all back at the hotel where I spent a very interesting night indeed. I almost forgot that Carine was even there as the passion of the moment overtook me. In the morning, Fabian went out to get us some croissants and orange juice which we consumed in no time and he was then on his way.

Carine and I spent the rest of the day wandering around the shops and generally relaxing. Thankfully no awkwardness remained between us although Carine told me that she felt embarrassed about her behaviour the previous night and that it must have been down to her hormones or something and simply wanted to forget about it. That was certainly all I wanted as well and hoped that things would just go back to normal for us generally. It had been a very interesting trip and I had experienced things I never thought I would get to, let alone even want to.

The following day, we headed back to London where I arrived home, gave my parents a brief overview of the trip and went up to my room to unpack. I thought more about what had happened between me and Carine, and knew that there was no way I could ever explain such a thing to my parents. I also tried to analyse how on earth I had managed to do what I had done. I came to the conclusion that the body was after all, mechanical and that arousal had been possible because I was generally a hormone-filled young man who simply responded to the kind of dedicated attention I had received. It was actually nothing to do with my sexuality fundamentally. In my gut and my heart, I knew this to be true.

I then spent the next hour writing letters to Jonathan, Caroline and Luca, telling them about what I had been up to recently. It was time to start getting myself into the right frame of mind for my last year at university.

# Chapter 27

The start of the university term was a flurry of excitement. It was the first time most of the students on my course had seen each other since before the year abroad, so there was certainly a lot to catch up on. Some of the girls had met someone special while abroad and were now boasting of being in serious relationships, in a couple of cases even having gotten engaged. We all found out what our new course timetables were and which books we needed to buy. This was also the year that we all had to write up the research we had undertaken while away and present our final dissertation to the entire group, followed by our final exams. It was going to be a very busy time and in many ways quite stressful. My future career opportunities would rely on how well I did in my degree and this alone was a daunting thought.

I caught up with Anyesa on the first day back and filled her in properly on my trip to France with Carine, including telling her about the sexual experience and subsequent voyeuristic arrangement with Fabian. She was surprised that I would want to do such a thing and laughed at the thought.

"You know," she admitted, "when I met Carine at your birthday dinner I could tell then that she had a thing for you."

"You could? How?" I asked, wondering why I had completely missed any signals myself.

"Women's intuition I guess," she replied, with a knowing wink. "Looks like she managed to get her wicked way with you in the end, but I'm not surprised it ended in tears afterwards. She really should have known better."

"Well, everything's fine now between us. Because we don't work together any more we'll just keep seeing each other as friends whenever we have the chance. I still think she's a really cool person, I guess she can get carried away with herself though."

"Well, as long as she fully understands the situation, that's all I care about," cautioned Anyesa. "I don't want you getting hurt or mixed up in anything complicated."

"Thanks Anyesa, I know I can always count on you," I said as I hugged her. We then went to find our course tutor to get information about some of the books we needed. As we walked along one of the corridors, we passed Simon. I had not seen or heard from him since Italy and as soon as he saw us he managed a quick hello to Anyesa and then scuttled off awkwardly. I marvelled at the apparent effect I had on him, being so ashamed at what he had done to me that he could not even look me in the eye. I hoped he would live with that feeling for a long time to come.

As the term continued, I started to focus on writing up my dissertation. There was so much research to include and it was hard to know what direction to take it in. The main topic was how the plight of the Jews changed under Fascist rule, from having been a relatively respected and safe community in the earlier days of Mussolini, to becoming victims of racist persecution as Hitler's Nazism took hold and affected Mussolini's thinking. I found the subject fascinating which is why I had chosen it and hoped that my final work would adequately reflect the effort I had put into it.

Things at home remained tense for me however. My mother still took every opportunity to try and 'change my mind' about my sexuality and became emotional at any reference to my gay lifestyle. One day, whilst trying to have a civil and uncomplicated conversation with her over a cup of tea, she reminded me about the rabbi that lived in Manchester who specialised in homosexuality issues. He had been the person that Rabbi Katz had recommended when he had come to see me before I went to Italy.

"Why can't you, even for my sake go and see this rabbi?" pleaded my mother. "If he really has a lot of experience helping people in your situation then you owe it to yourself, your family and your culture to look into it further, don't you?"

"I owe nobody anything, Mum," I replied defiantly, not wishing to be emotionally blackmailed into anything. "I'm gay and that's that. I am happy with who I am and happy with my life. Why do I have to keep explaining myself to you?"

"Please Evan, do this for me, I can't bear the thought that you wouldn't at least try everything possible to make things better! You think you are happy now but you're still so young and I don't want you to look back on your life years down the line and realise that you have made a huge mistake. I just want you to think carefully and change things while you still can."

With a look of despair on her face, my mother started crying again. These were reactions I had become very used to by now. Not believing that any kind of so-called 'help', would ever work, I was still moved by my mother's emotional state. I had lived for a while now with a fundamental sense of deep guilt that I had reduced my family to such a mess simply because I was gay. It was a hopeless situation. Despite my instinctive abhorrence of speaking to yet another rabbi for what was certainly a lost cause, I could not face seeing the continued damage that was being inflicted on my parents and siblings.

"Okay Mum, fine," I relented. "I'll go and see this rabbi and see what he has to say. Just don't expect any miracles."

"That's all I'm asking, Evan. I will feel much happier if you go and see him, it will put mine and your father's minds at rest."

"Well, if I can at least do that for you, then it's worth a visit in itself," I replied, feeling desperately sorry for the pathetic state my mother had been reduced to.

The following week, on one of my lecture-free days at university, I went up to Manchester. The rabbi I was seeing was called Rabbi Rubinstein and apparently he had carried out extensive research into homosexuality, what made people gay and how they could manage to overcome their inclinations to lead fulfilled and happy lives. I was interested to know what he would have to tell me and how he would come across.

At the end of the long train journey, I found him waiting for me at the station. He was a man of average height with blond hair and a rather wild looking beard. I wondered what had even led this man to be interested in researching homosexuality in the first place. After greeting me warmly, Rabbi Rubinstein drove me back to his home, a moderate sized detached family house on a leafy street. He then offered me a drink and some biscuits and we then sat down and got straight to the subject at hand.

"So, Evan," began the rabbi, "we may as well not beat around the bush here. You've come to see me because you feel you are homosexual and would like to ask me various things about this I assume. Let me be clear that you have come to the right place to discuss whatever it is you want to in this regard."

"Well, to be honest with you Rabbi," I replied, steeling myself for the inevitable confrontation I had come to expect with Orthodox rabbis by now, "I will hopefully save a lot of time here. I am doing this more for my parents than myself, as they are finding it almost impossible to come to terms with my sexuality and have begged me to come and see you due to your reputation. I personally do not have any issues with my lifestyle and have no wish to subject myself to any psychological analysis either. If anything, my only struggle so far has been with the Jewish religion and its apparent bigotry. Do you think you can help me with that?"

"Well, you seem to have started this on quite a defensive footing Evan," replied the rabbi calmly. "I have no wish to create any kind of awkwardness at all. I simply would like to hear where you are coming from and then share with you the insights I have into homosexuality, which you may find helpful. I also have no wish to change you, as that is purely up to you. As long as I can provide you with certain facts and information to help you make whatever decision you want to, then I will have done my job. I have a feeling that this is not the first time you have seen someone?"

"No it's not," I replied. "I have had conversations with other rabbis previously, which have all had the same outcomes, which is me being made to feel that I am some kind of misguided deviant obsessed with sex and that I have fallen from the path of goodness somehow. It's made me pretty cynical as you can probably tell and I have basically lost any respect for the Jewish institution as a result. I believe I am gay for a reason and that this is just how it is. God clearly had a plan when he created gay people and just because most Jews can't understand it, does not give them the right to persecute people like me that just want to get on with their lives and be happy like anyone else."

"I completely understand you Evan and I will not lecture you about the right or wrong of anything. You already know that the Jewish religion forbids homosexuality but you do have the free will to choose to live this lifestyle if you believe it is what you want and you will have to answer for yourself when the time comes. All I will do now is to tell you some things about your orientation that you might find interesting."

I was slightly surprised at the frank and open approach Rabbi Rubinstein was taking. So I was not about to get a lecture regarding how evil my lifestyle was, just some useful tips? This was worth listening to for sure.

"So," continued the rabbi, "there is much discussion about what the true cause of homosexuality is. Some believe it is genetic, that is, developed during pregnancy somehow. Others believe it is the result of certain environments or situations a young child faces in their development stages. The truth is, there is no one specific indicator that anybody can find. The fact remains however that even if it is the result of several factors, they would all be considered abnormal or unnatural situations that occurred whether during pregnancy or afterwards. From speaking to several people myself that have believed themselves to be gay and have wanted to change their orientation, it appears that the mind and psyche can play a huge part in rectifying the situation, if you only allow yourself to be open to it. I have helped several people overcome what they thought were their natural inclinations and through the correct focus and will to change their lives for the better, they have been able to find suitable women and settle down to a happy family life. I am not saying that the basic urges may ever go away, but every one of us has the ability to rise above our basic inclinations."

"Are you saying that human sexuality is really all in the mind then?" I questioned, feeling that yet again, this rabbi was not convincing me of anything.

"Well, I am saying that the mind is far more powerful than you think and although you may feel unable to change your sexuality now, with the right support you can achieve things that you may not appreciate at this time. A situation like this can also be considered as a real test of character and one of the main things you were put on this earth to deal with. I believe that the other rabbis you have spoken to before now meant this when they spoke to you but unfortunately may not have explained themselves very well. On top of this, the homosexual act itself is one that is fraught with danger. Not least because the anal passage has a multitude of delicate blood vessels that if ruptured through intercourse, can very easily become subject to sexual infections including, of course, HIV. As well as this, the penetrating partner can also contract any diseases that the receptive partner has, through the opening of the penis. As long as you are practicing homosexual sex, you need to be aware that you are in the most high risk category for contracting sexual diseases. Furthermore, due to the fact that homosexuals cannot by their very nature procreate with each other, means that it is not a community that can survive in the long term."

Having listened intently to what the rabbi had to say, I decided to explain my point of view. "Rabbi Rubinstein," I began, "I know that you are somehow saying that homosexuality is an inclination we may be born with in the same way as our inclinations to express our emotions, which we are able to control. The fact is I have never believed homosexuality to be like that as it is something that is an intrinsic part of you from head to toe, like part of your DNA. How can the mind actually change your genetic make-up? I don't expect anybody who is not gay themselves to appreciate what I'm saying. But think about this. Imagine if there was no issue with homosexuality in society and I asked you to try and overcome your heterosexual feelings and somehow force yourself to become attracted to other men, do you honestly believe you could do that?"

"Evan, that is not what we are talking about here... I am trying to explain that unlike heterosexuality, being homosexual is not a natural state of being..."

"No Rabbi," I interjected. "It is exactly what we are talking about. If you can't tell me that you could make yourself have homosexual feelings if you tried, then your whole argument is worth nothing. You were born as you are, just like I was born as I am. God intended for us to be how we are for reasons unknown to us. You have never had to experience the kind of hell I have been put through simply because of the gender of the person I am created to love! Can you not see just how ludicrous it is? As for your advice on sex, well I am very aware of the apparent dangers of it from having done my own reading. That's why condoms are so useful and provide protection from this. And as for procreation and dying out, well why is it that gay people have existed since the year dot and if anything only seem to increase in each generation? Clearly we are part of God's plan for the world somehow or he would have killed us all off ages ago."

"I am simply letting you know the facts, Evan and despite what you think, there is a huge difference between homosexual feelings and those of the rest of society. As I said, if you know what the reality is of the situation, then I do not intend to stop you doing what you want to do. Just know that homosexuality is not as you think God's design for the world and that you will answer for your actions just like we all will. Be under no illusion that the homosexual lifestyle is safe, either physically or spiritually."

"Rabbi Rubinstein," I replied, having had more than enough of this now and realising that despite a more laid back style, this was just more of the same and yet another anti-gay stance with no attempt to get to the bottom of my questions. "It seems that your research has not uncovered anything I am not aware of. You may well have loads of other things to tell me but if it's okay with you, I would rather go back home now and continue my life. As you said, I will answer for myself when the time comes and hopefully I will be able to finally get my answers directly from God." I then stood up, indicating that I was ready to be driven back to the station.

"As you wish Evan," said Rabbi Rubinstein as he stood up. "My only intention was to ensure that you were not in the dark about anything to do with living a homosexual life. If you do not wish to talk further then I at least ask you to carry out as much research as possible about the implications of homosexual activity. Other than that, it has been a pleasure to meet you and I wish you the best of luck."

The rabbi then drove me to the station where I caught a train back to London. That had been a complete waste of time, although the rabbi was certainly very pleasant. It was also the first time I had not been made to feel like some kind of scum by a Jewish authority figure and I was also thankful for that. At least I could tell my parents I had been to see this so called expert and hopefully they could finally leave me alone. I was exhausted emotionally and mentally from all of this. Just the fight to keep on top of everything under the pressure imposed on me by my own family was a struggle in itself, not to mention the internal struggle I had lived with for so long now. Would I ever find the answer to my life? I despaired that it would never happen. At least I had shown willing to be put through these ridiculous charades. But would it ever be enough for my parents until either I miraculously became heterosexual or crumbled into a quivering wreck? Life was just so unfair and I did not deserve this. When I arrived back home eventually, it was early evening. I went up to my room without speaking to anyone and went straight to bed, my morale in pieces.

# Chapter 28

The next day, after the family had finished having dinner together, my parents took me into the living room and sat me down to talk to me about my visit to Manchester. My mother seemed especially interested to hear what I had to say and had a hopeful look on her face. It was obvious that they both thought I would have suddenly woken up to myself after seeing Rabbi Rubinstein and I had difficulty deciding how to tell them that the trip was completely pointless.

"Your father and I are so happy that you went to see the rabbi, Evan," began my mother. "I know you didn't really want to but considering he is the best person to speak to about issues with sexuality, I'm sure you found it useful. Please tell us how it went."

"Well, Mum and Dad, I'm not sure where to begin really," I replied, knowing that what I was about to say would wipe the expression off my parents' faces; expressions of hope and anticipation that I had not seen in them for so long now. "The rabbi was definitely very nice and friendly, and spoke to me like a human being. He basically wanted me to know that being gay is something that can be overcome as the causes of it are correctable psychologically. He also said that he had spoken to other people that were gay but who somehow with his help had managed to control it and lead heterosexual lives."

"You see? Fantastic news!" exclaimed my mother, an air of pure relief and delight taking over her. "I knew it was the right decision for you to go and see the rabbi. Do you think he really can help you then? Your father and I will give you all the support you need, whatever happens."

"Mum, I hadn't finished. That's what the rabbi told me, however he couldn't convince me or back up anything he was saying. These people that he has apparently helped overcome their sexuality, how does he know if they really have done so, or if they could have been bisexual in the first place as opposed to gay like I am? He still thinks that sexuality is like an emotion that you can control. The fact is that it's not. I challenged him and asked him if he thought it was possible to make himself develop gay feelings and he simply couldn't answer me or discuss it. I just took the situation he had thrown at me and pushed it back on him because surely it's exactly the same thing but in reverse. His lack of ability to provide any real answers to anything was proof enough that there is no cure for being gay because it is not in fact a condition or just an emotion. When he knew he couldn't answer me properly, he decided to give me some facts about gay sex which I already knew and he told me to look into the whole thing further because it was still fundamentally wrong and against the religion. These are things I've heard many times before. In the end I realised that nobody can really explain anything and that I know exactly what my sexuality is and just need to get on with my life. So that's what I have to tell you both."

"But Evan," said my mother with an air of exasperation, "surely that can't just be it? Would you not want to try any possible method of changing things even to be in with a chance of turning things around?"

"Yes Evan," added my father for good measure. "You really need to try everything possible, we can't ever rest until we know you have."

"Really?" I replied. "Well I have officially decided that I will no longer entertain any more of these ridiculous situations. Don't you both see what it's doing to me? I'm twenty-one years old and I feel like I'm sixty! I'm exhausted in every way. My very existence is being questioned and through no fault of my own I've been attacked and emotionally blackmailed by you both just because you can't understand me. I can't take this any more! If you both don't go to counselling yourselves to come to terms with who I am then there's nothing more I can say to you. If it wasn't for this stupid religion, we wouldn't even be in this situation in the first place! Don't ever even try to speak to me about this again, I've had enough. I am me, and I intend to stay this way as it makes me happy. If you're both worried about me not getting married to some woman and being able to have children and stuff, then remember you have four other kids who can do that for you. I need to be left alone now."

I then got up and went up to my room, leaving both my parents to deal with their own reactions. I felt I was going to explode, I couldn't breathe. I had nowhere to go and no support to fall back on or anyone to speak to. Even Anyesa could not really help me resolve this. What was I to do? In tears, I went back downstairs where I bumped into my brother Lewis who looked at me like I had just crawled out of a hole. I continued going, went out of the front door and kept walking. I had no idea where I would end up, but I had to continue going because if I stopped then all my thoughts would catch up with me. As I walked along the streets, I noticed some other people from the community going about their business. None of these people would ever understand what it was like to be in my position. I resented each and every one of them, happily following their religious lifestyles, their cosy family lives continuing on with probably no greater worries than how their kids were doing at school and what kind of food to buy for the upcoming Sabbath meals. I knew that as soon as I was able to, I would choose to live in a place where being who you are, whatever that was, represented no issues to anybody. I knew that this immediately ruled out a religious Jewish environment and the sense of hope that this gave me was all I had to keep me going. Eventually I returned home having walked the streets for over an hour and went up to bed, a myriad of thoughts and feelings still buzzing around inside me.

Following the latest dramas at home, I had started to find it difficult to concentrate in lectures at university. My mind kept wandering back to my pathetic life and the hopeless situation with my family. I decided to buy a Dictaphone so that I could simply record my lectures and then in my own time when I could concentrate better, I would listen to them and hopefully be able to learn something. I was also struggling to continue writing my dissertation for the same reasons. This was my final year and everything depended on doing well. It was therefore the worst possible timing for my life to be imploding in the way that it was.

Anyesa had noticed the change in me and had become quite concerned. When I told her that my problems over the last couple of years had started to overtake me, she asked if I wanted to come and stay with her for a while in her halls of residence. She only had one single bed but did not mind if I needed to sleep on her floor for a few nights if it meant I would get a bit of a break. I seriously considered it but in the end did not want to make her feel that I was imposing on her and her privacy, especially as her room was rather small. I just wanted my parents back. I wanted them to understand me and to be there for me. It was all I really needed yet it seemed impossible.

The end of 1995 approached and I spent the Christmas and New Year period pretty much alone. Carine had gone back to France to be with her family over the festive season and Anyesa had done the same with her family who lived in Cambridge. I spent as many nights as I could out of the house, often going by myself into Soho, just to be anonymous and sit in some bar somewhere. I was never alone for long however due to the ongoing attention I would get from different men. I started to become very promiscuous, more so than I had ever been and took people up on their offers to go back to their place for sex at any opportunity. Sex became my way of connecting, of making myself feel wanted. It did not matter if the guy in question was especially interesting or not. If I received undiluted attention then that was enough for me. I was using sex as a tool, a way of escaping my life and bringing people closer to me. It was all I had that I could control.

As 1996 began I continued in the same vein, often going out at least four nights a week and always with the aim of finding someone who would want me. Along the way I met a new group of friends who in reality were only acquaintances that I could spend time with when we were out. They were fun to be with and uncomplicated. The fact that they, like my old friends Nathan, Toby and Mandy, were into recreational drugs, did not bother me this time. I just needed a social crutch. On a few occasions, I met up with Carine and we would go out together where I would end up leaving her alone in a bar or club to go off with someone. Despite having told myself I would never have sex in toilets again after the time with Juan, I found myself lapsing into it once more. Carine did not appreciate me leaving her in this way but I did not care. It was just the sense of intimacy that I needed, even if only for a few minutes in a urine-stinking cubicle. I knew I was going downhill and had begun to really dislike Soho and the gay scene in general, but I did not seem to be able to stop myself spending time there and doing what I was doing. Sex was becoming my drug, and my lack of self-respect was the driving force. I knew that if my parents ever knew what I was doing, they would not be able to handle it in any way, and for good reason. It meant that whenever my mother asked me about my social life or what I had been up to, I simply gave her a watered down and vague response. I did not have a truthful relationship with anybody in my family. How could I? Our worlds were simply too far apart.

One weekend, my parents gathered the whole family around. My mother told us that she had booked us all to see a counsellor so that we could have a family therapy session because there were serious problems that needed to be resolved. We were also told that we had no choice in the matter. Things really were going awry at home. My sister, Eva, still had not met anybody suitable and by now twenty-three years old, had become quite sour and cynical about the whole dating scene, often clashing bitterly with my mother over what to do for the best. Most of her friends seemed to have met somebody and were in stable relationships or even engaged to be married. I could understand how she must feel, yet I also knew that if she would only relax and stop finding things to criticise, she may actually meet the right man.

My brother Lewis had become very withdrawn and hostile, unwilling to engage with anyone in the family unless it was on his terms. At sixteen, Daniel was starting to get mixed up in the wrong crowds and seemed to have started smoking, which he had tried to hide from my parents to no avail. One evening my mother had caught him sneaking into the house and had discovered several packets of cigarettes in his pocket. As a staunch anti-smoker, this did not go down well in any way and caused major arguments between Daniel and my parents. Jonathan was now fourteen and although he had not been the source of any real concern as yet, my parents felt they needed to protect him from going astray by nipping any issues within the family in the bud before things got more out of hand than they already were.

So, one day the following week when we were all around, we went en masse to see the counsellor. Nobody spoke during the car ride there, the sense of resentment at having been dragged against our will being quite palpable. The woman who greeted us was middle-aged and pleasant looking with brown hair which was clipped up on top of her head with a hairpin. After we had been offered drinks and were seated, the session began. Marjorie, the counsellor spoke to us all in turn and asked us what we were doing in life and what we felt were the main issues we were dealing with at home from our individual points of view. My brothers did not say much, refusing to divulge their feelings to a stranger. My sister managed to explain that she was unhappy with her lack of progress at meeting decent men and that the atmosphere in the house was very depressing in general due to our parents' constantly interfering ways.

When it came to my turn, I decided to be frank and say simply that my parents could not accept the fact that I was gay and that it should be them, not us that the counsellor concentrated on. My mother then spoke, and the rest of the session was taken up with focusing on her issues. As my father was far more stoic and not one to be forthcoming about emotional matters, my mother was left to speak for both of them. My siblings and I were forced to sit there uncomfortably as my mother cried shamelessly and described her feelings of frustration, devastation and helplessness about my sexuality, and the fact that she no longer felt that any of her children were showing the least amount of respect for her as their mother. By the end of the session, it was clear that there was a lot more to do as far as my mother was concerned. It was agreed that the family session may not have been the most fruitful at this time but that my mother would continue to seek counselling for a while. I was extremely happy about this decision because it would at least mean that she got the help she so desperately needed. Something had to give in the end that was for sure, and I prayed that things would eventually change as a result.

I struggled through the rest of my final year, managing to complete my dissertation somehow and present it to my fellow students and course tutors. I felt I could have done far better but under the circumstances, it was a good effort. I had just about existed through my life in the last year, spending as little time as possible at home. My saving grace was Anyesa who was always there for me whenever I needed to talk. She was the quintessential agony aunt and great source of comfort to me. I also continued to spend time with my new group of friends as well as Carine and some French friends she was living with, who all provided a welcome diversion from my troubles. Although I had managed to catch up again with Alex not long ago, she was clearly preoccupied with her forthcoming wedding and so was not readily available. Nevertheless, she remained the only friend I had left from within my community. My social life in the main consisted of being in Soho, a place I now despised and felt had nothing to offer me beyond sex. However it was a means to an end as it was the only place I could be sure to find the men I so desperately needed to be with. I hated myself for my weakness, but at this point in my life, what was the alternative?

Simon seemed to have his strong clique of friends at university including Gemma and Miranda and a couple of others. Apart from having to see him at lectures, we had absolutely nothing to do with one another. I wondered how things would have been if he had never tried to molest me in my sleep. Would our friendship have lasted anyway? He was certainly a completely different person now than I had ever known before he came out; superficial to the end and entrenched in most of the stereotypes that had come to define gay people for the rest of society. Deep down I still felt very sad that our friendship had come to this and wondered if there was anything at all that I could have done to make things work out differently. Unfortunately, it was all water under the bridge now and too much had happened between us for us to ever go back. There was simply no way we could be in each other's lives any more, I just knew that in my heart.

It was 1996 and I was twenty-one years old. I was gay and Jewish and since the age of fourteen, had lived with a struggle that I could never have anticipated. I had not managed to find the true meaning of my life or any real answers as to why I had been put into the situation I was in. I had been strong enough to follow my desires and needs and remain true to my sexuality even though I did not feel at one with the gay environment. In the process I had lost faith in my religion and in the people that represented it. My family was in a bad way. My relationship with my parents and siblings had become severely damaged and I had no idea if things would ever be the same again. At least my mother was now having counselling to help her deal with everything. I felt that I was solely responsible for everything that had happened in my family, even though there was nothing I could do to change myself. A weaker person would have probably taken their own life by now, and although I had certainly considered this on a few occasions, I knew I could never go through with such a thing. Something inside me, despite everything, was telling me to get through this, that I was in fact strong enough to deal with it and that somehow things would change in the end.

Having gone through everything that I had experienced until now, I truly felt that I had no real meaning in my life and despite having spent several years pleading with God to bring me some enlightenment, this had still not arrived. Looking at where I had got to so far, there was not much I had to be proud of. I had made new friends while in Italy and in London who were people I finally felt completely comfortable with, which was of enormous value at least. By some miracle, my inner strength had kept me going until this point. It was now up to me to make sense of everything so far in my own way and turn things around somehow. I promised myself that despite everything that had happened I would become a source of pride to my family in some way, sometime. But first I would need to drag myself out of my pit of despair and regain some self-respect. I made a firm resolution to stop engaging in casual sex and to find a partner, someone that belonged to me and me to him. I did not want my situation to be an excuse for me to treat myself in such a disrespectful way. I would live more honourably, with morality and with pride. Otherwise I would be going down a negative spiral that may lead to depths that I could not recover from. I owed it to myself and to my family and my heritage. God was going to help me and I would continue to connect with Him whenever I could.

I also felt that I needed to create more distance between myself and my family so we could all get some perspective, and made the decision to move out of home at the earliest possible opportunity, probably when I managed to find someone I could be with. It may be the only way we could start to repair our relationship. I had to keep on going and I had to find my place. It was the only thing I was certain about.

What I did not realise at the time was just how different life in my twenties was about to become. I would finally be settled, and would enter a whole new phase of maturity and self-respect, along with entering an entirely different world altogether that brought a whole wave of new and unforeseen problems. That journey of course, warrants another book…